Sarah's Promise

⟨— *The Quest for Peace in the Middle East* —⟩

A humanitarian's journey of the heart

By Devra West, D.D., Ph.D.

Printed in Victoria, Canada

Published by
Fire of Mind Publishing
736 Fred Burr Road • Victor, Montana 59875

Cover Design: Eve Meng, ibid, northwest
Typesetting: ibid, northwest

National Library of Canada Cataloguing in Publication

West, Devra, 1950-
    Sarah's promise : the quest for peace in the Middle East / Devra West.

ISBN 1-55395-519-6

    I. Title.

DS119.76.W47 2003   956.9405'4   C2003-900165-2

TRAFFORD

This book was published *on-demand* in cooperation with Trafford Publishing. On-demand publishing is a unique process and service of making a book available for retail sale to the public taking advantage of on-demand manufacturing and Internet marketing. **On-demand publishing** includes promotions, retail sales, manufacturing, order fulfilment, accounting and collecting royalties on behalf of the author.

Suite 6E, 2333 Government St., Victoria, B.C. V8T 4P4, CANADA
Phone   250-383-6864   Toll-free   1-888-232-4444 (Canada & US)
Fax   250-383-6804   E-mail   sales@trafford.com
Web site   www.trafford.com   TRAFFORD PUBLISHING IS A DIVISION OF TRAFFORD HOLDINGS LTD.
Trafford Catalogue #02-1234   www.trafford.com/robots/02-1234.html

10   9   8   7   6   5   4

*Dedicated
to the Family of Abraham
and all the Mothers of
the Land of Milk and Honey*

Table of Contents

Sarah's Promise

The Quest for Peace in the Middle East

Chapter		Page

Maps

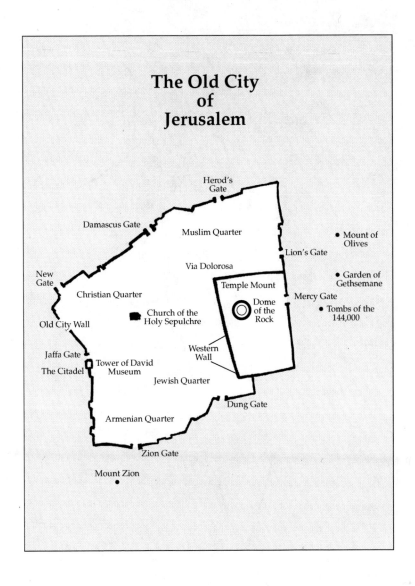

The Old City of Jerusalem

Herod's Gate

Damascus Gate

Muslim Quarter

● Mount of Olives

Lion's Gate

New Gate

Via Dolorosa

● Garden of Gethsemane

Christian Quarter

Temple Mount

Mercy Gate

Dome of the Rock

● Tombs of the 144,000

Old City Wall

Church of the Holy Sepulchre

Jaffa Gate

Western Wall

The Citadel

Tower of David Museum

Jewish Quarter

Dung Gate

Armenian Quarter

Zion Gate

Mount Zion
●

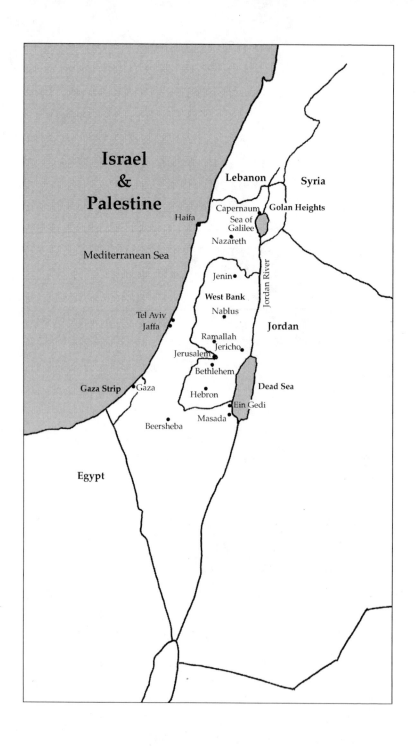

Israel
&
Palestine

Mediterranean Sea

Lebanon   Syria

Capernaum   Golan Heights
Haifa   Sea of
Galilee
Nazareth

Jenin

West Bank
Nablus   Jordan River

Tel Aviv   Jordan
Jaffa
Ramallah
Jericho
Jerusalem
Bethlehem
Dead Sea
Gaza Strip   Gaza
Hebron
Ein Gedi
Beersheba   Masada

Egypt

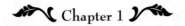
The Apology

Common Fears, Common Understandings

After a long, long day of dealing with the hard questions and high emotions that are common to this place, I am glad to be heading back to my hotel room for the night. It seems that politics plays a role even among peacekeepers and humanitarians, and even among the members of my own staff.

It has been a full day, more than full, full of challenges, full of possibilities, full of people who can help and people who can hinder. Several people got up and walked out anyway, despite my efforts to appease and accommodate, and left the table of coexistence, fed up with what they felt was too much risk or idealism, depending upon which direction, toward which polarity, the pendulum was swinging.

It was easy to understand how they felt. But it was hard to see them turn their backs. It was even harder to be the target of their anger. The measurement of rightness, political, religious and otherwise, is starting to eat at me and devour my sense of self from all the bending and appeasing. I feel stretched in all directions like the roads heading out of Jerusalem.

Feeling sorry for myself is short-lived. The chill of whirling, flashing lights in front of my taxi is immediately

1

followed by the whine of rushing sirens. My driver is grateful to take me wherever I want to go.

The only foreign passengers in taxis these days are activists, peace workers, journalists, government officials and a very, very few souls who are still willing to risk coming here for personal reasons, and even fewer who are sent here to conduct the few shreds of business that remain. The world of casual passengers has dried up and become barren.

But then the raw sound of the ambulances and quick response teams, that always grips my gut with the expectation of massive, larger-than-life and beyond comprehension tragedy, has taken a front seat to the trivia of the day. As I sit forward to see through the backed-up traffic, it's impossible to tell whether someone has had a simple fender bender or a heart attack or some such, or whether instead, entire families have been wiped out, with torn bodies and shattered lives strewn across the sidewalk in a mass bloodbath typical of another suicide bombing.

Like everyone here, as I crane my neck for a glimpse of the holdup that has brought traffic to a standstill, my first thought is the hope that no one I know or love or work with was caught in this crossfire of fate.

My cab driver, a young Arab man, shrugs his shoulders apologetically as if he knows what I am thinking. The pinched look on his face reveals his own share of worry. We sit lost in the private calling for the sparing of lives near and dear to us each. He sighs, I sigh. He runs a worried hand through his hair. I run both hands through mine, as if I can brush away the possibility of impending doom like raking leaves off a patio.

Neither of us can find comfort, as we both fidget in our seats, crossing and uncrossing legs or nervously drumming the steering wheel with prayers of anxiety and begging. I have already lost people that I have loved from both sides. I don't know anyone who lives here who hasn't.

Every day we live here in a strange tension of not knowing. Our prayers for safety volley with the heartbreaking news that a dear friend, or friend's child or mother or father didn't make it, was shot down or run over in the rush of insanity. The heartbreaking news comes often. It is the norm here.

Sitting captive together in the taxi, we wait, we listen, we watch, passing the troubled time like helpless lambs penned up for slaughter. Now we can see that this is no traffic accident. In this part of the world you have to be prepared for anything. More police and rescue vehicles join the shrilling of the ambulances.

The taxicab driver and humanitarian who, a short while ago, had exchanged the usual common courtesies between driver and passenger, now sit bolt upright for a better view, joined in the common experience of trying to make sense of what lies ahead, and whether or not danger, and possibly the worst of everything, is on the travel schedule.

As the noise gets louder, so does the thumping and pounding of our hearts as we sit suspended in an unmoving line of fire, a stone's throw from increasing mayhem. The fight-or-flight impulse has set in. Now we are visibly anxious and no longer care what the other thinks. Now we are turning our heads rapidly left and right to gain an advantage, twitching like animals, and getting into position to run for our lives.

More ambulances arrive on the scene, and we hold our breaths, bracing for the worst to come running down the street straight at us and crash into our midst. A warning siren louder than the rest pierces the intersection with an authoritative wail that warns all life to clear out and make way.

A police officer frantically waves the procession of cars around a blocked-off meridian. Now we are close enough to smell the fear. We are close enough to see the perspiration of terror taking hold of faces and bodies.

A rush of people has begun to pour out of the building up further on our right, like a torrent of madness seeking high ground. Running snapshot expressions of sheer horror bolt out into the street, wide-eyed with the burden of panic and terror, running for their lives with steps that may very well be their last. To witness this shudders the soul. To witness human beings running from the savagery of other human beings makes me grip myself with fingers of steel just to keep from screaming.

The scream is always there each time that I am a witness to the human atrocity that is running in the opposite direction of the promises of prophets. Screaming serves nothing, of course. I have learned to stay alert in these situations. You have to. Everyone has to.

But what if one day we didn't hold the screams at bay? What if the screams of humanity, of this place and its suffering, were broadcast all at once in a single tormented call that cries out in its truth of knowing?

What if the scream of all screams, that knows the violence must stop, was heard around the world? I know that this thought will stay with me as a companion of sanity. And I know that the voice for a better world must continue to be heard. It must precede the hands that will rebuild.

Up ahead, chaos is clearly taking over and echoing in all directions, reverberating off gathered groups of frantic people and limestone walls. I can see the Old City of Jerusalem in the distance, as domes and spires of holiness look down upon this moment of decision and the internal screams that will never end from those that endure the unbearable.

An elderly woman with a little boy in tow is literally dragging the child by his arm with such forcefulness that the child is grimacing, eyes squeezed shut and teeth bared, partly from fear and not wanting to see and partly from the hot sensation of his arm being yanked from its socket. An evacuation is in progress. Getting out of the building has become an emergency reality, and now panic and pushing has ensued.

A woman falls on the concrete and cracks her head wide open. She tries to get up but she stumbles, helpless. Someone else rushes past her, knocking her over again; someone else stops and helps her to her feet and gathers her, limping, to a safe distance on the other side of the avenue's meridian. The concrete slab is the barrier, the safety zone and the line of decision.

Now many people are staggering behind her, competing for the attention of emergency workers, some from pure panic and some from minor injuries that have come from being forced to evacuate a large building. It looks like one man is collapsing and clutching his chest, perhaps from a heart attack. Suspicion has given rise to the expectation of insanity and the bombs that insanity so ruthlessly wields.

The rescue workers and the bomb squad saviors will cross that line of decision, leaving the safety zone behind to stare, with stark determination, at the possibility of their own death. They are brave Israelis, trained to save lives. They must become ruthless in their courage.

They are called to go in, no matter what, to die to their own screams, and simply do what must be done. They don't know what they will find on the other side: machine guns, suicide bombs, toxic gas or a combination of the unthinkable.

The woman with the head injury sinks to the ground and collapses into the kind of stone-faced shock that precedes losing consciousness, saturated with the gushing bright red of her own vital fluids. People are being lined up and grouped and herded on the side of the intersection that has been assigned to safety.

Some are craning toward the building they have just escaped from, because someone they know and love hasn't made it out yet. Some are shaking and crying and are nursing their wounds of emotional trauma. Some are being treated and made ready for transport to a hospital. Some are limp with shock. The ones who just stare into a frozen vacuum are the ones that I reach for, as a witness, as a mother, as a passenger from a foreign country sitting in the backseat of a taxi.

More bomb squads have arrived and are assembling for the assault. They are decked in their battle gear of helmets, gas masks and chest plates like modern day gladiators. The air around them is tense with ominous and grave deliberation. As if a silent alarm has gone off in the midst of the already deafening clamor, the panic suddenly surges and accelerates.

The police are desperately trying to direct what has now become an onslaught of humanity running from the building's orifices, like cattle on the verge of an outright stampede. This does not look good, I think to myself, and

I wonder who will get hurt, how many and why. What if the bomb is on a timer and blows everything in sight to smithereens? It could be a dirty bomb, or worse. Who picks the lottery number that determines who lives and who dies in this place of Russian roulette and volatile politics?

The taxicab driver reaches around and locks all the doors, front and back. I'm not sure why. His entire face has changed. Before, he was sweet and pleasant and humble, almost apologetic in an endearing sort of way. Now he is steely and visibly hardened and anything but humble. He is ready to do whatever it takes to survive.

This adds to my nervous alarm and I gather myself into my own hardness. Outside, beyond our presumed safe haven of the locked doors of a dilapidated old taxi, it seems the experts have a plan. They pass the word down the line to the assembled saviors and gladiators.

The group of men suddenly stand up tall, like trees in a forest, sure of their ability to weather a bad storm. A knowing look is exchanged among them, and in a single turn the bomb squad team bolts in a unified lurch straight toward the door, straight into the jaws of danger, straight into the off-limits building, single file, pushing past the fast-moving stream of screaming people who are still filing out.

My driver shifts into high alert and has broken out in a visible sweat. His eyes have become small, dark, beady and intent, like a cornered wildcat looking for a way out. He darts a glance in my direction and seems to steady himself.

And then without a word, he slams the engine into reverse, knocking over a fence railing, and lurches up onto the sidewalk. Thrown forward, I grip onto anything I can grab a hold of, stuck in the backseat without any say whatsoever, frantically wondering what he has in mind and where he is headed. Jerking and bumping and hitting the ceiling of the car with the top of my head, I manage to yell above the din and demand to know what he thinks he is doing.

Still straddling the sidewalk with the wheels of the taxi, he swerves missing a pedestrian by less than an inch, as I am forcibly flung to the other side of the car. He is clearly in a sweating panic himself now and is intent on escape, swerving sharply to the right again and slamming into the gray wall above the cement, swinging hard and full on into an alley full of crates and boxes and shipping gear.

Everything is flying every which way, and there is no way that my young driver can even see what's ahead of him. But he steps on the pedal and guns the engine, forcing every last drop of speed from the old excuse of a rundown rig.

Now I register that I had hesitated to get into such an old beat-up vehicle when he first pulled up to the curb, at the same time I was thinking to myself, "Why am I traveling alone in a place like this, anyway?" Now I am asking myself, "What was I thinking? How could I have been so out of focus and absent-minded, not to have taken more precautions? I know the unspoken rules here."

The crashing noise of ramming everything in sight on both sides of the alley adds to the fury of the moment, as the taxi leaps through the next thoroughfare and heads down another alley, and then another and then another. It seems the plodding worn-out mare has become a racing stallion.

The taxi has found its reserves of strength and speed despite its age and condition, suggesting that the adrenaline of an emergency can affect even inanimate objects. Meanwhile, I'm plastered to my seat, head thrown back and horrified.

The ride is getting rough and abusive. I'm wondering now if I will be taken hostage or something wild like that, even though I have always trusted myself and divine providence to be here, even though as an American, I am highly unwelcome by the vast majority of the Palestinian population, and sometimes even by the Israelis. I grasp at the door handles and try to hold on, still shots racing through my head of all the people who had warned me not to be here.

Shouting in Arabic, and wildly gesturing to garbage cans to get out of the way, he makes his break from the immediate scene of flashing lights and emergency vehicles, zigzagging across town on winding, cluttered side streets. I have lost track of which part of Jerusalem we are in, and I search for something familiar to get my bearings. We are going too fast to see much of anything, and the white limestone buildings whizzing by all look the same. Darkness is coming on now, and I feel like I am sinking.

What if I really am in danger, what can I do? This question is urgent, more than relevant. But something inside demands that I not give in to full-blown panic. I must come to terms with this: am I being taken hostage or am I just sharing a lousy situation with a fellow human being?

And then like a flashback that has emerged from the subconscious, I think back to a day of reckoning, a day of brave revelation and the proving ground of faith made real. I had been teaching an interfaith course, and in the afternoon after the session I had felt compelled to take a walk in the Arab section of Jerusalem, near the American Colony Hotel where the course was being held.

This was a significant decision, because the day that I strolled away from the safety of the hotel was a day of observance for the Arab people to commemorate what had been for them a literal slaughter. The day was actually understood as Riot Day.

All over the land of Israel and Palestine, Arabs were out in force demonstrating, protesting the brutality that they suffered, and in some cases striking back in whatever way they could to avenge their plight and the loss of loved ones, which is a cultural and traditional mode of ethics and response.

Maybe it comes from the "eye for an eye" belief system that takes matters into its own hands when the justice of the land turns its head and refuses to comply with either ancient law or modern civility. Lives were paying the dues for pent-up rage on both sides of the conflict. This day was a designated day of planned and deliberate rage throughout the land.

And so I ventured out alone with my blond head uncovered into the Arab neighborhood, a decision that was foolish or brave or both. Perhaps I too was insane, but it was a test of my mettle. Thinking back to why I did it, from my resolution to be in the thick of things to prove that most Arabs are good and kind people, it's like I had to prove this to myself as a condition of my own faith.

I didn't tell anyone that I was heading out into an area that was very definitely off limits to any foreigner, let alone an American, let alone a woman, let alone a woman walking alone completely exposed to the whims of whoever was encountered, let alone to walk straight into a danger zone on Riot Day.

As I ventured farther into the Arab neighborhood, I was met with cold, snarling stares and grimaces of hatred. I could feel the age-old heartlessness of prejudice that is rent upon so many people just because they are not the right color, or the right religion, or the right economic privilege. I was clearly not the same right color, or same right religion, or the same right economic circumstance.

As a lily-white American from the suburbs of the heartland, I was suddenly feeling the harsh sting of prejudice and the very real danger of my audacity. For the first time, I knew what it felt like to be tried and judged and sentenced as sub-human and not deserving of life, all in a single piercing glance.

I walked in clear disfavor, wrapped in the imminent harm of the loss of body and limb, into a neighborhood that struggled with poverty and despair and the rage of desperation. A few men, obviously Arab, stood ahead on a street corner and I remember that my stomach clenched into a knot and turned upside down just to walk in their direction. They stared long and hard at me and then at one another, and convened to decide my fate. It was their call. This was their territory. I was clearly on their turf. Anything was possible.

But just as I felt that I might be accosted and dragged off into the devouring darkness of hateful revenge, two young boys came running up to me out of nowhere, bright-eyed and curious. They wanted to know where the foreigner was from, and did she speak English. At first I recoiled, thinking maybe this was a trick or a trap. I was visibly shaking. Common friendliness was suspect. Nothing could be trusted.

But then like a miracle or a light turned on in a dimly lit cellar, we began a cautious exchange. Soon the prickly testing with hackles raised became shy smiles and the tentativeness of strangers. Eyes and bodies questioned life and death with the probe of intuitive instincts and gut level assessment. But then as if a white flag of surrender had been raised, the initial standoff eased into an easy walking side by side.

I told them that I was sorry for all the trouble of their people, that many Americans were sorry. They were still young enough to feel that I was sincere, and I was obviously alone and not a threat to them. Nobody really wanted war.

In an unbelievable scenario, they forgot to hate. They forgot it was Riot Day. They seemed to understand the paradox of politics versus the lives of real people and shifted the attention of our talk to practicing their English. They asked questions about America, which to them was like the land of milk and honey. Of course their fantasies were fantasies, and not what America really is.

We walked on, still tentative but in good spirits, exploring each other's lives with the powder keg of Riot Day going off all around us. Demonstrations and explosions and riots had begun early in the day throughout the land. Booming flashes and wailing sirens had taken over Jerusalem by breakfast.

As if we were in another world entirely, I received their eager attention. They received ample praise from me for practicing their English and doing so well. It was a good exchange of simple humanity, even though the politics of conflict continued to bristle with hostility and missiles and planned invasions, as if war had become a permanent fact of life, a business-as-usual planetary condition.

We walked past another cluster of men on another corner who eyed us with glaring suspicion. And again I felt suspended between the death sentence of vengeful hatred and the innocence of these young kids who were jabbering like magpies, oblivious to the seething stares.

The boys surrounded me now on all sides, and some were half skipping in glee down the street. We walked past the men who stood posted on the street corner unscathed, with the exception of the tactile sensation of hot stares hitting me in the back between my shoulder blades. It was like walking through a minefield, surrounded by innocent babes who miraculously made it to the other side, as if aided by some higher power.

Farther on down the way, we stopped by a little shop that was still struggling to stay open, where I bought the boys some pencils, some treats, some candy and a few other trinkets to stuff in their pockets as small trophies for practicing their English on an English-speaking stranger.

A few other boys joined us, and then a few more, and then a few more, as we proceeded through the eerie reality of death and danger on the one hand and peace of life on the other. Soon I had an escort of young Arab boys and youth completely surrounding me, as if I was a long lost family member.

As we passed onlookers on the street, the hateful sneers from before faded into non-committed questioning glances, shrugs and a "live and let live" attitude. Soon glares and menacing slit-eyed glances became stares of curiosity or indifference. I felt like a kind of pied piper, holding court with a handsome gaggle of Arab kids, all male, and all having a good deal of hope in the light of their eyes.

And this was the day of riot and revenge. During my time with the boys, some fifteen or more in number, as we made our way through the neighborhood, I did a lot of apologizing for the ignorance of the world, mostly for the ignorance of privilege, which included my own. I apologized for the way things are. They took deep breaths, as if what I was saying was some kind of remedy for the cross they were assigned to bear in their young lives.

I hoped that maybe they wouldn't grow up to be suicide bombers, or worse. I hoped their homes and families wouldn't be bombed and bulldozed. Perhaps that was a presumptuous thought on my part, but it was a hope, plain and simple.

The boys walked me all the way back to my hotel, where we saluted one another a good-hearted farewell, wishing health, wealth and prosperity to follow all the days of our lives. I would continue my prayers, and so would they. Praise Allah, they said in parting.

Praise anything and anyone that can stop this madness and bring humanity back to goodness, I thought as I watched them run and skip back to their neighborhood and back to their lives of uncertainty, along with the very real and painful certainty of poverty, danger and struggle. And I walked through the doors of my hotel, back into the world of seeming privilege.

And then, as I came back from the fast-forward review of mettle testing and faith-building, I sharply registered the fact that I still sat in the back of a runaway taxi with streets and buildings whizzing by.

And then with all of this rushing through me, I came back to myself and was no longer afraid. I did a 180° turnaround from the moment that had seized my soul and caused me to fret about whether or not I was going to be kidnapped by a taxicab driver turned terrorist.

I came to my senses, back to my heart, back to my humanity and back to the wisdom of apology. I remembered why so many Arabs are outraged, at the same time that I had just witnessed the tragedy of Israeli citizens who live in the horrid grip of terror every day.

There I sat in the midst of the impossible polarities of two sides of the same coin. I had just witnessed an emergency evacuation of the elderly and young children because a bomb was expected imminently to take innocent Jewish lives.

I had also witnessed the poverty and atrocities of the living conditions of the Palestinians on many occasions. The grief and struggle they endured were an overload to the senses from a humanitarian point of view. Inwardly I apologized to every human being that had ever lived for anything I had ever done to add to the insanity of lost human values. My prayers became vehement, although I prayed to myself in silence.

As if he has received my silent prayer, my Arab driver begins to slow down. He begins to return to normal. My unspoken apologies seem to have an immediate calming effect on the terror that had consumed us both just moments before. The young man in the front seat, the driver's seat, who had metamorphosed into a half-crazed madman or a fleeing bank robber, tries to regain his composure by assuming the facade of just an ordinary taxicab driver once again.

Out of breath, he has begun to calm down a little, although he is still on the lookout, routinely sending darting checks in all directions, surveying his surroundings, like radar scanning for the enemy. White knuckles are still gripping the steering wheel. He is trembling and mumbling to himself and the whole of the world for the life he is living.

Finally, looking startled and surprised, he turns his sweaty face in my direction, straining his neck to look back at me, as if he suddenly remembered that he had a passenger along for the ride. When our eyes meet, his entire demeanor rolls on a dime, and he visibly cowers in apology, but this is an apology that holds within it the embarrassment and sorrow of an entire culture. The high chase, the runaway race for survival, gives way to the humanity between us.

I in turn give voice to all the apologies that have raced through my mind and my prayers and begin to blubber, tears streaming. The litany of all the things I am sorry for pour into the backseat where I am sitting until I am close to swimming in "I'm sorry... I'm sorry... I'm sorry..."

I'm sorry Americans are so clueless. I'm sorry we don't see the suffering that we contribute to. I'm sorry big business has become the politics of war. I'm sorry that greed and exploitation have been allowed to run amuck for so long and to leach out humanity to the extent that they have.

Thoughts race side by side as I continue to blubber one apology after another. I'm sorry that business leaders, who care about the planet they live on, are not given more due for doing the right thing. I'm sorry Wall Street's "sustainability index" doesn't carry the real weight that it should. I'm sorry that the lost lives of thousands upon thousands of citizens in other countries are but questionable numbers, just hearsay. I'm sorry that the human heart is dying on the vine of heartlessness.

I'm sorry that there are rotten eggs in every basket that ruin even the most well intended plans and ideas: good soldiers, bad soldiers; sincere peace workers, hell-bent crazy radicals; corporate leaders doing the right thing, corporate leaders doing the unthinkable; leaders for a better world, leaders who don't care and aren't leaders at all. It's all so mixed up, good and evil vying for control of an entire planet.

My driver seems stunned. He seems moved. He seems touched, even in his own moment of bare-naked survival. He pulls over to the side of the street and stops the taxi, speechless and overcome. Despite my unanswered questions of, "Where are we going and what in the world are you doing?" I can't help but notice how young the driver is, when suddenly reduced to an unveiled vulnerability.

He is terrified and in a geared-up, hyper-survival mode, but he is also terrified, like a child who has just awakened from a nightmare, rumple-haired and disoriented with the meek utterance of the word "Mother," not far behind on his lips.

There is a distinct innocence in his eyes that seems to plead to be taken into the softness of a mother's comfort, and a far larger, greater, more insistent pleading for mere acceptance of his humanity by another human being. Clearing my throat of uncertainty and self-centered judgment, I ask him if everything is OK.

Clearing his throat of childlike innocence, he musters his remaining masculinity and tries to appear in charge. "This is just how it is," he says, "No big deal, had to get out of there. Don't want to go to jail. They'll take you in for nothing. Sorry, misses, to give you a scare. I'll get you back to your hotel right away, no charge." The only thing I can say in return again and again is, "I'm sorry."

He pulls back into traffic and after driving in silence for five or ten minutes, he ventures, in a small voice that has the power to move mountains in its smallness, "They took my father and my brother away and they never came back. They were innocent, my family never was involved in anything, and we kept to ourselves, nothing at all, nothing, none of us.

And then my mother died. She got sick. Things were hard for her. There was no money and no medicine. There was nothing I could do. I've been on my own ever since. My uncle looks after me. He helped me buy this cab." A faint undercurrent of a smile softly waves across his cheeks.

Reaching his hand out, he pats the dash of the old beaten taxi lovingly, as if stroking a cherished treasure or a beloved friend or a favored palace horse of distinguished breeding. This cab is all he has left.

I call back my previous judgment about the taxi being a junk heap and swallow it down in the hard light of the exchange that has just transpired. With another gulp, I swallow down the self-pity about how stressful my day has been, with so many meetings and my worry about the compromise of my illustrious intellect.

I am now the one who feels apologetic, for myself rather than for the ills of society. Now I feel the impact of the realization that becomes authentic apology for dragging the self-absorbed lament that had accompanied me into the taxi, when I first flagged him down and got in, into this man's only prized possession. His taxicab is no doubt his castle. I weakly offer up another apology.

Pulling up to the curb of my hotel, the driver shrinks in his seat just enough for me to notice the instantaneous change in his self-confidence, as the glass doors swing wide to the gracious, high-ceilinged, chandeliered lobby inside, and the way is cleared for me to enter a world far removed from my rough ride of circumstances and sharing of apologies. I am about to step into a world that clearly intimidates my taxicab driver. This is not a world that welcomes him or any Arab. And I'm sorry for that, too.

I have a handsome tip ready for the Arab youth, thinking that's the least I can do, upon realizing up close, that he too has been caught in the crossfire of fate, like the lady with the cracked-open head and the brave Israeli men of the bomb squad who may not finish out the night.

His pride is stronger than his obvious need, though, and he vehemently refuses to take my money, shaking his head and sitting up tall now. "Sorry for what happened," he says again, "Sorry," leaving the meaning of his comment trailing like the wake behind a speedboat that spreads out in a wide fan of effect all the way to a faraway shore of unknown possibilities.

And so we part company with mutual apologies for everything that a soul can be sorry for. Reaching for his eyes one more time, I shove a twenty dollar bill onto the console and take the hand of the doorman, who guides me like a prince guiding a princess out of the pumpkin carriage into the looming castle of a hotel, and into a glistening world just beyond the world of taxicab drivers and Arab boys.

Inside, under the bright lights of the lobby, I must look a bit ashen. The doorman, who knows me by name because I've been there for weeks this time, asks if everything is OK. "Yes," I muster, "Everything is OK, everything is fine, just a hard time getting through town, and there was another bomb scare or terrorist attack, you know. I guess we'll hear about it on the evening news. Looks like there was a good chance they got everybody out in time."

Unlocking the door of my white-walled room with the ever-so-pleasant pastel embellishments, I let the heavy door slam itself shut and stumble shaken into the plump and waiting chair next to the balcony windows. It's the kind of internal shaking that is not specific, a kind of short-circuiting of the nervous system that can't find a name for itself.

Wishing I could just disappear into the fat cushions, I am grateful for the simple sanctity of being alone with the heavy door shut between my flesh and the rest of the world. Looking toward the TV, I consider turning on the news, but think better of it and let the thought go. I've seen enough, no more, no more tonight. I guess I'd better pray that the power doesn't go out, that there aren't more bombs. On that very real and practical thought, I decide that I'd better clean up and take a shower while I can.

Taking a deep breath in an effort to calm my nerves, I gather the will to unwind from the jarring realities of the day. Dropping my head back in a confession of giving up, the demands of the ordinary and practical are vying now for the mind space of the extreme.

It seems the rites of the day have to play out and unwind on their own terms before I can return to myself. My joyride and personal face-off with my American ego and with the misfortune of the Arab boy is still oozing and washing over the rest of my life.

I conclude that this is exactly the kind of thing that I can't tell my father or anyone who loves me, those who in their well-meaning appraisal have already passed judgment that I'm "crazy" for coming here. And yet, the look on the taxi driver's face, the way he patted his car and apologized to a stranger for the mess that is so rudely beyond his youthful control, that he has no choice but to live in, day in and day out, has struck a chord. The chord is still vibrating, rushing inward into everything that I am.

I have been praying for answers all day, even as careful words tumbled upon my breath with articulate accuracy, skirting the unpleasant whenever possible. I sat at large shiny tables with aspiring politicians, psychologists, spiritual leaders, relief workers and activists. We were highly engaged in high thoughts and high ideals and the high ground of still trying to navigate the all but impossible.

In the midst of concrete decisions and conscious conversation and loud debates and an occasional pounding on the table, accentuated with a few rude departures, prayers tumbled from my mouth in silence. This wash of prayers known only to me, the sacred that runs through my life when I least expect it, is like a gentle stream of sweet honey. Prayers for every life… Prayers for every soul… Prayers, prayers and more prayers… Silent prayers that no one hears but me and hopefully the Divine to whom I cast my calling…

Today was an ordinary day in the midst of extraordinary circumstances. Today was a day of small victories and small defeats and a blood-rushing race through the back alleys of Jerusalem's Arab section. Sirens screamed just on the other side of the line that was drawn to warn all the people in a Jewish-owned public building to run for it. Like the galloping horses of the pharaoh thundering toward the Red Sea, everybody was running.

But my legs won't run any more. I contemplate what I would do if my hotel caught on fire or the loudspeakers in the hallways announced another bomb scare. I've already been evacuated myself once this week, as my security team herded us all away from glass windows that could come crashing down in an instant.

Weak-kneed and limp-limbed, I only have the strength to dribble prayers into the empty room where I sit alone and exhausted, prayers that move from this day and all the others, from the time I first set down in naive excitement at the airport in Tel Aviv over eight years ago. It has been a full day, more than full, full of challenges, full of the mundane and the unexpected.

The prayers are all I have, offered up in the fragile hope that the answers of the ages will still come, and that the remembrance that I have been waiting for will break open like a coconut giving sweet water to sailors who finally crawl to shore after having been lost in the undrinkable bitterness of haunting salt-laden waves.

Prayers, sweet honey, taxicab drivers, little boys grimacing, bomb scares... this is life in Jerusalem, this is my life, and this is my reason to remember what is essential and to reclaim myself each time that I forget.

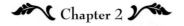

Chapter 2

Jerusalem

City of Promise, City of Tears

Sleeping, dreaming, waking... past, present, future... hope and futility... These are the thoughts that linger on the landscape of troubled slumber as I open my eyes to another day in Jerusalem. It is just after 5:00 a.m. and the fragile beauty of the dawn sky has begun to spread an ancient red hue over the emerging silhouette of the Old City.

Here I am once again, returned to this place of whispered secrets that carry the wisdom of the ages and screaming sirens that inevitably follow yet another bombing. Here I am once again, all too familiar with the tossing and turning of a sleepless night.

Jerusalem might as well be dubbed the city of supreme paradox, the stealer of sleep, the thief in the night, and the gateway to both heaven and hell. I know for myself from what I have experienced here that she is a holy, heavenly place, remarkable in every way and beyond compare. I also know that there are days when she exists as if all holiness has been extinguished, every time violence breaks out and riddles the air with machine gun fire.

It is indeed a paradox when priests and rabbis and sheikhs must stay indoors out of fear for their lives, hiding from the world in their respective sanctuaries. Lethal weapons do not distinguish between the holy and the unholy on the really bad days when the tide of revenge spills over its banks and floods the Old City with terror and tears.

If she is indeed the heavenly and holy place that I surely know her to be, then she often masquerades as a decidedly hellish place of perpetual conflict, struggle and grief. Her beauty is as complex and beyond words as her wretched problems of strife are beyond definition. There are families who have lived in and among these shifting sands of fate for generations. They continue to carry the banner of a crest of family surnames like Levi, David, Benjamin and Dan, and Hussein, Rahman and Assad.

They are the heirs and masters of this land. They live by a different set of rules, sniffing the air for the threat of impending calamity, rather than watching the weather for approaching storm clouds.

If more than the usual number of soldiers gather on the street corners, this could mean the word is out, that expectations are high and an unspoken red alert is flashing. Like frightened animals running from a forest fire, people rush home to nervously wait out the inevitable. In this place, the Holy Land, the possibility of trouble and annihilation is more likely than not these days.

Outside my hotel windows a tentative broadcast of early morning light is drawing the darkness of the night into itself molecule by molecule. Pondering the question of her fickle identity, I wonder if the first tender glimmers of dawn can tell us what we will witness by day's end. I read in the news yesterday that Jerusalem is now considered the most dangerous city in the world. Over half of Palestinian children are suffering from serious levels of malnutrition. Statistics tell us that 65% of Israeli adolescents are suffering from posttraumatic shock syndrome, and yet the polls tell us that 65% of the people want peace in the region. And I would guess that these numbers will be in a sharp increase in the days to come.

It is as though two personalities are vying for control of a single body, as if some kind of fate-laden battle between good and evil is playing out a royal drama of even more than Biblical proportions. This battle for religious supremacy, for land and limb, for control of the past and possession of the future, for goodness taken or severity given, is an embroiled and titanic waging of life and death. Little does the average person, who perhaps lives halfway around the world from here, know of the heavy weight that this place can and very likely will bring to bear on his own precious life. I shudder and sit bolt upright in my bed to regain my hold on my own existence.

In a rapid assessment, I glance around my hotel room just to register my surroundings. I notice that a subtle but familiar sweetness is wafting in through the window. The horrific weight of old wounds and bitter resentment is seemingly absent in the fragrance of the honeysuckle flowers that wrap around the balcony a few feet from where I sit.

Their existence is an unnoticed paradox when helicopters beat angry wings above sleeping villages and slice any semblance of peace to shreds, and the loveliness of honeysuckle is lost and forgotten in the clamoring rage of opposing forces.

Today these clusters of tiny flowers bravely offer a salutation of intoxicating balm to regional events, no matter what the outcome of the swinging pendulum. It is as if they are willing to blend their unconditional goodness with all manner of smoke or stench that might rise in their midst, unchanged and uncompromised in their slender, white-petaled beauty.

If goodness could weep for itself, it surely would each time that it is forgotten, forgotten in the most terrible way, forgotten on the edge of annihilation. Like an endangered species, goodness may be nearing extinction in a place where goodness was said to be born, and born again.

On my last trip here we were evacuated from our rooms twice in a single day. During these bomb threats, as whistling sirens, loud speakers and police walkie-talkies surrounded us in a panicked and confused emergency; our security guards rushed us to the concrete floors of the lower level, below the ground floor of the hotel. My first evacuation took place some time before that, when the US and Israel jointly walked out of the summit on human values in South Africa. In response to this, Arab and Palestinian sentiment was explosive as their plight continued to take a backseat in western political ideology. Their suffering was not quite important enough, all suffering not quite important enough, including the suffering of Jews.

Since then, it seems, hope has been meager and feebly holding on, if at all. Life in the Holy Land, on both sides, has all but fallen into complete dysfunction. Like many days since then, the days just after the walkout in South Africa were days of sporadic rage, and being here in the midst of it was an eye-opener for me, setting the tone for future trips here.

The Hezbolla bombed an array of targets and the Israeli choppers quickly hammered down on suspected perpetrators, strike for strike, hit for hit. Soldiers across the street from where we stood wrestled a suicide bomber to the ground, de-bombing him with only a whisper to spare, de-bombing, de-fusing, and disarming a young boy gone mad.

It's gotten so even I can smell the eerie foulness of imminent attack in the air. I remember watching television one evening after a particularly exhausting day of organizing the details of our first peace conference in Jerusalem, when the big fighter birds gathered ominously in the sky like vengeful vultures, and began to spew streaks of blazing booming gun power into an Arab settlement nearby.

I knew the bombs were not headed my way, as I watched the flash of exploding lives billow upward upon impact, as vicious decisions and beliefs and claims clashed for survival. But I knew someone's life was being annihilated, someone who would be missed and mourned.

Being only a few miles away from the display of victory and destruction, I had only to decide whether I should watch the drama outside my window or the drama of a news report about the conflict on television. There wasn't much difference visually, but you could smell the hatred floating in the air, falling on the olive trees like snow coming down in a blizzard.

The volatile environment outside crept up on the television screen that I was watching with the acute and cutting edge of the cold-hearted calculation of military maneuvers, of strategy and strikes, sending waves of fear and bewilderment through my heart with a visceral intensity that even the television, no matter how graphic, could never hope to duplicate.

People across the globe have grown numb watching violence on television, especially the never-ending saga playing out between Israelis and Palestinians, unless it happens to be their own backyards going up in flames. But I was far from numb and this was as close as it gets to my backyard.

The experience of bombs and death, up close and personal, that moment, that ticking of the clock, was one of the life-changing events when the mind and the body fought for control. The sound of the bombs roared through me from head to toe. Gasping in short darting breaths, an instantaneous panic set in like a deer frozen in the headlights, while my mind watched, meekly murmuring that there was nothing to fear, nothing I could do.

After a while, who knows how long, I returned to myself to register that I was still staring blankly at the television set as fighter choppers roared off into the heaven-bound sunset, having achieved their mission, having played out a stealthy game of predator against prey. Two hours later, the whole thing repeated itself on the evening news, and I got to watch it again like a spectator at a sports event, only I had already felt and smelled and tasted and shuddered at the atrocity in action.

Watching precision-coded fighter choppers, that were more than likely made in the US, belch streaks of death-laden fire power into old mud brick villages was hard on the heart and the nerves and the whole of my body. The ancient little city of Jericho, as an example, is reputed to be over 10,000 years old, and most sites of destruction are also hundreds and hundreds of years old.

I sat there shaking, even though I knew at a mental level that my hotel was not the target. The Israelis were after a terrorist leader, someone who spurred on the killing of innocents in the name of no other alternative than the revival of the spiritual warrior extraordinaire. There probably hasn't been this much fervor in "religious warriordom" since the Middle Ages. And yet my experience of angst and frozen terror is pale and shallow when compared to those who lose loved ones, those who lose limbs, those who lose their lives.

Putting that day in a hard matter-of-fact perspective, I turn to the present, to the day that lies ahead that must be navigated to avoid trouble, to avoid the unavoidable. With an effort of breath and gaze, I reach beyond draping honeysuckle vines to seek solace from the Old City's graceful spires and golden-domed rooftops that reach skyward in the gentle dimness of daybreak.

She is nectar to the weary. She is soothing to the eye. Jerusalem's medieval visage never fails to mesmerize her onlookers. I stare in awe at this spectacle of beauty that remains beautiful despite everything, and the tears just come.

Sadness and longing for a long-held promise that has yet to reveal itself nags at the edges of my desire not to care and not to be so affected. Jerusalem holds me in her grip, it seems, and I know with an absolute sense of inescapable destiny that there is no point in trying to break free. The feeling of hope and futility from before has begun to swell in my throat, as I bear witness to the emerging outline of the famous stone rampart wall that encircles the Old City, the wall that refuses to give in, and vows never to give up or give way.

I can't help but break down and weep as an internal need to wail in utter grief takes over. This inner sense of collective wailing is larger than my own life and drowns out any anger, any rage that is left, because this place, this ageless beauty, Jerusalem, is so dear to me that I can't bear to see such sacredness become the object of the worst of human traits.

The burdens of thousands of years seem to haunt me and add weight to my soul, as if there was a single answer to be found, and if I were to find it, beauty would survive. Jerusalem would be the world treasure that she is, sparkling high above infantile insanity as if the dark side of the human mind and heart never existed and never even dreamed of anything other than pure beauty in the form of a sanctified city of peace. A single answer haunts and seduces and holds in an indefinable silence, the answer to all questions and the promise of all futures. But there I stand in the thick of it, seeking the illusive.

Pulling myself together, drying my eyes with my nightgown and stacking emotions like towels on a shelf, I notice that enough light has broken through the edge of darkness to illumine the procession of ageless stone that holds Jerusalem in its solid embrace. Stone walls, golden domes, massive archways, turrets and towers are her special beauty. I am reminded, and profoundly so, that she is nothing less than a fine aged wine to the most studied palate, the Mona Lisa to an artist's eye and celestial honey to the soul.

Even though the sun is not yet visible on the horizon, it is casting delicate fingers through the great stone archway that rises above the wall not far from my hotel like a monolith of history. Even though a dull, aching angst continues to rise and fall on my breath like the tides pulling at the shoreline, this gateway to the past always enraptures me, as if it knowingly extends a mystical invitation with my name on it to enter into a nether world of phenomenal, matter-defying, immortal proclaiming of holy sites and antiquity.

Its arched expanse is oddly familiar, as if I have some kind of one-on-one intimacy with each enduring slab of limestone that links the present with the past and streaks across empty space to protect what is secreted inside.

The old archway that looms in full view just beyond my balcony is called the Jaffa Gate, because the road that empties itself at the gate's entrance has made the winding journey through the arid desert hills that ramble all the way to the ancient seaport of Jaffa, lying south of Tel Aviv. Jaffa is the oldest of all the seaports along that stretch of the Mediterranean. The harbor town is still a charming fishing village most of the time. It was named after Japheth, son of the Biblical Noah, in the tradition of Noah's Ark, and the finding of land at long last, after being tossed and turned in the flooding deluge that became an endless sea.

It was Japheth who stood by Noah's side as he first spotted the white dove with an olive branch in its beak and the rainbow that cast its arched beauty across the sky to herald the promised shore of a new future. Arcing on the horizon, the celebrated rainbow was beheld as a sign from above.

The metaphor goes well beyond the Biblical story of surviving the Great Flood for forty days and forty nights in a wooden ark, while the entire world in its previous form was said to have been swallowed by the wrath of rising waters. Like the ark, the dove, the olive branch, and the lineage of Noah, the Jaffa Gate stands proud of its origin.

The self-possessed arch to the ageless serves as the portal for what was once a dust-embedded dirt road, now a paved, smooth, white-striped modern highway, that has brought generations upon generations from the edge of the sea to the defining perimeter of the Old City, and continues to do so now. Each eager pilgrim, weary traveler, or stressed-out taxicab driver who has ever reached the unspoken authority of the shadowed archway of this massive stone gate, shares the commonality of having passed through a time shield or a spiritual portal that is beyond common comprehension.

Towering above the road and the Old City wall like a loyal sentinel, the gate looks and feels immensely substantial and formidable. It easily conveys its jurisdiction as a sort of silent record keeper of all the human lives that moved through its outstretched arms to define the inner sanctum.

From my vantage point on the balcony, I feel such smallness, as if I were nothing more than a lost speck of dust watching the Old City wall make its indelible mark on the future. The wall is a defining edifice that Jerusalem depends upon, and visitors marvel at. Its mere existence having been built and rebuilt over thousands of years is an invincible statement that surrounds what has survived for all the world to see. I stare transfixed, looking on from my meager little vantage, and ponder the humanity that engaged itself in the mighty wall making.

An image of the sun-browned hands that once built each stretch and turn of the rising rock edifice flashes across my mind's eye. The backs that had bent over in aching labor reflect off its chiseled surface. I imagine what it must have been like in the days of King David and envision the tenacious human strength that lifted the huge newly cut blocks of limestone into their places, next to the ones that already waited for a place in history that no one can deny, even now. So many rulers have shaped the wall to their purposes and liking.

So I tell you, this rampart wall is not just any wall. It is a wall that surrounds the microcosm of Old Jerusalem, countless lives, bloodlines, reigns and kingdoms, an unparalleled human drama that as yet has no conclusion. It is a wall that has been built and built again many times over, to encircle the pageants of the ages in this magical yet perplexing place.

The wall has taken shape, and has expanded under the command of many rulers, but the enormous blocks of stone have ever been the same silent dutiful servants of the power at hand. The shared humanity that spilled itself in triumph and defeat alike, as walls were raised in unabashed jubilation or brought down in bitter anguish and searing defeat, has always been the same.

Some of the slabs that hold the memory of passing empires are over forty feet in length. They lie in wedged overlapping layers deep beneath the surface of present-day Jerusalem, like soul mates dreaming in eternal slumber. Layers upon layers of the sifting sand of past generations have settled into cracks of time, in an organic coexistence with the immovable rock behemoths that endure as an archive of human experience. If only the wall that watched the coming of conquerors and the ascent of holy men could speak and tell the stories that are imbedded within its stony hold.

I imagine that each and every limestone block is like a numbered vault that carries within its girth a finite point in time that defined the people who lived and died here. Perhaps it is a willing repository of solid stone, archive and record keeper to the minute occurrences of everyday life that continue to unfold within its unyielding circumference, interwoven with the twists and turns of past ages, the tales of which have found their way into our ancestral holy books and sacred scrolls. It defiantly holds Jerusalem in a time warp, like a great and impenetrable force field that stands between the silted flood plains of the past and the solid ground of what is yet to come.

The wall has eight monolithic gates in all that have ushered wide-eyed and hopeful visitors from around the world into its interior of intrigue. With names like the

Lion's Gate, the Damascus Gate, the Dung Gate, each one conveys a sense of this place and its roots of origin. Each gate can hold its own in terms of historical significance, and can boast of having arched over the heads of kings, prophets, saviors and conquerors.

One of the most revered of the gates is named the Golden Gate or the Mercy Gate. This one has always won out over the others for my attention, as if it, too, has a story to tell of long-lost secrets and faraway futures. It has great double arches, which have remained sealed shut for hundreds of years, to be opened, according to prophecy, only at the appointed time of the return of the long-awaited Messiah of the Judaic faith. Many evangelical Christians believe this prophecy too.

I can tell you from what I have carefully observed, that once a soul enters the confines of the old rampart wall, he has not just entered an ancient city of historical heritage, he has entered an otherworldly realm. He has entered a living deity with a mind of her own. For everyone who comes here, the impact changes their lives forever. It is one of those places that defy all the normal laws of relativity.

Jerusalem is a mighty vortex, an absolute reality of reckoning that both separates and joins heaven and earth, while at the same time holding court to the judgment of souls, one by one. Coming here takes you beyond yourself and turns you inside out. There is no way of escaping it.

I have often seen people stop dead in their tracks, weeping openly in the narrow, cobbled streets, overcome with a moving power that cannot be defined. Tourists and clergy alike collapse in remorse and shake with ecstasy. Hearts are opened and souls are cleansed, as tears flow like floodwaters breaking over the edge of a dam of pent-up longing. Our collective humanity seems to spill and empty itself here without restraint.

Some beg for favors for loved ones in the torment of their suffering, as the edifices of historic shrines loom overhead. Their prayers are written with love, with hope, and oftentimes with fear on scraps of paper folded, twisted tight, and wedged into any remaining crack in the Western Wall, a remnant of the Temple of Solomon.

Just to be there where countless prayers have expressed the longing of humanity made me weep, so I took to going to the Wall in the middle of the night, alone with my own tears and my own tiny pieces of paper, given to the stone keepers of ancient promises.

But I am an onlooker, a non-Jew and a foreigner. I watch as dark eyes, both Arab and Jew, watch back, resenting that I am here. Some welcome me, hold my hand and shed their own tears just to witness mine, knowing they pour from the same heartbreak and grief of human anguish. Some wail and lament their personal condition. Others give their hearts to their creator in unabashed and sincere dedication, like cosmic virgins being sacrificed to the solar power of fiery suns.

Brides dressed in long white veils join together in procession before the Western Wall, flowers in their hair, watched over by machine-gunned soldiers. It is a coveted tradition to be married at the Wall, but even brides must be protected from the enemy on their wedding day. Getting married in Jerusalem is a holy thing, auspicious for the betrothed couple, and equally dangerous.

It is common to witness people breaking down in open view, in fits of raw emotion that are normally confined to private moments of deep personal rendering behind closed doors. In fact, in years past when Jerusalem was filled with the faithful, this kind of display was a daily occurrence. The locals who live among the numerous holy sites appear to have grown accustomed to seeing grown men in business suits, soldiers with machine guns slung over their shoulders and camera-clad tourists drop to their knees in unabashed reverence, sometimes weeping and wailing and overcome.

It makes no difference what walk of life the visitors to the Old City come from, whether they are young brides or elderly grandmothers, or what country or nation they call home. The amazing native-born, who live in and among this religious clamor, seem to nod inwardly at the procession of pilgrims who come here, all the while going on about their lives as if nothing out of the ordinary is taking place.

This scenario reminds me of emergency medical workers who have no choice but to get used to blood and trauma. In a similar vein, the natives and local people of this land bear the spiritual phenomena as just more clouds in the sky, even as they too seek an auspicious sign among the wisps and billows that might speak of deity speaking to its human counterpoint. This is a place where thousands seek revelation or at least some small token of divine favor.

Seekers searching for a pristine point of return or a glorious moment of spiritual immersion come from all directions, like countless streams converging into a single body of omnipresent holy water. They come from Asia and Europe and South America. They come from everywhere.

The scattered lost tribes return here like prodigal sons and daughters coming home to the hearth of their early days. Even now, with the entire region in turmoil and groups of tense and watchful Israeli soldiers standing posted at every street corner, you will still see a few brave souls inexplicably drawn to the spiritual experiences that are so profound here.

Several years ago, I observed a group of perhaps a hundred Muslims and Hindus dressed in white robes paying homage at the site where Jesus was crucified. They were rendered speechless and weak-kneed as they approached the rock where Jesus is said to have been laid, a rock that is now surrounded, protected and sanctified by the mammoth walls of the Church of the Holy Sepulcher.

Many of my own major life revelations have cracked open, wide gaping and grateful, while sitting side by side with the holiness of this extraordinary treasure house. My own knees were made weak. My head felt a holy presence, and knew it for certain.

It was as if the churches, holy springs and gardens, mosques, synagogues and winding walkways that channel through this microcosm, had each had a hand in turning the key to setting free deep places inside my psyche. Some of these experiences left me humbled and shaking. Some left me feeling lightheaded and overwhelmed. Some were simply an intellectual comprehension. All were essential to who I am now.

And so it is that pilgrims from around the world make the journey of a lifetime to the Old City. Many souls return again and again. I am one of those who keep returning, drawn like a lemming to the sea. Jerusalem never quite lets you go, once you have walked through the gates of the ancient wall that has conquered time.

Stubborn, awesome and frightening is this seeming obstinacy that holds Jerusalem to the tethers of the past in a way that controls the present with a ruthless insistence.

It seems that there is no future here that will ever be allowed without first resolving every last particle, every single atom of betrayal and heartache, every drop of spilled blood.

It is as though Moses himself is demanding retribution with a determination that is far beyond the power wielded when he bade the Red Sea to part as a demonstration of the Almighty Will of God.

The conflict of who "rules" this city has been constant and tragic from generation to generation. Each king, ruler, tribe, religion and nation has claimed the right of ownership. It could almost be said that the parched skin of the desert land that surrounds Jerusalem has traditionally received more moisture from human blood than from rainfall.

More recently, new bloodshed has mixed with the spending of the old, especially since the Palestinian "intifada" first cried out in avid protest of the defiant agenda of the new regime of the old war general, Ariel Sharon. Beloved to some, feared by others and hated by the Palestinians, he sees the protection of Israel as his moral obligation, his soul mission and his career duty all rolled into one absolute noble agenda or angry vendetta.

Who knows? I for one will not judge him. The scope of it all is just too much to gather in and analyze. Only God knows the heart of this man, or any man, woman or child. To the shock of many world leaders and the delight of some, Sharon, either unthinkingly on the one hand or strategically on the other, made his stand at the holy site of the famous Temple Mount, inciting Palestinian wrath and right-wing Israeli support and jubilation simultaneously. All the while the world looked on.

I can't say which is true. I am in no position to surmise whether he innocently claimed his birthright to the resounding agreement of his compatriots, the "chosen people," or whether he instead deliberately shook his fist at the enemy to rub salt in the wounds of the disinherited. I can't even begin to say. There's been enough judgment and analysis to fill the Sea of Galilee until it curdles, stews and simmers.

One thing is for sure: he chose one of the most revered as well as one of the most conflicted spots on this earth to give a press release. Surrounded by TV cameras, he stood on the same holy ground as all the revered ones who had come before him, taking a stand and carrying out a twist of fate that has yet to subside. The Temple Mount is hotly disputed and vehemently coveted, with both sides claiming it as their true and rightful due from none other than the God above all Gods.

In the days of old, the clouds had parted and the heavens had opened in the skies above this site of the Temple Mount again and again. This same profundity is true of almost all of the holy sites in Jerusalem, Israel and Palestine. There's hardly a rock or the withered remains of an olive tree stump that doesn't claim fame and fortune as something that can be clutched to the breasts of possessive, zealous or otherwise impassioned onlookers, stewards or pilgrims.

The shrouds of past prophets are draped everywhere. The religious significance of so many of the sacred sites is woven together like a tightly bound weft and warp of a single blanket. The Word of God has combed the wool and dyed the fibers.

It is almost too much holiness for any blanket-clad shoulder, people or religion to bear. The colors that run the blanket's length count the twelve tribes of origin, along with famous battles between mighty armies, and between a giant and a mere boy, as young David slew Goliath on behalf of a grateful King Saul.

How could David have known that a slingshot and a stone would ignite a destiny that would cause the people to exalt him, or that he would be persecuted soon afterward, by the jealous King Saul, the patriarch in power who would torment David with a vengeance? How could he have imagined exaltation becoming life threatening? He would flee for his life across the sands of the Sinai, growing stronger in the fleeing. Saul's armies remained hot on his trail for several years, which ironically taught him the art of outsmarting Saul's best generals.

And yet they reunited in the bond of the heart eternal when David spared Saul at Ein Gedi. This is a tale of compassion and mystery when David found Saul asleep in a cave and slew him not, but rather left his cherished sword lying by the sleeping Saul. This same sword had been given by Saul to young David, to demonstrate his domain and his surrender. It was a royal coup of regal and kingly dimensions and many implications. Not long after the incident at Ein Gedi, David wore the crown as King of the Tribes of Israel.

The cave where Saul and David surrendered to one another in the bond of a higher calling, all of Ein Gedi which overlooks the Dead Sea and the site of many historical references from Jerusalem to Jericho, is considered sacred by some. Sacred sites like this one mark the births of Biblical reference and kingly assignment, the blanket that covers hill and dale.

The more striking tints and hues draw the memory of thousands to the luster of the Holy Land. It is woven into a cultural casting out of the sinful or unwanted, and the sin-filled slaying of innocents still swaddled in their mother's milk. These pungent shadings of human theatrics drape the bowed heads of present-day thinking and hang tightly around the necks of the faithful.

The once-sharp lines of contrasting color and distinctive pattern defined kings and kingdoms, great and small. Old patterns of warp and weft have begun to fade and soften over the centuries, as past archenemies have gathered together in shocking new alliances.

Where once upon a time, the Romans conquered, raped and pillaged; now the Pope from present-day Rome visits with a VIP escort and with considerable pomp and circumstance, and has even been known to apologize for past rampages through the Holy Land on the part of Christianity and the Church.

It all goes back too far to sort it out by means of conventional thinking. The Holy Land plays every possible role, adorning herself as she sees fit; queen one day, slave the next. Sometimes this blanket of God's people takes the form of the royal robes of high office, sometimes the humble sackcloth that changed the world. She is ever a coat of many colors, a single soul, and a single bloodline, woven from the lives of all the weavers, whose hands and mouths and eyes and ears shaped the future of their offspring, envisioning a future known only in the highest places of divine knowledge.

With this flow of thoughts, I look out over the still-sleeping city and I worry that the very fabric of reality here is pulled with such a taut and terrible tension, a terrible and demanding tension, that the blanket of origin, woven from the birthright of all souls, may very well be so torn to shreds as to be unrecognizable.

What then of the children who will be left with nothing but frayed fragments falling through the space between outstretched fingers? This is no ordinary blanket, despite its tattered edges, strained threads and blood-soaked fibers.

It is a magnificent altar cloth that adorns the throne of life in this part of the world. Jerusalem sits at the center of this vortex of paradoxes, the heir apparent to the throne, the altar itself.

The eyes of hopeful children burn with the memory of the robes that once shawled the shoulders of the saints, taking shape at the very Mount where spirit descended into matter. What then of this landscape of tribes and peoples, and its dreams and promises, its tapestry of miracles and beauty? Who or what will bring the dove of peace to rest upon the shoulders of the innocent, the brave, the faithful and the young?

From what I have seen, it will take more, far more, than ordinary solutions to resolve such an extraordinary set of circumstances. The chaotic hand of conflict and the ruthless rage of revenge cannot begin to salvage the sacred that has been betrayed here of its own accord by mysterious lessons meted out at its own expense.

Platitudes cannot be traded for recriminations. It will surely take a supernatural, divine genius of some kind. It will take the awesome hand of divine providence to bring peace to Jerusalem, to lift her up to her own holiness.

Surely she has earned divine intervention of some kind, given all that she has endured throughout the ages, all that she has endured at the hands of saints and soldiers, all that she has endured... all that she has endured...

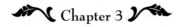

Chapter 3

The Past

Land of Milk, Land of Honey

Still sitting propped upright in a mass of tangled sheets and weary pillows, with the questions of the ages exchanging glances, I gaze out through the floor-to-ceiling glass doors of my hotel room. In the dim light that surrounds me, they seem like crystal clear windows to the Old City's soul. Beyond them the sunrise continues its waxing generosity of light.

I glance at the clock on the bedside table and register the fact that I have been immersed in thought for over an hour. It's headed toward 6:00 o'clock, and the first pale colors of the sky have begun to deepen into bright golds and ruby reds on the horizon.

The skyline silhouette of rooftops, turrets and towers has grown more vivid as the Old City rises from beneath the long night just passed, a night that for me has been spent tossing in an eerie unrest of fast-turning thoughts and unsettled emotions.

Still feeling bedraggled rather than lifted up, I continue to watch the fragility of dawn grow into the bold strength of a clear morning, one of the clearest in a while, as present-day Jerusalem bravely takes her stand beneath a commanding sky the color of pomegranates, oranges and lemons. I think to myself that I am witnessing the colors of heaven meeting the colors of earth, and take a small measure of comfort, a tiny but acknowledged upliftment. I peer more intently at the emerging images that I could almost touch, if only they would stand still long enough to be truly seen.

Once again I am sorting out the past, sifting through fine sand, paging through swatches of past recollection, accounting for who said what and who begot whom, searching for bits of lost evidence like a detective trying to solve a murder mystery or like an archaeologist carefully examining every fragment.

This type of meandering through the vaults of recorded history has occupied a considerable chunk of my time of late, sometimes to the point of embarrassed distraction. I've spent years studying the accepted archives of the Bible and Qur'an and Torah, as well as keeping an open mind and ear to the mystic archives that offer the stories and legends that color the pages of history with humanity's dreams and visions and versions.

But the early morning hours are a good time for reflection, I tell myself. Maybe I will discover a crack or a fissure, a crevice that has gone unnoticed, a pot shard or sun-bleached bone that has found its way to the surface of things, some shred of something that will give way to a revelation of spilling secrets. Maybe I will find the answers to elusive questions, as if a soul can put a finger on a single, solitary issue, or illusion, or person that in the end will sum up the past and the future in one infinite brush stroke of inevitability.

This desire is as sincere as my heartbeat to find the key to the overwhelming largeness of the problems here, as if a root cause at planetary levels of significance can be found. At the same time to do something useful, even a single meaningful contribution that offers a little hope, is the practical intention that motivates each day's efforts.

I, like many, feel personally compelled or assigned to be involved in the resolution of conflict here, a rather absurd and even self-aggrandizing thought, even if the intentions are large in humility. Can I find a path of effective action and wise contribution of my time and effort?

It is as if a tug-of-war is going on inside between the mysterious magnetic attraction that I have to the whole mess here, and the very logical point of view that sees no earthly reason why I should have any such involvement or concern with it whatsoever. For years logic has presented an, "After all, this is someone else's problem. It's a cultural, political, religious problem going on halfway around the world, far removed from my comfortable life in America," type of rhetoric chattering behind the struggle of this work. But for the past year or so, now that more and more people are finding it difficult to deny or ignore the problems in this part of the world that affect us all, this rhetoric, this excuse of supposed logic, has lost its voice.

Very clearly, the problem here concerns everyone. It is everyone's story and everyone's problem. And yet, who am I to think that I, an outsider, could in any way influence what so many great minds have already striven to understand? I repeat to myself the obvious, that for centuries a long succession of noble attempts have failed to unify the warring factions. This fact of history precedes my meager glimmers of do-gooding intention. Even the legendary reigns of King David and King Solomon and other rulers and conquerors who achieved some semblance of unity among the Tribes of Israel were short-lived in the grand sweep of things.

Despite all this, despite the blistering obvious, a stubborn hope with a definite mind of its own stirs itself into a determined response. It rises up and brushes itself off before the dust of doubt and despair has even settled to the ground. It runs on automatic whenever the logic of conventional thinking begins to circumvent the search for the Lost Tribes of Israel and their secrets.

The project plan of peace among nations and tribes and peace workers takes form. The fundraising efforts continue. My small story echoes off the walls of the big story, even when I am awash in the scrutiny of my own doubt. Even though there are moments when I am convinced that I am the fool of mythical dreams and unproved sagas, that I am standing on nothing solid, that there is no Mount of Olives under my feet, that there is no dove of peace flying into rainbows above my head, that there is no hope this morning because I had a bad night.

The voice of hope emerges from the dusty debris to take a venerable stand all its own, calling with an insistent, "Don't give up, don't let go, look deeper, find the way, find the key, open the door. The ultimate answer to the ultimate question will be found."

I am caught in the glamour of questing, it seems, as the turning of the mind and the hunger of the heart rise like formless mists from a primordial swamp of history books and intuitive surmise, as if the longing for truth is the single ingredient that can surmount the barriers of grief and darkness and bring the life-giving waters of knowledge to the thirsty. The mists refuse to die. I cannot deny them if I am to have even a few moments of peace, peace and well-being, our collective and rightful longing. Somehow, somehow... there must be some answers, clean and far-reaching, that can shed light on this ragged and wretched reality of warring tribes and opposing religions; the quarrel between them, as old as time itself.

This 4,000-year-old saga that holds me spellbound began, or at least was marked in the religious history of the prophets, when Abraham and Sarah, the mother and father of the renowned Tribes of Israel, first embarked upon their journey through a formidable expanse of desert rubble, to seek an unknown but "promised land" of milk and honey. They hailed from the legendary Ur where their future already seemed sure and prosperous.

As with all historical accounts, who really knows the true circumstances that unfolded? All the "what if's" and "how's" and "why's" feed my mind with the desire to understand the human experience and essential elements that may have influenced their personal story and its effect on future generations. My intuitive thoughts may very well fly in the face of accepted belief, but something strong inside calls me to listen with the wisdom of the heart to the subtle voices of the past that gather in response to my litany of questions.

What moved them in the early days of their historic betrothal to leave behind a comfortable ascent to vast wealth and power? What caused them to leave their given lives of prominence in the lap of relative luxury, such as it was in their day? Sarah, the youngest daughter of a well-loved King, ruler of Ur, respected by even the rulers of faraway Egypt; Sarah, a fair and exceptional beauty, the virgin daughter, purity incarnate, who had already been promised to the Temples of the Goddess to live a life of celibacy.

And Abraham, the eldest son of the only living priest whose bloodline poured directly from Noah, who was himself one of the last remaining priests from a previously great and noble lineage to have survived the Great Flood. Some consider that ancient priesthood to have hailed from the lost civilization of Atlantis, and this rings a bell for me internally. Abraham's own father was such a powerful figure in the esoteric traditions that he exacted awe from those in the highest of places. Abraham, who had been promised to the priesthood since his birth, was by blood the son of an initiate and was thus a link to the archives of wisdom of origin.

What caused Abraham and Sarah not only to marry but also to strike out on a grueling march through brutally arid and hostile terrain? What inspired them to leave behind a familiar landscape and loved ones who grieved their departure to initiate a journey that would bring so much hardship, a hardship that has yet to end, but has affected the lives of souls for over 4,000 years? What rhyme or reason did they follow? What vision or compulsion drove them out of such a Garden of Eden and into the jaws of jackals, ruthless pharaohs and endless desert tribulations that bore only the hard-shelled fruit of hardship?

Were not the swelling hillsides and pregnant valleys of Mesopotamia a jewel beyond compare, already full of promise? Was Ur not a rich and civilized kingdom, whose bountiful harvests stretched on the horizon like sparkling gems on a royal crown? The echo of their reasons seems to be laden with some sort of otherworldly force that is beyond all possible human grasp. These same and similar questions have been asked in every possible formulation since the very first steps of Abraham and Sarah directed their destiny west of the Euphrates Valley and the rich delta of Ur.

For the hundredth time this week, I muster the now feeble question, "What influence could I possibly have on a situation of such mysterious and studied magnitude?" The question timidly tumbles from my mind, never reaching my mouth, as conventional thinking loses the wind in its sails, and I grow inspired just to fathom the possibilities of the whys and wherefores of the lives of Sarah and Abraham and their unfinished legacy that has been the subject of the Bible and the Torah and the Qur'an alike.

I am intrigued indeed, and gathered up into the pages of their larger-than-life drama as mother and father of a nation, as husband and wife who were subject to displays and demonstrations of divine dispensation. I would be happy to wrap myself in the prayer shawl of Abraham's reverent prophecy, and drink in the stories of Sarah's grandmothers, sitting raptly at the feet of her wisdom as she dispensed the untold stories that the scribes of holy books could never know.

Meanwhile, in the 21st century, we gather, march, meet, rally and convene on all sides of society, on all sides of the conflict, whether debates are held in parliament or around kitchen tables. Here in the Middle East, here in Jerusalem especially, one must get used to the fact that the past arrogantly, seductively lingers in the air.

One must also accept that the keys held by the past are as yet hidden from practical, modern view. They will not be handed out to just anyone. The keys are as sacred and golden as they are hidden. It is as though the secrets buried deep within the problems of the Middle East are like a primordial guardian of sorts for the world, at least for the part of the world that is at risk of moving too fast into the future.

From the point of view of the average Arab citizen, the Western world is running like a frothed and panting out-of-control racehorse gone wild to an unknown finish line. From the average Arab's point of view, if there is such a thing as an average point of view, the Western world is full of flaws and bad manners. From the devout Islamic mind, and probably the true believer of the Christian and Hebrew minds as well, one's word is one's honor, if one is true to the Islamic faith. The Western world is like a fickle maiden that glances from suitor to suitor, making promises to anyone who will allow military bases or some such to be built in their midst.

The unchanging lofty heights of Mount Sinai, where Moses received the Ten Commandments, look on with wisdom from their motionless vantage, having the essential pieces of the past firmly in their knowing grasp. At the top of the mountain is the memory of a pillar of light and a fiery blessing that blessed the prophet Moses. It still burns with the truth of the ages and the solar heat of unseen stars, shedding light on all things present, all things past, and all things future without condition or haste. It burns unseen to the eye of mortals. It burns yet and forever to the eye of the deep seer. It is the grand knower of all things that must be known. And it is calmly biding its time of reckoning. Such is the stronghold of the secrets of the Holy Land.

Those of us who are caught here in the demand of the modern Israeli-Palestinian drama are still looking for passage through the desert, as if we are reenacting the 40 years of wandering, as if we are still praying for manna to feed our empty bellies and nourish our weary souls. We are caught in a dangerously intoxicating dilemma. We are strangely eager captives, despite our lament that so little of what goes on here makes any sense whatsoever.

Most of us suffer a sense of powerlessness in the face of stone walls and demons and political agendas that are rooted in the fine line between the survival of the fittest and the outright unforgivable. Peace workers, humanitarians, feminists and relief aid workers alike are at the mercy of the shrewd seductress of unsolved mysteries and dilemmas. We are drawn into this ancient fray like half-starved children, hungry for forbidden candy. We are shown just enough to inspire the noble search, to put crumbs on the trail and carrots in front of our noses.

And yet the keys to the past must be found and very surely will be found. I am sure of this. Such is the convincing hold of this place on the vulnerable soul. Such is the work of the unseen power within the wedded questions of eternity and finite reason, and the surreal reality of Israeli school children who have gas masks handed out at class like pencils and crayons. Inspiration in the face of this insanity bolts from the starting block like a lean Olympic runner, running the race that will open new doors or shut them forever.

Maybe my work here, my purpose, is of a different nature than I had originally thought. Perhaps there is something more that I am destined to undertake than merely a humanitarian stand in the midst of crumbling convention. Perhaps there is a secret code to be broken or a puzzle to be solved or a mystical formula to abstract.

There is an unknown thing here that reaches back into time like a passionate lover grasping for dear life to save a beloved from drowning, awakening an ancient desire to retrace the steps from origin to now. In my smallness, an even smaller light, so tiny as to be barely perceivable, beckons. But is it light? It seems so, so dim, so faint in the onset of a gaze, but yes, it is recognizable as light. And which way does it cast its knowing glance or affirmative nod?

Hope endures even here, carrying the spark of the prophet, the heat of the bush that burned with the vision of Exodus, the pillar that carved the Word of God into stone tablets, and the Fire of the fiery worlds into the ugly pall of daily bombings that may very well build sufficiently upon itself to smite not only the enemy but also all life on the face of the Earth.

Nuclear threats have become commonplace in recent months, hurled casually back and forth across the breakfast tables of negotiating nations like the posturing of old married couples vying to gain advantage. Countries are locked head-on in a vain and unwinnable power struggle that is spreading to the underdog worldwide. My body doesn't like these threats. My hands want to cover my ears. My eyes want to squeeze shut.

I feel like a fragile child, forced to endure the piercing bitterness of a failed marriage that suffers from its own self-inflicted toxic environment, except that all humanity is the victim of the failed marriage of nations. Their refusal, ignorance or inability to get along and coexist and get on with the wedding march down the aisle to peace and prosperity is the shared grief of all humanity. Sadly, there is nowhere for the innocent child to go, nowhere to hide, as the fight outside the wedding chapel continues and spills in pandemonium out into the street, nowhere on earth. The threats of impending annihilation permeate the very walls of existence.

Perpetrators and innocents may very well be partners in eternity, bonded through a shared apocalypse. Even the child's angst and anger at this inexcusable indecency is extinguished in the grief that mourns the possible death of a future, any future. But even drenched in gloom, the holy spark of life struggles to sustain its light.

Cold winds stalk the heat of origin, and wolves pant at the heels of the last remaining innocent lamb. In some distant reality, I am the child who collapses into numbness, but I am also the child who is called by the whisper of angels. "Look little one," they say, "open your eyes, it is there. You can find it, but you must look with the eyes of the heart. The wolves are shadows that stalk the fears of humanity, but the true human spirit cannot be touched by wolves. You must look with the eyes of the heart."

Sometimes I feel split in half by the schizophrenic nature of Jerusalem, the epicenter of dispute, even though neighboring countries vie for attention by rattling their sabers of dirty bombs, chemical agents and other such means of immense destruction. The little guy is thumbing his nose at the authority of dominant nations with increasing boldness. Like flashes of history on fast forward, I mark in a tidy succession the events, which presumably led to all the controversy of our present-day turmoil. How did we get from holy visions to gang warfare on an international scale?

Back to the Sarah and Abraham story, the Christian Bible records the time when the patriarch Abraham had laid his son Isaac upon a large slab of rock at the top of what is now the famed and fought-over Temple Mount. There he surrendered to a higher calling than his own human heart, willing to sacrifice his very flesh and blood. To lay down the life of his beloved son Isaac unto the Lord's almighty Will was a pivotal moment in all religions, it seems to me.

Perhaps through his obedience, Abraham set into motion a new order, a new pillar of light connecting to a higher world. Perhaps his perseverance and surrender to God was the first seed of a New Jerusalem. Perhaps the age-old tradition of animal sacrifice was turned on its heel and uplifted by his purity of heart. Perhaps he fulfilled the ultimate test and on that spot christened a place in the future, perhaps far distant from now, that would one day usher in a new purity between the human soul and its creator. Perhaps, he simply returned to the Will of God as it was in the Beginning.

With a soft hand lightly on my heart and hanging onto that thought with newfound brightness, I wonder about the far-reaching arm of cosmic influence. Maybe, just maybe, that noble act on Abraham's part had set into motion the higher and greater expanse of the concept of sacrifice, elevating the seemingly punitive need for a sacrificial lamb to new and unimagined heights of the altruistic giving of one's self to the greater good of the whole.

For example, perhaps the once noble sacrifices of soldiers on the battlefield could be made in a new light altogether, the nobility of sacrifice for one's own family and country taking on a new form, shape and meaning that embraces the whole of the world. Perhaps an ultimate supreme sacrifice would be extracted as the price for peace, one that is neither animal nor human.

I surmise in my pondering that indeed the greatest sacrifice for many would be their beliefs, especially those who shut out the rest of the world before the particulars of religion, materialistic pride, and the politics that lead to the shady dealings of big business and big money. And in the headlines of the *Jerusalem Post,* the death toll is still rising on both sides with each lofty surmise that passes through my thoughts.

Perhaps such a sacrifice cannot be imagined from our present-day viewpoint, but will in the end become crystal clear, perfectly plausible, and knowingly as obvious as wind and rain in springtime when its day and season have come. Perhaps nobility and a happy ending would go hand in hand, like a bride and bridegroom leaving the altar after exchanging vows, or the soldier who turns his sword into a plowshare. Surely anyone can see, even the most stubbornly, righteously angry on both sides of the conflict, that there can be no land of milk and honey without the nectar and holy ground of peace.

There are many human stories that comprise the story of humanity's walk in this region of the world. Bearing equal due in the historic succession of things significant and phenomenal about the Temple Mount of Jerusalem, which began with angels and fathers and sons, is the tradition of Muhammad, the Islamic prophet and messenger of God, who received revelations that became the holy scriptures of the Qur'an.

The story Muhammad tells us of his ascension with Archangel Gabriel through the heavenly realms to the Throne of God, Himself. This gave birth to a Muslim nation that has grown to populate the world with more than a billion believers. In a feat of coincidence that vies for complexity with the best of all reason, Muhammad's ascension to heaven is said to have taken place while standing upon the very same rock that had served as Abraham's sacrificial altar.

Built on this site some 1300 years ago, the Dome of the Rock is an exalted mosque for the Muslim world and stands in majestic prominence against the skyline of the Old City. It rises like the shining swell of a gold-cast bubble, a turquoise jewel of mosaic architectural brilliance, a shining gateway to the face of the prophet Muhammad.

Sometimes flashes of blazing light reflect from its round-domed presence like spiritual electricity. I've seen it with my own eyes. I've felt the white-light fire of it. Its reflective expanse looms for all of Jerusalem to see, rising from the very same spot where Abraham's prayers lifted him into the grace of God, where King David composed his psalms, where the songs of Solomon proclaimed the completion of the first temple, where the illumined Muhammad gave his body and soul to the higher realms, where Jesus taught the multitudes.

If there ever was a Rock of the Ages, the Temple Mount is it. This rock is not just a rock. It is a bridge to the Word and the Light and bears the imprint of hallowed footsteps. And this is also the revered site, a mere few feet from the dome, which is likewise claimed by the Jewish faith as the home of homes for their faith, the sweet earth that is their personal and chosen due.

Defining its borders is the famed and cherished, debated and fought over Western Wall that has drawn untold thousands, and more likely millions, to its cherished side. The Wall, as the locals call it, is the last remaining remnant of the sanctified Temple of Solomon. The Wall still stands today, as a symbol of the enduring presence of God and His promises.

The same is true of the nearby Church of the Holy Sepulcher, built on the site where Jesus is said to have been crucified. This church is the mother of all churches, and it too beams a radiance throughout the Old City of Jerusalem that cannot be denied. It too draws countless souls to its exquisite artistry, architecture and inner sanctum of spiritual power.

I myself was barely able to walk away on my own two feet when I entered the sepulcher where Jesus was laid. I was overcome with the presence of love and staggered beneath the weight of it, tears running down my face much to my surprise. These sacred sites are potent; all of them, and from my own experience the cause or source of spiritual power does not favor one tradition more than the other.

The sites of Hebrew, Islamic and Christian impact radiate with a presence that can be felt whether or not a visitor is a Jew or a Muslim or a Christian. These sites draw the long march of souls to the sand that they sit on, to the breast of Mother Jerusalem. The spiritually-bent flock takes in these sites according to its calling, with reverence or irreverence, depending on the religious affiliation that is assigned by those who look on and judge, as if they were descendants of Herod, turning their thumbs up or down in response to the clock of cultural belief.

Footsteps, whether soft barefooted impressions in the sand or the gouges left by proud combat boots, are driven by some kind of incredible conviction, indefinable compulsion and spiritual emotion. Warriors and peacekeepers live in the same skin.

Some karmic-bound souls have been stationed here for a lifetime, and eat their breakfast with a view to the Temple Mount, the Western Wall and the Church of the Holy Sepulcher day in and day out. Some were born here, having been placed in the midst of this powerful whirlpool by the benevolent and mysterious hand of God. Others have been drawn here, just as soon as an unreasonable reason could prevail to magnetize their young and impressionable hearts to this place of paradoxes, to live out their lives and raise their families.

Jews come from around the world. Pilgrims come from every nation. Palestinians come from where they are and always have been, trying to stay; while others long to go, if they could only get out. Some people come and go, but always return, like myself. Some have received their call only recently; they have just arrived, luggage in hand, hopes still basking in the longing of idealism of some kind or another, whether peacekeeper or defiant land settler. Some arrive with strong convictions and have dug their heels in for the long haul, bringing their past with them, and dropping it like bundles of firewood at the altar of an eternal flame.

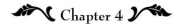

Chapter 4

The Citadel

Fortress of Faith, Fortress of Antiquity

Finally rising from my own version of a rumpled, war-torn battlefield, I lift myself out of bed decidedly on my own strength of will. Glancing at the cluttered dinner tray left over from the night before, I reluctantly note there is no radiant presence or pillar of light or holy making phenomenon anywhere to be found in this room. There are only ordinary remnants of the past week, a non-stop ordinary week of too much to do and ever more that could and should be done.

Mildly grumbling at the lack of either ascending or descending forces in my life of late, I gather myself and with determined effort shove open the oversized glass doors to the balcony, and step out into the kind of brightness that is rare in other parts of the world, but common to these arid desert hills dotted with limestone homes and settlements that shine like scattered pearls, spreading out in all directions. Squinting from such intensity of light, I sweep in the vista and breath deeply, letting the smell of coffee brewing, bread baking, and flowers in clay pots strike chords of normalcy.

Ironically, I am on the seventeenth floor of a modern hotel overlooking the famed Citadel or Tower of David, a major landmark of Jerusalem, known for its rather imposing guard tower that rises above everything in its midst. The brightness, coexisting with fat white clouds, has gained a firm claim on the mid-horizon, as a visual grace bestows itself on this formidable fortress that replicates the palace that once housed, in relative luxury, the privileged court of King David's wives, priests and counselors. An old fortress, a duplicate of what was or could have been, has become a commanding presence among the antiquities and edifices that still yield and shudder from the hands that built and destroyed them. Some remain; some were built again and again.

A break in the clouds has made way for several rays of light to shine like spotlights on the main tower, a massive statement in stone that enjoys an undefeated prominence that has overlooked the surrounding visage for centuries, as if to say, "This Citadel is hereby anointed with the light of the ages and the promise of the future."

Maybe this is a sign that positive forces abound after all, although I quickly reason with the fact that the fortress was originally built to ward off aggressors from foreign lands and protect the virtue of the fair city. Now, in modern times, the Citadel is a stately edifice that holds within its walls and watch towers many, many sagas of love lost and love won, intrigue, conquest and surrender.

Inside this wind-worn reminder of a time long past, is an exquisitely orchestrated museum, one of the most intelligently designed that I have ever seen. The Citadel houses the progression of the history of Jerusalem in a display of artifacts and miniature replicas that capture tourists and academics alike into its web of political and religious epics, the two being mixed together like blood brothers. An impressive visual of the coming and going of victors and their spoils, and the plight of victims and their losses, the museum is a masterpiece.

60

At the heart of the museum is the Temple of Solomon, exquisitely rendered, just as it once stood in all its splendor as the protector of the Ark of the Covenant. Seeing the temple in miniature brought all the larger-than-life accounts of the House of David into a physical replica of believable fact, a firm foundation of non-fiction in solid white marble.

In an eerie sort of way, in a profound sort of way, the temple might as well have been a super-magnet, as I found myself back in front of it again and again. Every time I wandered off to explore a different decade or century, I would wind my way back through the corridors of the museum, to the room where the temple was displayed, as if my footsteps were being directed by the temple itself. I was literally mesmerized. It had some kind of spiritual power over me, this tiny reflection of what the past might have been.

Taken by the mystical properties of this House of God, this sanctuary of stone, this exalted chamber for the Holy of Holies, I was awakened to its soul. In my mind's eye, I could see all that had been planned from the beginning, and all that had been hoped for and all that had risen and fallen. It was as though I had held the divine plan for the temple in my own hands.

I could feel the smooth texture of papyrus scrolls and I could see the brown-stained ink of the architectural renderings. I could also see the lives that brought the temple into being and the visions of the faithful and favored, as spiritual genius flowed from the heart of God into the minds of men, to awaken the memory of an ancient oath like the revelation of sacred water from a desert wellspring that remembered to gurgle and gush to the surface.

I could feel King David's passion pouring through the psalms as he lamented for aid and protection, calling forth to the heavens for divine intervention to smite his enemies and cause his people to love him. David longed to serve even as he longed to conquer, control and stay in power. I could feel his anointed brow turned upward in supplication, even as he plotted and schemed and summoned the power to slay and indeed smite his enemy.

I could feel his ecstasy when he brought the Ark of the Covenant into Jerusalem, dancing before it, stripped of his kingly robes. Half naked, somewhere in-between holy priest and God-intoxicated madman, his life teetered in an identity crisis for much of his reign. To fancy one's self as king and warrior, judge and ruler, priest and oracle tipped the scales of what any soul could expect to balance. I could feel his fanatically honest heart solemnly making a promise to build a temple from the vast spoils of his victories, the wrath of the divine favors, and the weight of his gold coming to rest where it truly belonged.

I could feel the faithfulness of Solomon's proud promises to his father, David, and the straining of the flesh that pulled prayers and promises asunder in the lives of both father and son, the tales of wine and women, betrothal and betrayal surviving the centuries. I could feel the ruthless taking of power, and the bonds of lonely hearts obsessed with their objects of affection, as well as their desire to be loved and to trust at least one single person among the thousands who prostrated before them.

I could feel ever so strongly, Solomon's purity of commitment and nobility of purpose during all the years that construction was underway, and all the years that the white marble laid out its claim on what is now the Temple Mount, and all the years of both favor and rebellion that marked Solomon's reign.

A ten minute walk from the Citadel, are the remnants of the Wall that once protected the Temple of Solomon which still stand in the Old City center. This Wall of all walls rises in proud and unending testament of the golden days when all the tribes came to Jerusalem under the as yet dreamed of Star of David, and swore with swollen hearts that they would always give her their all, their allegiance and their lives if need be. How often did the crowds gather, roar and cheer when the King and his army stepped high through the massive arched gates of the old city wall, victorious.

It is well known that the reign of father and son was one of the greatest and one of the longest, eighty years and more, and stretched from Egypt to the Orontes River, of modern day Syria and Turkey. David and Solomon, both of them wedded to celestial visions and beautiful, beguiling women, both of them anointed with the burdens and rapture of the throne. The House of David was said in the writings of scripture to be granted blessings from above that few mortals have enjoyed. The prophets of the day gave testament that God had proclaimed that the descendants of King David would be blessed with divine favor. "And thine house and thy kingdom shall be established for ever before thee: thy throne shall be established for ever." II Samuel, 7:16

I remember staring at the details of the museum temple model as if transfixed; losing all track of time, until the museum's guards politely asked me to be on my way, as it was closing time. I remember having to gather myself, tugging at my far-flung imagination, like bringing a resistant child in from the playground of its dreams.

I wanted to stay there, to become miniature myself, to lose myself in the halls and gardens of the temple, to pray in its sacred chambers, and write psalms in its cool clean innermost corridors. I wanted to feel the cold smooth marble under my feet at midnight as the altar lamps were lit.

I wanted to command the weight of warm, golden vessels filled with the oil of olives that made my hands holy at dawn. I wanted to stand in the scorching, uncompromising, high noon sun and read aloud the scriptures that proclaimed the advent of heaven on earth. I wanted to remember everything that Solomon had promised to David and everything that David had promised to God, and everything that God had promised to the House of David.

I haven't visited the Tower of David Museum for several years now, and so I make the mental note to go there in the near future. Perhaps if I walk in the rock-walled gardens or stroll through the rooms of the miniature realities, some significant piece of the past will be jiggled loose and find its way home to my heart. For weeks I have been meditating, contemplating and obsessing about my purpose here in Jerusalem, while my days are filled with the tasks of organizing my small contribution to the peace effort.

I am hosting another peace symposium in less than a week, which will bring together people from all walks of life: peace makers, academics, politicians, UN representatives, spiritual leaders, women activists, and humanitarians for an active dialogue and three days of presentations and discourses. It is a conference of hope and remembrance, and of networking possible alliances among like-minded groups and leaders.

It's the least I can do. For my small part, I am sometimes overwhelmed with how difficult it is to organize something as simple as a three-day talk, not an easy feat in this part of the world, and all the while in the back of my mind I remember what the colossal effort of raising a temple from barren sand must have required.

Shafts of light continue to move across the walls and towers of the Citadel, in the interplay of fleeting moments that shadow the canyons of time, and play hide and seek with an elusive past and even more uncertain future. Each morning since I have arrived I have been caught in a spinning wheel, repetitively turning over spent thinking and empty questions, lost of answers. I have to admit that more often than not my pondering is as deeply distraught as it is inspired.

All the while, day after day, the Citadel stands as an immovable witness. The invincible fortress looks on in noble silence, as I add my pained and musing thoughts to that of the innumerable minds that have engaged the continual give and take of power, which cycles through this land like the inevitable changing of the seasons. The Tower beckons above all the clamor of honking taxies and the vendors and hawkers that are desperate to sell olive wood rosaries, hand embroidered yarmulkes, and plastic toy camels to tourists who have all but become extinct, because the Holy City and Holy Land are dangerous places to be.

Tit for tat... the exchange of accusations between the Palestinians and the Israelis goes round and round. Ambassadors from the world's nations are assembled here in constant challenge. I have had my share of meetings and lunches and tea and coffee with a good many of them, and the one thing they all have in common is that they are bone tired and on the verge of collapse. It's a tough job just to be here; exasperating. The embassies have become their home away from home. Due to the likelihood of danger their wives and children cannot be with them, so they work here alone, going back to empty apartments and hotel rooms at the end of the day.

Their wives and children could otherwise enjoy one of the most richly imbued treasure chests imaginable. They could be waiting after the workday was over to offer some kind of normality to the lives of foreign diplomats who are fathers and husbands. But the workday is never over, the meetings stretch to midnight. Wives and children are forbidden to come, even though Jerusalem is considered to be one of the wonders of the world that travel guides feature in highlighted claims. They could even visit the Tower of David Museum as a family if things were different, if wives and children could risk being here.

But I still thank God for all the shrines and historic landmarks that grace this city, looming in stubborn defiance above all the heartbreak, violence and insanity. The tower of the Citadel has become a comforting fixture that I look to as a sign of stability in an otherwise highly unstable situation. These are places where God is said to have smiled down upon the innocent, given strength to the righteous and uplifted the faithful with His own mighty hand. They are the enduring redeemers for those of us who seek some shred of solace from this place while we burn the candle of our mental and emotional strength at both ends.

It is amazing that any remnant or replica of the House of David still exists after three thousand years of human clamor and confusion, or that his place of burial could be identified or speculated about. It's amazing that the garden walls of the old Citadel are still standing, even if it solely exists upon the pages of prophecy and written account.

With this thought, I make more of an effort to drink in the luminous beams that are still washing over the massive bulk of the Citadel. Perhaps it will be a morning to remember, this morning of exceptional and unexpected light; perhaps it will be a day full of promise after all. Taking several more full-lunged breaths, the air of Jerusalem is like nectar. If only the "war of religions," of conflict, of modern circumstances can be silenced in my mind.

The air is clear, the breath is sweet. On an empty morning stomach I summon my culinary imagination and can almost taste the savory breakfast stew that was once prepared for the favored guards of King David's elite army, those who were willing to give their lives in an instant to protect the King, his assets and his fair city. In this spacious moment the worlds are overlaid, one upon another.

An ancient atmosphere remains tangible, drifting through the eternal ethers from a distant sunrise that spread its glory upon the landscape several thousand years ago. I can smell the aroma of simmering lamb and onions hanging in the air, even though the twenty-first century that I live in is the defining reality.

There is loud clanging and doorbells buzzing from the hallway of my hotel as waiters begin to bring breakfast to hungry guests. Modern life surrounds the lingering echo of the iron stew pot of the king's kitchen with a surreal backdrop that doesn't quite measure up with the richness of a palace repast. I imagine that I can feel the pride of the soldiers who ate like kings themselves because the King loved them, loved their loyalty and knew only too well that his own survival rested in their hands, just as much as theirs rested in his.

The intertwining of fate was, no doubt, the unspoken bond of the soul in those days. Sweet savory stew for the first meal of the day: only the best for the king's personal guard, a small price to pay for the laying down of the flesh in the name of loyalty and allegiance. These were the days when Jerusalem was first carved out of the surrounding rock hillsides, an arid and primitive place trying to be civilized, as new walls rose up from the desert dust to usher in the plans of ambition. Kings and priests collaborated and convened in secret alliances that would become the tales of mystic lore.

Yes, Jerusalem is a queen of destiny, born of an anointing oil endowed with powerful spiritual properties and mythic proportions. Yes, she will endure all things and will remain the virgin bride of a new beginning for all the world to behold. I believe this or cling to this hope on the days that are especially difficult.

I think King David knew that her life would be long and rich with a profound future as he set about the task of building his citadel. I think he knew this during the long stretch of his prosperous and fateful reign. I think he knew it even in the sorrow of his last days, many years later as he lay old, spent and feeble on his deathbed. He knew that she would prevail. Yes, I am sure he did. He knew this as his life lived on after his death, to become a living legend that has been handed down through the generations, even in foreign faraway places that he never knew or even dreamed about.

I am deeply relieved to take in this moment of visual sacred landscape, to forget my self-important angst and myself. Seeing things from a newly minted perspective, I admit that the gentle breeze that is wafting through my hair and rustling the bougainvillea that shade the balcony is a thing of God, a blessing that can lift me up if I allow it. The sweetness of simple pleasures, like the beautiful vista of the Old City skyline, manages to coax a smile that speaks of holding on.

I am being granted a precious moment of reprieve after a dreadful night, my long and soulful dawn-breaking cry that cleared the cobwebs, so that I can face the day and muster the resolve just to be here. Even though I can feel the sting of red swollen eyes, I have no difficulty seeing that Jerusalem is indeed a sight to behold, a fair beauty of incomparable charm, anointed, like David, with an ancient promise that sheds the life-giving essence of the ambers, reds, and roses of a womb-like fertility, and strength enough to slay giants in the Valley of Elah. If David as a sixteen-year-old boy could slay the seasoned warrior Goliath who was twice his size, then maybe there is hope for us all to defeat our self-created odds.

Our next symposium will be held at a location with a view to history, overlooking the battlegrounds and valley bottoms of legends. The expansive windows of the conference room where we'll be meeting look out over the very site where David stood tall in victory over the Philistines. As I hold onto the hope of also beating the odds, great odds, I am thankful that the rasping sounds of emergency sirens are not tearing at the web of Jerusalem's heart this morning, to defy the miracles of legend.

This is the first morning in a long time that dawn has graced the city outside my balcony without the wailing cry of ambulances and rescue teams rushing through the streets below to yet another tragedy of human crisis. Still she clings to her promise and, despite all that she has witnessed and endured, she remains a rare and breathtaking beauty. Of all the cities in the world, Jerusalem is the fairest of the fair, even though she has become pitted and defiled with the scars of bombsites.

On the ride from the airport in Tel Aviv to Jerusalem, when I first arrived for this trip several weeks ago, the driver of my shuttle van pointed out all the latest destruction as though he was pointing out tourist attractions. He pointed and shook his head, marking the locations once identifiable as restaurants, homes, market places, plazas or businesses that now remain partially standing, if at all, like lonely hulks no longer able to hold themselves up.

He gestured every so often at roped-off gutted storefronts that stare faceless onto the street, or places once thriving with children and shoppers, now virtually empty and deserted or leveled to a flattened pile of rubble. Each time I come here from America, I am a witness to a landscape that must survive being battered on a daily basis. Lives and buildings, hopes and dreams have been shattered, over and over again. The pain runs deep within these scars. Nothing is safe. Nothing is sacred. The bombs and tanks have become masters of the land.

There is a sense of unspeakable sacrifice that the people have endured here. It doesn't matter whether the ancestry is Christian or Druze or Jew or Arab or an ancestry I've yet to consider. The word "endure" seems to be rising to the forefront of my thoughts, as if an important message is pulsing beneath the surface of circumstances. Endure. But how can you ask young children to endure lying terrified in their beds at night? How can you live with babies and infants being fitted with gas masks not long after they are born, in the hopes that their little lungs can elude bio-chemical warfare?

I recall my efforts to hold back tears of emotion at a peace symposium that I orchestrated in Jerusalem a few years ago. I couldn't exactly fall apart in my foreign shock, as I was host to the succession of speakers. Watching the haunting images of Arab children fleeing for their lives as Israeli tanks rolled into their villages, I sat frozen and stunned in my seat, desperately tying to control the urge to well up and sob. Meanwhile as the host of the symposium, the one who must stand on the stage and speak into a microphone to introduce the next speaker, I battled for ground. I fought hard, gritting my jaw tight to hold back my own sobs of anguish, just to contain myself and not break down completely.

The slides and photos were part of a presentation of a well-respected professor of psychology from the Tel Aviv University, who had done a study on the dreams of Arab and Israeli children. He had attended the symposium as a featured speaker. His study had documented the lives and dreams of the region's children, who endure the daily bombardment of a hostile war-torn society.

The piercing images were forever imprinted on my mind, when one photo frame after another had flashed the unforgettable faces of mere babes on the stage screen. His presentation was so vivid, so incredibly heart-wrenching. The unheard screams of the innocent sent shock waves and tidal waves into the auditorium; waves that crashed headlong into hearts that wept.

Still standing on the balcony and holding my gaze steady on the Citadel, a flood of new images claims my attention, coming out of recent violence nearby. A child is running through the streets, running for his young and expendable life, as a military tank looms on the horizon, a hulking shadow that engulfs his small frame of a body. Another small child is bent over her dying mother. As she squats by the woman's limp and lifeless side, her tiny feet

71

are swimming in a pool of her own mother's spent blood. The look on her face cannot be described with words that I have ever seen or heard.

Another child, a little boy standing alone in a market-place, holds his hands to his ears in an automatic response to the explosion of a suicide bomber. A baby stroller is lying on its side next to him. The baby, very likely his little sister, is gone. He is standing there shocked out of his skin, frozen in a nightmare he will never comprehend.

As I witnessed gasps and shudders move through the audience, this image comes to me as if to say, as if to scream and roar, "Something must be done. Something must be done. No matter how much you doubt what you are able to do to make a difference, something must be done. This cannot be allowed to go on!"

The psychologist from Tel Aviv had spent his adult life specializing in the science of the mental and emotional well-being of children. I'm sure he never dreamed during the years that it took to earn his Ph.D. that he would be doing studies on destroyed villages, grieving families and the anguish of an entire nation's children less than a hundred years after the holocaust. His study was a visual story that should go down in history, side by side with the holy books of the future. It was a plea for compassion from all the world's citizens to stop the terror of children.

What faces, what expressions. The photos of Israeli children were frozen with the same horrific terror in the aftermath of suicide bombings as the shocked Arab faces of the small souls who picked through the rubble of their bulldozed homes for the bodies of family members or tiny remnants of their destroyed lives.

If only this video could be shown to the US Senate, the United Nations, the politicians of the Israeli Knesset, and the Palestinian Authority, instead of being limited to a peace symposium of already sympathetic viewers. I make a mark in my mind with a wide sweep of will, to see what I can do to get the video into the political arena, where it most needs to be seen. Maybe then sanity would prevail. Who could witness these images of innocence turned to horror and not feel remorse of some kind? We as adults stand responsible, every one of us, especially those of us who live in the wealth and privilege of the very same countries that wheel and deal in the name of American interests that give license to twisting truth to fit our greed like a glove.

Even someone who was obsessed with their own self-importance would have to be swayed by these freeze-frames of wounded and horrific moments in a child's life that prove, without a question or doubt, the criminality of our present planetary approach to our shared birthright. All but the most hardened of hearts would have to respond and think twice, I tell myself.

It's time that all adults from privileged countries snap out of the complacency of privilege and make it their business, their personal business, to find out why our planetary politics is allowed to make huge mistakes that undermine life for all of us, while lawmakers in so many countries look the other way. How often are modern interests a façade for the financial advantage of the very few? It's time we hold ourselves accountable for the way we do business around the world. Neither a single child nor our entire planet can endure our irresponsibility much longer. No child should be expected to endure this, no matter the cause. No child, anywhere.

Endure... with the decision in place to get this video shown in political circles, a new strength finds itself within

my heart, the piercing from before finally eases and I notice something unusual. It's been quiet all morning. As this
occurs to me, the gentle quiet washes over me like a welcome balm. The silence is a soothing Godsend.

Today, the transition between night and day is unbroken. Light has blessed the Citadel. Dawn has come as a
simple testimony of new potential. Today all the normal
sounds of a city waking up can join in with the innocent
chirping of the songbirds that scamper in the olive trees. I
pray that there will be no need for sirens and ambulances
today. I pray that today can be a peaceful day. I pray to
remember everything that is given to me to remember.

O, Ancient of Days that lives in my blood, I ask that
you find me. In this moment I am standing still. The Tower
of David is tall on the horizon in testament to a clear bright
morning. I turn my thoughts to the hand of goodness and
give myself over to that enduring grace. Remembrance. I
am in God's hands. What will be, will be. With renewed
conviction, it is time to start the day, surmise and assumption, musing and pondering, visions and prayers running
alongside the mundane.

Chapter 5

The Call

Voice of the Profound, Voice of the Ordinary

As the bustle of modern life weaves in and out among walls and gates and towers, I find even the traffic and honking horns comforting. The schoolyard across the street has filled with the motion of children arriving for their classes, and the usual bustle of kids doing their best to be kids, even though they live in the midst of warring nations. There is a tenseness and an air of caution not normal to kids. Everyone is doing their best to maintain normality in the everyday stream of things, even though life is far from normal in this part of the world.

Polarity is the law of the land, the ruler of opposites and opposition. Opinion holds opposing views, usually at 180°. Ask any two people what happened in a given incident and you will surely get two different stories. My own story is a story of polarities as well, serious and profound on the one side, and laughably far-fetched on the other.

Today, taking the humorous side of how I got here, and what moved me to keep returning, helps to keep things in perspective. I think in the large sweep of things, God, too, must have a sense of humor. Getting dressed and stacking all of my papers into my day bag in one sweeping motion, I conclude that the chain of events that has led to the past week would indeed sound on the edge of the ridiculous or absurd to most people. I myself see the almost comical nature of it, a saga that defies the confines of convention.

Humor in the midst of the profound and even the tragic is a good thing, a thing of wisdom, lightness and survival. Sometimes the sacred and the profane, the ridiculous and the profound wrap around each other like twin vines. They make good companions and bring balance to the tendency to get carried away with an exaggerated sense of self-importance, or a depressing sense of doom, or whatever else seems to be the uncontrollable and inevitable.

But we cherish those life-changing, world-altering, cause-creating, religion-generating moments when all things are possible, when the very gates of heaven, glowing and golden in their majesty, are flung wide open to reveal the essential and the pure, perhaps even the seemingly far-fetched. In our desire for joy and bliss, we also seek those moments of reason when we are brought to our knees, weeping at the revelation of truth.

We couldn't live without ample doses of the extreme moving through the collective human mind from time to time. All the great prophets and great minds from Jesus to Einstein were initially viewed with suspicion. But it cannot be denied that when the profound is unleashing itself upon the ordinary, it is as though the wellspring of origin, of life, of God, of heaven, of word, of The Word has broken free from its high place above and beyond all things and, in its freedom from sanctity, descends like a riptide upon the unsuspecting. The unsuspecting, the blinded, who thirst after having thirsted for an eon of agonizing, dreadful thirst, who are gathered up into a virtual bliss of unlimited horizons and the nectar of bountiful, sweet revelation, become the prophets of profundity.

Gandhi reclaimed India from imperialist Great Britain wearing a loincloth, using his humility and sense of absolute truth as his only weapon. He was known to show up in London for meetings with heads of state with his milk goat in tow, tethered with a handmade rope.

And we all know the story of Moses and how he brought the great Pharaoh to his knees with the Will of God and the locusts and plagues that shook the ground under the feet of slaves and aristocracy alike. We have all stood in the wake of the desert wanderer, Abraham, who became the mercy and example of extraordinary faith that seekers still seek 4,000 years later.

"I Have a Dream" and "We Shall Overcome" became the battle cries and public prayers of Martin Luther King, who fought for human rights in America to become the roaring crashing tsunami, which changed the course of history, and maybe more than that. It doesn't matter that the wave is five hundred feet tall and is headed for the shore like a thousand freight trains, churning and foaming, racing and lunging at the speed of light. Revelations are worth every drop of blood or sweat that is given to them.

It doesn't matter that sacrifices will be made, that lives will be changed and uprooted, that nations will tremble, or that the mothers of nations will cry. Only nectar, sweet nectar, blissful nectar exists when the wellspring of revelation is unleashed. It has no other face. It is the "great cause" speaking to us humans in the language of the all-powerful origin that seeks its reflection of effect. The effect of heaven upon the unsuspecting is the cause of new creation, and new creation is the thing of promise.

This unleashing of heaven upon earth is what we live for, and is what we need now in gigantic doses. As we flirt and cower at the thought of this war of oil and religions, a dangerous mix of motivations holding us all in its grip, we need the profound in a very big way to set us straight.

I for one would prefer the trumpets of angels to blood and guts. I am calling and praying and calling and praying for revelation, not just for myself, but for us all. Many would give their lives for a single moment of genuine revelation and the promise that breaks upon the hallowed dawn of all tomorrows.

Just ask Jesus and Buddha and Gandhi, and be sure to ask Muhammad, and the many modern day prophets like Mother Teresa or Nelson Mandela. Any doubt that was cast upon them was outlived by the larger-than-life effect that followed the glory of their visions. I'm sure all great souls would tell you of the struggle and the sacrifices that they endured, and yet "the call" moved through them and shaped their destiny.

When the angels fan their wings in our direction, all the "what ifs" of human imagination are purged from the surface of longing, and from the subconscious, and even from the unconscious, and deeper yet. There, in an infinite timelessness and an unspeakable wide-eyed trembling awe, all the ifs and maybes and hopes and dreams of divine ideal are answered with a greatness of affirmation that is undeniable and yet also beyond definition. Revelation is the great call for greatness. The angels gladly fan with golden wings for the occasion.

But alas, I have found that as the profound draws back into its holy place of origin, back into the mysterious cosmic wave from whence it came, the ordinary quickly leaps forward to claim the day, sometimes ruthlessly. It is as if the ordinary concrete of accepted convention of societal belief is a jealous lover, who plots and schemes to be the fairest in the land, filling every available waking moment with its self-assumed grandiosity. A swift and fatal grabbing of innocence lashes the recipient of otherworldly light into submission, like monstrous talons appearing out of nowhere to steal a newborn lamb from its bleating mother.

Do not rock the boat. Do not tell the truth. This is the voice of societal convention, of the chains that bind the human spirit, which great souls break free from but then suffer the effect when the truth is indeed told. Where does the profound go after the benefits of revelation subside? Where are the once-glowing gates of heaven? Revelation is always destined to have a rendezvous with the concrete walls and barbed wire fences of the everyday. But when we persevere, when we hold the vision, when we overcome, revelation gives us the power to break free and move in a new direction.

One has to see the humor in this atrocity, this cosmic practical joke. Even I, after a wretchedly hard night and a good cry, feel a solidly hardy laugh rumbling head-on into the mixed bag of full-grinning pleasure and unabashed skepticism that have taken up partnership before my feet have so much as touched the floor this morning.

I shake my head just to recall the seeming insanity that alternates between reverence and what might be described as a complete loss of control. Once the profound rolls back into the deep, deep sea, or the high heavens, or the golden cosmic dust of its origin, it's hard to tell whether human reality ever touched the hem of the robe of its golden, swelling majesty or not. Or whether you have only been the victim of an overactive imagination or are intoxicated by some kind of idealism.

But the truth is... There were moments in my life when I touched the hem of the robe: more than once. I am sure of it. These have marked me with a dusting of indelible gold. They swept my life clean, if only for a few precious moments. That is why I continue to search, and perhaps even bore you with sunrise and sunset commentary. That is why I watch the sunrise for hours for even the faintest of clues or traces. That is why I post myself before the sunset, like a sharp-eyed eagle looking for tender morsels of faith.

Setting out on foot, I decide to leave earlier than usual today and walk the distance between my hotel and the place where I have an appointment to meet with a diverse group of scholars, conventional thinkers, and esoteric thinkers, both Arabs and Jews who live in the Old City. Ironically, the centuries-old building where I'm headed sits squarely on top of the dividing line between the Muslim Quarter and the Jewish Quarter of the Old City. Half of it faces out over the Islamic stronghold and half of it faces out over the Jewish stronghold.

I allow myself a leisurely pace, passing through the cool expanse of the Jaffa Gate and turning right and winding past the stately Citadel and the Church of the Last Supper, I make my way, comforted that these places have become familiar to me. Heading in the direction of the Academy, I weave my way through the Armenian sector and the old Roman Cardo, past kids going to school and mothers beating rugs and preparing for the day. So far so good: all has begun and remained calm.

Walking along the rampart wall, the old wall that defines and contains the past, I drag my hand on its surface for reassurance, and take a moment to climb up where I can get a good view, pausing to rest and collect myself.

It is a perfect morning weather wise, not too hot and not too cool, a miracle of non-polarity, although as the sun heads toward noon, the desert heat will raise the temperature to extremes once again.

As I look out over historical ruins of white toppled stone blocks and pillars of once grand buildings and the black asphalt byways of modern life below, I search for memories and the inspiration of some long lost truth. I can't seem to stop looking for any shred of evidence or clue. I can see numerous Biblical sacred sites from where I'm standing. This vantage point of abundant antiquities is common in Jerusalem.

I search for the promise that lives in the blood of all the tribes, and the footsteps that later became Christian, Jew or Muslim. I search for the golden treasure that is buried in conflict and hidden from the light of day and the sight of sanity, almost forgotten forever. Almost. And yet so much beauty fills the day on both sides of the wall.

I offer up "thank yous" and promise to make my share of necessary phone calls, a practical thing, even minuscule, but every communication any of us can make on the side of sanity and peace is vital. The Academy has been a gracious host to all efforts. I do well to hold my own when I count my blessings and retrace the steps that brought me here, or at least bravely review the wave of revelation that carried me on its mighty swell, and just as mightily tumbled me like seaweed, and left me in the wake of the ordinary, to grapple with the details of a self-assigned mission of sacrifice and remembrance.

And so with a steeled effort I recall how it was that I first came to Jerusalem, still staring out at the soft, rolling hills and resting my elbows on the warm surface of the stone ledge that invites foreigners and seekers like me to

81

ponder and reflect. It began with a decidedly divine revelation in the most unlikely of places. I call it a "divine revelation" because what happened was not the kind of experience that is a daily occurrence. It was a golden gate wide-open kind of experience. It was the kind of life-changing experience that defines one's destiny and frames one's future.

Like it or not, receiving a call, "the call," the Almighty's Call, the call of a lifetime that has your name on it, cannot be easily tossed aside, no matter how ridiculous it might seem in the aftermath, when surging revelation recedes into the need for a practical plan. Upon trying to construct anything practical, the glory that could move mountains can barely find a hold in the rubble to find a way to make sense of it in ordinary terms. And yet you have to.

Here's my story... I was flying home from a lecture trip and had to change planes at an airport midway. I was somewhat absent-mindedly moving along in the rushing stream of passengers who, like me, were caught up in the task of looking for their destinations.

I was changing gates, hurrying to catch my connecting flight, and had to make one of those split-second, seemingly meaningless, insignificant decisions. There before me was a choice between the moving conveyer belt walkway, where travelers roll through long stretches of terminal hallways, or the solid ground and tiled passage that followed an expanse of windows that ran the entire length of the terminal.

I chose the windowed path that looked out over airplanes and runways, but also mountains and eye-catching vistas. I stopped, faced the horizon on the other side of the glass, and took a moment to just stand still. I hadn't stood still for days. I was in a hurry, but I needed to stop. So I stopped and stood there.

The sun was setting. The sky was amazing. It was more than amazing. It was so amazing that it gathered me up into its awesome splendor and cracked open a part of my soul that had been sleeping for hundreds of years. Just like that, all at once. There in the midst of a busy thoroughfare between terminals, I received an anointing. The Golden Gates had opened. The tidal wave rolled in. The light poured through and through.

Rendered speechless and unable to move any further, I stood motionless in my earthly tracks like a pillar of stone, a pillar of light, a pillar of the purest love, yes love, as the flow of travelers rushed past me. Time had opened, time had stopped, time had begun again and accelerated to a reality beyond time that left this one and entered another.

Suddenly I found myself in the throes of an otherworldly experience. Pulsations of light streamed through my body. I was swallowed by bliss. I was immersed in a presence of benevolence and wisdom. It was like the future had opened and God was showing me visions from the Throne of All Creation. And the promise of eternity was whispered ever so faintly, barely audible, but a promise nonetheless. It was pure and perfect in its faintness, subtle in its whispering mystery and half-told utterance.

The subtle is always the most profound. The abstract nature of the love of all existence hit me with a palpable blow, as if a bolt of lightning had struck me in the chest, still subtler but omnipotent in its impact. And then I understood. With ancient tears streaming down my face, I made a promise of the soul to exist in a purity of heart and good will in return for this otherworldly blessing.

No sooner had I offered up my promise than terrible visions also came into view, frightful and horrific. Although my eyes were shut tight, I could see what I clearly sensed as the future. Crisis, war, bombs and bloodshed filled my mind's eye, as I saw the entire Middle East region and then all the world in utter turmoil. The upheaval of all normalcy was rampant. Many lives were being lost. It was as though a fire-breathing, dagger-clawed dragon was scorching the land and holding it captive. The whole world seemed to be dangling by a thread from the dragon's teeth.

I was shown that I would be standing at the center of it, in the streets of the Old City of Jerusalem, even as missiles were being launched overhead and the dragon swooped and ravaged side by side with the age's evils. This sounds a little drastic, no doubt, but that's how it was; that's what I sensed; that's what I was shown.

Somehow, even as I watched the horror that I was given to see while standing there, holding onto an airport handrail, facing busy runways that led to the rest of the world, I was also given courage and solace more than enough, because I wasn't scared or upset by what I saw, the blood and guts of it. It simply was the way it was. There was a matter-of-factness to it: nothing more and nothing less. Because from the unimaginable horror would come unimaginable redemption. I already knew this, even as the images of destruction depicted a time of chaos and suffering and hatred and revenge and the falling of souls into the very bowels of hell.

I was also shown that there would be peace and a wondrous hereafter made manifest for earth and her people. I was shown that horror would be followed by a planetary choice for peace and love and brotherhood and decency. I was shown that I would be working with other people to bring hope to the difficulties and I was shown something else as well. Something profound but as yet unrevealed, a promise that would no longer be subtle and faint, but rather would become a fiery flame before all the nations, a flame that warmed the souls of all the world with hope and goodness and more. The "more" was the secret within the promise that, when the time was right, would be opened like a gift from God on high, the Holy of the Holies, in a thanksgiving beyond comprehension, absolutely beyond comprehension.

And then, still holding the hands of rapture, I was shown something more. I saw myself standing with a group of people whom I had grown to know well. We were gathered together in the final hours before something of great importance was about to happen. We had worked for years together and had grown intimate. We had had our ups and downs, our quarrels and our joys. I could feel all of this. I could literally feel the future.

There we stood as one heart and one soul out in the open in what was the center of Jerusalem, in the very same plaza that shares history with the Wailing Wall and Solomon's Temple and Muhammad's Night Journey. As I looked up beyond the crowd, it was sunset, a sunset to remember for generations to come. A soft glory was all around us. I could feel the unforgettable grace of it. I could feel the noble bond of having met incredible odds with perseverance and faith.

We were shaking hands, hugging and patting each other on the shoulder. We were an international circle of collaborators, who had given our all. We were thanking everyone who had assembled. Hands were pumping up and down with wide grins and sweeping gestures. Each of us had played an important role. Each had contributed something essential. The camaraderie was hard earned and deep-seated. Happiness was the prevailing mood among us, along with a relief that spoke of risk and close calls and ultimate sacrifice. This moment had been a long time coming, a moment we had all prayed for.

And then, as if a great bell had pealed to ring in a new day, a new world, a new era, we turned as if called by an unseen telepathy to cast our common gaze of faith upon the face of our most cherished dreams. It was a face of magnificence. As a group of planners, builders and architects beholding with a single eye, we drank in the grace of stone and glass and gleaming metal. A temple, an international place of convening nations, a building of celestial appearance, majestic proportions and exquisite beauty towered in the background from where we stood, like the Taj Mahal, only far grander. A golden spire reached for the sky, like a message of the prayers of humanity.

The building's scope and purpose and beauty were the wedding of all paradoxes of heavenly and earthly beauty. It was in this perfect light, silhouetted by the flaming reds and golds and purples of a sunset that could be the grandfather of all sunsets, for the unveiling of a temple for all nations that stood tall and regal, broad and purposeful. The heavens were splayed across the horizon touching down on Earth in folds of vivid and soul-rending color, like a royal robe of the richest velvet draped around the temple's domed and golden shoulders.

The Temple was built. It was finished. It was ready. It was real. The war was over. The floods of fire dragons had come and receded. The dove of peace had an entire bouquet of olive branches in its beak. The United Nations for Peace on Earth had found a home.

And I had found my purpose, profound and ordinary. I had received a vision. I was shaken and breathless after this display of mightiness. I had been holding on for dear life to the airport guardrail that ran the length of the terminal windows. My knuckles were white as snow, almost blue. I had hung there for the entire duration of the experience of future worlds. My clothing clung, sweat-soaked to my body, as if I had just run a marathon.

Hard reality returned as I remembered with a jolt that I still had a flight to catch. With deliberate command, I unwrapped my fingers from their frozen grasp on the guardrail, adjusted my bag on my shoulder, and struggled to my senses. Gathering myself into the ordinary, into the bustle of airport traveling terminals and departures and gates, I continued on my way.

On the flight home I pondered into the night. Staring at a sea of deep black outside the tiny portal of the airplane window, I sat close to the night clouds and the night stars that were flickering and fleeting past the airplane. None of the grandiosity of what I had been shown only a short time ago made any sense. It seemed so oddly out of sync, out of place and detached from my present world of endeavors and small-scale thinking. But it had engulfed me with a totality of certainty and I was grateful.

When this vision of the extraordinary took place, things were fairly peaceful in the Old City and tourism to the Holy Land was at an all-time high. Back then, several years before the intifada, even my mother was planning a trip to Jerusalem with members of her Baptist church. Outside of hearing her share a few of her travel details, I hadn't really given Jerusalem or the Middle East much thought. Previous to that fateful change of airport gates and the choice to take the path less traveled, with the sunset that shown through the windows to the heavens, I had only a vague association with this part of the world.

Nonetheless what happened, happened. I couldn't deny it even on my worst days of doubt and despair. I was duly anointed and granted the rapture of revelation in the middle of a busy airport terminal. Like wet cement that has dried hard as a rock, it was fact, perhaps spiritual fact. That's the best that I can describe it, looking back.

But I soon learned to be careful when talking about "the call to Jerusalem." Back then before peace work, peace rallies and the like that now give the human race a new voice were a thriving reality, I was oddly alone in being called to the unseen front lines of peace that I sensed would be so crucial. People responded with incredulous expressions.

My closest friends, even my very closest friends, doubted me and openly wondered if I was losing my grip on reality. And so there wasn't much support for the revelations of the heavens or the sweeping hand of fate in the aftermath of what quickly became the ordinary as the speed of light screeched to a halt. There were mostly skeptical reprisals and conventional platitudes tossed my way with casual but deafening effect.

A part of me, the part that had been buried, the part of my heart that had fallen asleep and finally at long last had taken its chance to resurface wide awake, was sorely, sadly dejected after having been so exalted. But I endured this changing weather of the mundane and began packing my bags for the unknown. Come what may, sunny skies or stormy seas, I was headed for the Holy Land.

Like most people who feel called to come to Israel, I eagerly anticipated my maiden voyage. And like most people, I was naive and even a little starry-eyed. Landing at the Ben Gurion Airport in Tel Aviv, I instantly began to gain a visceral sense of the importance of my links to this part of the world, as if the human saga of thousands of years was running through my veins, and perhaps it was and is. I hadn't expected it to hit me so immediately or so square on. I was indeed profoundly touched just to set my feet on the ground.

Pausing for just a little while longer, years later after receiving the call, I linger to register the vista beyond where I stand, and I feel renewed to remember. Sometimes we have to go back to the beginning or retrace our steps to the fork in the road that changed our lives. Patting the wall with love and with a new sense of dedication, I turn back to the day ahead, and the winding little path of stone that will lead me to the center of things, and the meeting of minds that will transpire just a few steps from the walls and temples and churches and burial grounds that make Jerusalem what she is.

Perhaps there are a few molecules of Bedouin blood in me, after all. Perhaps, if I reached far enough into the vaults of my family tree, I would be able to trace my own roots all the way back to the sheepskin tents of Jacob's wives, Jacob, son of Isaac, son of Abraham, and the brood of children that they bore who branched out across the face of earthly existence as the Twelve Tribes of Israel. Who knows? Maybe my blood is filled with the hopes and dreams of wandering ancestors who still watch over me, and have for their own mystical reasons called me back to the desert.

Perhaps the Biblical matriarchs of the sun-blistered nomads, Sarah and Rebecca and Rachel and Leah, mothers of the past and mothers of the future, the women who stood as pillars of faith and suffering and nobility throughout the pages of the Bible and the Torah and the Qur'an, would initiate me into the sleeping secrets of their long-held wisdom.

Perhaps they would part the sheepskin doors, like Moses parted the Red Sea, and beckon me to enter the tents of antiquity. I imagined that inside the dusty tents of the desert mothers, the billowing walls would be white and luminous, the whiteness of promise, the whiteness of a pure womb, and that I would be welcomed and absorbed into the folds of a sisterhood that has been forgotten by the modern world.

Called or not called, past or present, white or black, I would soon live to admit that my own private paradox was not so dissimilar to that of the rest of the mystic realm of the trial and tribulation of the Holy Land. I would come to realize that the ups and downs that I fought with inside myself were not so different from the Armageddon of opposing sides.

If paradox is the ticket for entry at the Tel Aviv airport, then I had that end of things covered. And so I became one of untold thousands who have made the pilgrimage to Jerusalem, searching to remember, and longing to find a starting point. And I arrived with my share of baggage, packed tight with my own polarities of every shape and size.

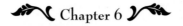

Chapter 6

The Unity

Bones of Light, Bones of Dust

Having finished our morning meeting at the Academy, a round of warm exchanges are shared over a spicy meal of the local fare, prepared by the wife of one of the scholars and very humbly and beautifully served. The building that has been home to the group of refined and innovative thinkers is situated in a cluster of some of the oldest buildings in all of Old Jerusalem. Limestone and mud walls form curved shapes, arched hallways, and circular courtyards, the stone and dust of living.

The central meeting room boasts a large domed ceiling above a grand round conference table, some twelve feet in diameter. Cobalt and sea green mosaic tiles, the artistry of careful hands, has graced the rooms and windowsills for hundreds of years. The colors have softened and muted with age and the passing of humanity of that has filled this little paradise with the roundness of life. The architecture of the cultures that crafted the Old City brought such a feminine influence of beauty and flowing design to the harshness of the desert.

The humility and graciousness of the women who serve our meal also carries a quiet wisdom that radiates through the food that is eaten. The tradition of this part of the world, where women cook and serve, is strong and

91

enduring. These women make pure beauty out of what is expected of them, and I feel privileged to be among them.

They are the salt of the earth; hands are weathered; faces are soft and hearts are deep. I want to follow them back into the kitchen, to share their world. It feels like an age-old feminine society is alive and well among them. It contains them and creates a web of living sisterhood that I too need and long for.

The meeting went well; views and plans were exchanged with an easy tone of conversation accompanying our noontime repose. Suggestions for the symposium were brought into a last minute plan and refinement of action. The daunting problem of getting Palestinian speakers, professors and humanitarians out of the occupied territories was addressed, additional petitions and appeals were made ready and organized, and lists of immediate follow-through phone calls to the UN, national and municipal agencies, and the Palestinian Authority were assigned.

While espresso and tea end our meal, details are brought as far as we can manage them into yet another degree of agreement. Bright, wise faces share the table today from many backgrounds and religions and professions. This has truly been a meeting of minds, with several people present having crossed the lines of convention to come out of the closet and express their sincere views, views that cannot be expressed openly among their own professional circles.

Talk turns to temples. Brilliant minds turn to history. Visions turn to what might be if a temple of the prophecy is to be built. Many have envisioned the legendary promise of the third temple. Some have brought dreams and visions into the black and white of architectural drawings and graphic renderings. Virtual journeys of the temple of the ages are being designed for an internet project.

It seems that the factor of visions has impacted a surprising number of minds present, that cannot deny it and pretend otherwise. Jerusalem is a place where the unseen magnitude of existence is seen at many levels of seeing, as if the phenomenon of visions was given birth here.

I turn to the world of ancient landmarks just outside the large arched windows of the Academy as the discussion becomes saturated with the wistful surmising of a great work come to pass. I try to imagine what the great edifice would look like that would unite the Tribes of Sarah, that would unite the East and the West, that would unite every nation into the common purpose of "peace on earth, good will to all, prosperity and abundance to all."

Intrigued and wanting to stay longer, I reluctantly check the time and realize that my next appointment is in less than a half hour. And because I had walked, I really need to say my good-byes and leave talk of peace, plans and temples for another time.

As I step outside, the mid-afternoon heat hits me with an impact, a reminder of severity, as I retrace my steps on cobblestone streets and find myself irresistibly pulled in an unexpected direction. Something within tells me I just have to follow my intuition. Looking at my watch I wince and break free in a single moment of knowing. I call ahead on my cell phone to say I'll be late and to start without me. It is midday now and the hot desert winds move through Jerusalem, causing a kind of shimmer in the air.

To the east of the Old City, just beyond the fortress walls, lies the illumined Mount of Olives, the Garden of Gethsemane, infamous site of that kiss of betrayal that sealed the fate of Jesus, and the immortal burial grounds of the legendary 144,000, who's fate lies in rising up in a kind of resurrection of souls and prophets. Both sites lead to one another with deep rivers of mystical and esoteric whispers that many have tried to coax into speaking.

And this is what draws me like a magnet, despite appointments and schedules. A sense of certainty begins to guide my steps, crossing over to the other side of rational thinking that knows when something important has defined a set of new priorities. I just can't say no to this potent little piece of God's dear earth; only, in this case, it's a considerably thorny place, scrubby, scarred, barren and beaten. Here the scars run deep while angels sing. In this place, the illumined shine and ascend while the mortals betray and sink deeper into the abyss of illusion.

If you see only the physical surface, you would never guess that this is the land of milk and honey the prophets wept over. And so I shift into the kind of keen-eyed observance that is essential so as not to miss what needs to be seen. I am seeking the unseen that I might see whatever it is that I haven't seen before.

And so it is that multitudes of seekers, the curious, the pious, the bored and the overexcited, have filed side by side through the highlighted Holy Land destinations of the tour guidebooks. For years I have witnessed the ones who collapse in reverence at the Garden of Gethsemane and the ones who check the film in their cameras and wonder why they came. Some fight back the tears successfully, others unsuccessfully. Some even become hysterical.

Making my way in the general direction that I feel is calling me, I conclude that we are a strange lot, we humans. The morose and morbid, the tragic and profane seem to draw us in every bit as much as the sublime. These places of tragedy and ascension lie together as if they are two sides of a coin, forever joined in a single fateful point in the scheme of things, where molten metal becomes its own alchemist and decides to fuse.

Before the regional fighting got so bad, the tourists came by the tens of thousands to the gardens and mounts and burial sites, as if a director had boomed the word, "Action," to modern day walk-ons in a filming studio, costumed in full tourist regalia. Now almost no one comes. The streets are nearly empty.

Yes, Jerusalem and the Holy Land have always been a place where congregations have gathered around the demise of the helpless, the sites of battles, atrocities, betrayals and crucifixions, like crowds gathering to stare transfixed at a gruesome traffic accident. The more grotesque and shocking to the nervous system, the more awful the imagined sight of blood and guts, the more unbelievable the twist of fate, the more we are drawn to the site of final judgments.

It is as if we fancy ourselves as the judge and the jury, and the judged and the condemned all rolled into one huge emotion, as if going through the motions will make it an easier transition when our own day of reckoning comes hard on the heels of the unexpected.

These places of antiquity are like halls of judgment; preceded by the anterooms that one must inevitably pass through in order to secure passage to the other side of the mysterious duality of heaven and earth, a duality that seems to feed off of itself and eat itself alive. The feeding frenzy goes on until nothing is left but naked, silent bones of what had been, which I would guess is the point of it all. From there, you can make of it whatever comes to mind. From there, the accounts of what come to mind, shape what follows.

In the end, there is a cold, strange beauty to the bare white bones of the souls who have given up the flesh. They stay in the shadows of the stories that are told about them, until dust becomes their long-sought absolution. The prophets, saviors, yogis and sages have always shared eternal life and immortality as a common theme of their teachings.

Those who give up the flesh on purpose, or at least in full knowing, are considered to be the triumphant, although the air of tragic consequences still wraps around them like an invisible shroud. For the onlookers, the tourists, the cast of thousands, the floodgates are unleashed wherever the tourist sign points. Oceans of tears fall upon these shrouded bones, or upon where the bones are thought to rest.

What shrouds these are, and what they must endure! You would think they'd come crashing down from their invisible assignment in the ethers, unable to bear the weight of human assumption any longer.

A single tear shed upon the fibers of their folds, one drop more, even a weightless molecule of saline and salt more, could tip the scales of fate forever. What would happen then?

Would some sort of spiritual avalanche loose itself upon the slippery slopes that mark the divide between fact and fiction, between the mortal and the immortal, between the bones of the favored and the bones of the forgotten? Would the Shroud of Turin, subject of argument and object of devotion, drop out of its lofty sanctuary beyond the physical to suddenly, miraculously, manifest before the eyes of the innocent? Would the ethers be torn apart and cause some kind of time warp?

Would the shrouds of the all prophets descend from invisibility and come alive simultaneously to proclaim what the prophets in the flesh proclaimed, unified at last in a single voice of victory and a single story of salvation, accompanied by the trumpets of the angels of the Elohim? Would they finish the job, bring peace and promise to the land of promises and hope to nations, especially the down-trodden, Third World places where tragedy is the norm?

The shrouds are saturated with the tears of the grief-stricken, past and present, as if the dead could still feel the hand of unfinished business weigh heavily on their hides, on an expected day of judgment.

This is what the Buddhists call karma, and the Old Testament calls an eye for an eye or the final evaluation of deeds and destinies between creator and creation. As far as shrouds go, there are mortals and then there are mere mortals. The bones of the prophets are of a different sort than the bones of mere mortals.

Here buried bones are held in the highest of regard. They are judged to be instruments of redemption relin-quished of human conditions and things like ordinary karma. They are held in high regard because maybe, just maybe, there is redemption, if one becomes a pilgrim and follows the footsteps of those who are said to have died or risen in divine favor.

Just maybe a power of grace is still to be found in bones and shrouds that are thousands of years old and in the art of divine dying and are a necessary link for those of us left behind and still struggling. These bones may hold the mystical key to the survival of one's own flesh and blood. Some of the most awed fights in the Holy Land are over the bones of the prophets and their presumed burial sites.

Of course, there's considerable argument over whether, in fact, certain bones are to be found in certain places. I wander through this line of thinking as a past note to taking stock of my first trip to Jerusalem and the numerous trips that followed after the addiction to this place of existential pondering began in full-bodied demand.

Mulling things over, looking back, and squaring off with the circumstantial and maybe karmic hand on my own hide, I am more painfully aware than ever that I was drawn into the clutches of the past and held fast by life and limb, belief and gullibility just like everyone else.

I was no different than any other seeking pilgrim tourist as I made my way along the paths of dust and denial that led to all the places that bore plaques announcing with authority: so and so slept here, so and so was born here, so and so was baptized here, and was risen from the dead here, or is now buried in this hallowed ground for all eternity right here, absolutely right here, where the sign points.

I was no different. I followed the signs, took in the sites, and let it all hit me however the watchful eye of the lords of karma would have it.

Except that I had been touched, and there was no way I could deny it. I didn't need a sign. The heavens had opened one time too many to bury my head in the sand. I had received the call of the mysterious. A pillar of light had descended in my midst and set me straight.

Nonetheless, I followed the signs like everyone else. Some days were revelatory. Some days were sticky hot, grinding, gritty and tiresome in this place of wonder and holiness. Some days were beyond anything I could have ever imagined and well beyond what I can find words to describe. Now as I weave my way along the pathway that runs through and connects the holy sites, I wonder what will be revealed.

Today I look for signs of a different sort than in the past. I look carefully in the eyes of everyone I pass along the way. In the past, encounters with locals and native sons also ran the gamut. Some were truly sages in their own right, like modern day saints. The light poured from them and caused me to take note and remember reverence.

Others were running scams, selling camel rides and plastic trinkets, hustling anyone and anything that walked. I say this as if I need a reminder of the nature of things and the difference between fact and fiction.

Leaving convention, schedules and appointments behind, I enter into the magnetic pull once again, only this time I do so wide awake and acutely watchful. Today will mark my soul with something that's difficult to describe, especially its effect on me. I can sense it.

I can describe and account for the weight of it. It is what it is. Yes, I have visited all of these places before, some more than once, during my first few visits to Jerusalem and the surrounding Middle Eastern countries.

But today is different. Today the pull is different; my steps are on different ground, the ground of the unexplainable that becomes certainty. It is like breaking free, in a way. Today I am not a tourist or even a pilgrim. Today my feet know the soil and remember why I've been called here.

It happened at the burial site of the 144,000. This is a hillside of gravestones that look like long waves of white mile markers, a mere stone's throw from the Garden of Gethsemane, where Jesus was betrayed by Judas. I swallow the dry air and recount to myself that with a fatal kiss he was handed over to the hand of fate. It was a kiss of death and resurrection, followed by the Roman soldiers who took him away.

By the next morning, Jesus carried a heavy wooden cross on his back and, with a crown of thorns on his head, stumbled with the weight of it, the weight of all the world's suffering, far beyond his own, as if his burial shroud had already been prepared for him eons before, before the kiss of death, before the Last Supper, before his Sermons on the Mount to the multitudes, before he was even born or conceived unto Mary, the Virgin Mother.

And by day's end Jesus was hanging on a cross of timbers, crisscrossed with the lives of the trees that had been cut down in their prime, just like him. Each place he stumbled is marked with a plaque, fourteen stations marked with plaques in all, along the Via Dolorosa where he reputedly carried his own cross to his own waiting crucifixion.

The exact route itself is yet another hotly contested subject, but I too have walked the 14 Stations of the Cross and was brought to my knees more than once. Before the intifada, the Via Dolorosa was flooded with the faithful who came in small groups and large congregations to carry wooden crosses, to remember the sacrifice of a noble savior, to remember their own forgetting, and weep 'til the Stations of the Cross glistened at midnight and send up prayers, heaven-bound with promises of the heart to save and be saved.

Today I stand on the edge of an expanse of gravestones so old as to be crumbling and sinking into the sand, remembering the theme of sacrifice that Jesus had spoken about, and in the end, or the beginning, depending on how you look at it, died for in order to be born again.

Today it still amazes me that with the springing leap of a grasshopper, you can straddle the holy ground from the garden of the kiss to the gravesite of prophets. Jesus and the prophets very likely walked on this hillside, before it became the burial site of the souls who came after them.

The tombs of the 144,000 have had a similar, strong and seductive magnetism on my soul, just as the Temple of Solomon and the Golden Gate. In the heat of the day, I find myself meandering among its weatherworn wind-whispered gravestones, instead of attending yet another planning meeting and taking care of the business of present day responsibilities.

It's a site that is a little off the beaten track of the usual tourist stops, even though it is right next door to once heavy human traffic that pours through the Church of Gethsemane that commemorates the night Jesus prayed all night beneath the stars and olive grove branches, communing with God, presumably, or perhaps on the nature of his "soon to be realized" fate.

This is not the first time I have ventured to the gravesite of the 144,000, but today the tourists and the locals are nowhere to be found and there is no one there but me. I take note of this, looking around in all directions several times. I am alone. I am alone with the exception of a sea of buried lives and the power of prophesy that would have 144,000 souls ascending on the day of judgment or the dawn of a new era, or the opening of the Golden Gate or the moment the Messiah walks among mortals.

I am alone, except for all that can possibly be possible in this place of fate and miracles and life-changing points in the infinite nature of time and matter. Not a single tourist, not a single souvenir hawker, or anyone else is to be found. For me this is profound in and of itself.

Back before the sentiments boiled over, and before the razing of Arab villages began, the crowds were thick and bustling, so this emptiness in places that were usually full of throngs of people strikes me. It feels like a miracle of major proportions just to be alone. And here I am completely alone with only white grave markers and the white dusty bones that rest beneath them.

One could write an entire book about the 144,000, on the possibilities of its meaning, not the least of which is decidedly beyond what could even be considered esoteric, deeply so. I quickly become weak in the knees from the power of the place.

I know in all certainty, in an immediate insistence, in an instantaneous absolution, that beneath the limestone rock and sand, my own bones are among those that are buried here. I feel like I have lived and died among these rocks and hillsides before. I just know it. It is a "chill down the spine" kind of knowing, yet at the same time it is simply a matter of fact, like the looming presence of the Old City wall that rises up in undeniable testimony in the near distance. The urge to find my place in history is indeed magnetizing.

Perhaps the pull of karma was at play after all. I could have immediately begun to hunt for my long lost plaque or marker, if I had allowed myself that indulgence. But my purpose here is not about the question of the possibility of past lives, or even any slim comprehension of the vice-grip of karma, at least not consciously, not in the way that I understand it. It is about something else.

I know from things that I have read that one version of the fate, purpose or karma of this hillside of bones is fairly well agreed upon, at least as far as anything can be agreed upon. Tradition has it that on the day of the Great Tribulation, the souls of the illumined 144,000 will "rise from the dead" to serve as the attendants for the coming of the Messiah in the Hebrew faith, or, as Christians see it, the second coming of the Christ.

Perhaps there are other versions as well. I try to picture this, but instead what I see in my mind's eye are souls in present-day bodies coming back to Jerusalem from every corner of the world. Instead of spirits rising from the dry earth of buried bones, I see real live warm-fleshed people bringing the promise of their love and hope back to where so much began and where so much will perhaps end, to begin a new beginning.

Instinctively, I sense that there is far more going on here than can be understood through conventional thought on this matter, written, proclaimed, trumpeted or otherwise. I come here to this place in peace and wisdom, drawn by a certainty that I might come to rest in a different sort of way, perhaps to begin again in some way.

It is blisteringly hot now; the day has become a severely hot afternoon, with temperatures soaring over 100° Fahrenheit. In this piercing intensity, I stand and endure it, and for a long, long, long while look out over the endless sea of glistening white stone grave markers that dot and sprinkle and grace the gentle roll of the sloping hillside that spill in the precise direction of the legendary Golden Gate.

Heat waves shimmer off the gravestones like halos of light. The entire hillside is illumined as if it could explode, as if the whole hillside would ascend if the light were to get any brighter. Even though the sun beats down in the full force of a midday heat that can roast chilies or coffee beans, the spiritual light that reverberates from stone to stone is stronger yet.

Knees still weak, I collapse where I stand, which is conveniently close to the sparse but welcoming shade of a struggling bougainvillea that has vined up like a canopy at a bus stop. Thank God for this flowering branch of leaf and color.

I don't know how it managed to grow in the hardpan and sand, but there it is like a gift from heaven above. And just in time. Thinking back I might otherwise have passed out from the glaring heat and the ascending light. As a foreigner the desert heat is a fierce reminder of my frailty, especially today. I can feel the heat through the bottom of my shoes. A speck of shade is like finding a diamond in an expanse of rubble.

Once under the boughs of brightly colored purple and pink, a new vista comes into view. The tender blossoms remind me of the vestments of priests and goddesses respectively, with the heat of both sun and spirit drawing out the color from their depths in both instances.

Before me lies the outstretched embrace of the Old City, yes the Old City, where the Christians, the Jews and the Muslims all claim special rights and favor in the sight of God in a clamor that must be tiresome to the lords of light by now, making even angels weep and saints lose their tempers.

Each stubbornly making its claim on a living thing that belongs to no one but itself, I can still feel the purity of reverence that existed within each claim, a purity that has been all but buried beneath the burden of possession and the booming voice that says, "This is mine, not yours." I say this in all due respect to the innocence of my ignorance and to those who feel themselves to be caretakers of the sacred.

I contemplate the history of the land and flesh and familiarity of the dynasties that were laid to rest on this bone dry, arid white hillside. The generations that have lived on after Abraham and Sarah's passage into legend continue to commingle in the dust beneath my unintentionally irreverent and woefully overwhelmed and bended knees.

Entire families, the descendants of Biblical and historical significance from Jacob to Job, as well as the bones of the much loved and sometimes equally hated King David, are said to be among the remains of the 144,000. This is just too much past for one place to hold, too many bones to pay homage to, too much karma, too much holiness, light and heat. There seems to be a fire burning in every direction.

Sheltered from the glare of it all, I shudder at the thought of bones, and death and resurrection. Parched and thirsty, I must appear somewhat in need, even desperate, still at the mercy of the demanding, midday heat and the insistent flames of white burning secrets.

As if in answer to my unspoken, unconscious prayers, an elderly Arab woman, rotund and radiant with a comforting, earthy vitality, appears out of absolutely nowhere, and peers at me through the bushes with dark brown questioning eyes. In a heartbeat I am startled and relieved, jolted and comforted, as is the ongoing paradox of the Holy Land.

The questions of the heart seem to strike us both, like twin clocks, or two souls ascending side by side. Draped in traditional garb, she lifts the canopy of vines with a swishing, sweeping gesture that mimics the throwing back of the grand drape of a floor-length wedding veil, and with notable command of her considerable girth, sits down next to me, hard and deliberate, with a dust-raising thump.

Gathering her skirts with an air that is satisfied and confident, she extends her hand, gestures with the whole of her ample body and offers me a small glass of lemonade. My mouth instantly begins to water. The possibility of the flavor of succulent tart lemons touches my tongue without a fight, no fight whatsoever, and a longed-for sweetness seduces me and I submit on the spot to her generosity or her enterprise, both of which are welcome.

Reaching for my tourist coin purse, I assume she wants money but she refuses to take my shekels. She also has a glass of lemonade for herself, smiles, heaves and grunts, as she rearranges her weight to gain comfort, positioning herself closer yet, as if I were the daughter of her own breast that she has come to offer suckle.

I drink down her lot. I feel relieved and cared for as the wisdom of her eyes embraces me. She seems like an ancient grandmother sent from the past to remind me of my true heritage.

As my thirst is quelled, she just sits there next to me, staring out over the hillside with obvious gratification at having offered exactly what was needed, exactly when it was most needed. But her eyes seem to be fixed on the arched entrance in the distance that spreads itself on the neckline of the rampart wall like a large diamond brooch on an evening gown. The direction of her gaze and the intensity of her focus give her away. I am duly alerted.

It is one of those "more than meets the eye" kind of moments. My esoteric radar becomes instantly activated. This particular gate, the Golden Gate, the one that has been sealed shut for hundreds of years, will one day arch over the head of a great white horse, upon whose noble back will be riding the prophesied Messiah. This gate grabbed me the first time I laid eyes on it seven years before this moment.

The old Arab woman is staring at the Golden Gate, the Mercy Gate, the same gate that ran through my dreams, as if she wants me to join her in an odyssey of time travel, to somehow pass something on to me.

The conspiracy is out in the open. She looks straight into my eyes, seeking the windows to my soul, with a knowing that chills my blood to its cool immortal state and warms my heart in all of its humanity. We share our glasses of lemonade in silence, drawing the drinking out as long as we can to make it last. And the lemons are tart and sweet, just as I had imagined.

But what is shared is beyond time, beyond everything. The camaraderie of heart and the bond of bones that crosses all boundaries begin to ring loud and clear. It is then that I realize that my parched tongue is being quenched with more than just lemonade.

I begin to also drink from the cup of a sacred lineage that my soul longs for. The hair stands on end all over my body, as the old woman, who appeared out of nowhere, gathers herself to sit even closer, even closer than before, really, really close, intimately close. She sighs and closes her eyes. From there, who knows? Who can say?

I close my eyes too, and the heavens break loose. The avalanche of shrouds that I pondered and anticipated just an hour before is upon my very soul. I guess the lemonade shared in such intimacy must have tipped the scales of fate or pleased the lords of light and karma, or maybe her grand girth and tart lemons are more than the shrouds of the prophets can take.

107

They shake free from the shoulders of the angels and drop like exploding fireworks of ecstasy, running through my mind's eye and heart of hearts like a stampede of elephants, trunks held high, trumpeting as the heavens reveal new designs and displays of color and vastness.

Light descends and the eye of God opens wide. Vivid revelations begin to roll upon the landscape of my mind's reflection remembered as knowing. Sequences from different lifetimes begin to coalesce like watching a movie on fast forward.

I see myself in innumerable circumstances, on all sides of the fence. I have been Bedouin, Arab, Jew, and Christian, and even Egyptian before that. I remember the calluses on wise hands that dipped clay pots into scarce springs of cool water. I remember breathing in the fragrance of the oil-laden hair of the other women of the tribe that I love like sisters.

I remember the cool and lavish courtyards, and glaring sun burning in the eyes of priests and oracles that guide entire kingdoms. I remember the prayers for the child that sucks life from my breast and the tiny hands that play with the strands of gold that hang from my privileged neck.

I remember hard, hard times of never-ending trudging and council meetings in sheepskin tents that are held into the dark night of doubt and rebellion.

I remember the time of Abraham and Sarah as clearly as if I had been there, seeing with eyes of wisdom that are as keen as a desert falcon, feeling the texture of every nuance in my surroundings with fingers that have grown sensitive to the weft and the warp of life, from both hardship and gratitude, smelling the smells of campfires and simmering stewpots, and plump fresh-picked olives in baskets, and babies being born in the middle of the night, while frankincense and myrrh are burnt as offerings to the Goddess of Fertility.

But more than anything I remember Sarah, beloved wife of Abraham and matriarch of future generations. Sarah looms larger than life, larger than the Old City wall and just as solid, just as real. Sarah... Sarah... Sarah... Sarah of Abraham and Sarah who began her life as Sarai... My mind turns over the sound of the name. It is music to my soul; like hearing a favorite lullaby that I haven't heard since childhood, if I were lying withered and fading on my deathbed.

That's how sweet it is to think her name out loud. How profoundly resonant is the sound of the name Sarah. It is as if the song of Sarah rings through the chambers of an inner sanctuary that is mine, and mine alone.

The chords of remembrance were struck by a celestial symphony. I swear it. Retrieving the name Sarah through the sensing, feeling, shivering understanding of the soul that draws memory in a non-linear knowing is like hearing the sound of truth, voices and wisdom, echoes bouncing forever off canyon walls.

The canyon walls that I speak of are the experiences that seem to be part of me. Ancient archives open as if some kind of floodgate has broken free, unleashing a familiarity that makes certain the question of faith. Cascades of wisdom roll through my consciousness as abstract links pour into a concrete foundation that would stay under my feet forever.

I am astounded at the clarity and impact of this visioning. It is as if it were being orchestrated by the arch-dean of cosmic wisdom, to be sure that no stone remains unturned in my understanding. My blood rejoins the past in reunion.

All the while my Arab grandmother holds me soundly in her gracious girth, patiently holding open the veils of time, while I, the white woman from faraway America, remember what needs to be seen.

Bloodlines of the desert tribes of the past are transformed into ley lines of light of the present. Sarah has called me home. Tears of joy spill down from the perch of angels, giving moisture to my parched surroundings, like the water of life springing from a mysterious cascade.

Sprigs of young olive tree seedlings spring up everywhere with the first glimmers of an eternal sunrise as the visioning continues. Palm trees sway to the lilt of harps and flutes and the clear pure notes drift in upon the soft breezes of high noon, like the sound of the spheres reverberating in a celestial amphitheater.

Flowering vines flourish and give generous fragrance to the night air as the stars above open wide for voyages to distant suns. It is the Garden of Eden: The garden that Sarah and grandmothers with lemonade know; the garden that Sarah shows me. And I had been there, too.

A branch snaps. Small pebbles scatter. Dust furls in the air next to where I sit. I reluctantly peer through the meager slit of an eyelid that wants to disappear in the garden of Sarah's breath. When I open my eyes wide, the round, robed Arab woman is gone. She vanished in silence, in mystery, without a trace. I feel the ground next to me, just to reassure myself that she had actually appeared and sat next to me.

Yes, thank God, the ground is still warm and still bears proof of her existence. A slight indentation where the ground had given way to her hugeness, not only of body but of spirit as well, is evidence enough.

And I still hold the empty glass in my hand. The empty glass is proof. It might as well have been the chalice from the Last Supper, as far as I am concerned. It still has bits of lemon on its rim, from the last swallow that had eased my thirst and soothed my soul.

She left me with the empty glass that is full and overflowing and far more. It is as if an unknown grandmother of the Twelve Tribes of the Universal Israel, the Israel before the definition of Jews and Arabs took hold of the human heart and shook it loose from the rib cage of Adam and the womb of Eve, has found me, embraced me and suckled me as I sit all alone in the graveyard of my ancestors.

The grandmother who came to my side was Arab, definitely Arab, or so she seemed to me, pointing the way to Sarah or the gateways of her memory.

Or perhaps she was a descendant of Hagar. Hagar had been Sarah's handmaiden and had lain with Abraham at Sarah's request. She bore Abraham's first child, Ishmael, when Sarah's faith had ebbed, believing herself to be childless.

Hagar had served Sarah throughout the drama, love, betrayal and banishment: the same Hagar, whose son Ishmael was asked to leave the tribe, never to return. And Hagar tasted the bitterness of banishment, when she too was cast out, no longer favored, and was forced to face the future alone. This story is an old one but pivotal to our present day circumstances. Where did Hagar and Ishmael go and what fate did they meet?

The bloodlines of history tell us that Hagar is the mother of the souls who became Islam and that

Muhammad sprang from her Tree of Life. What of Hagar, what of Sarah, what of women around the world? She was not likely to be given any due in this land of the chosen few and the ascending many, and even Sarah is barely mentioned in scriptures.

But for me she had entered my life from the past or the future, I couldn't say, but she had entered, she had opened and she had revealed. Like an atom bomb going off in all directions, I exploded with all that she gave me to make this recognition loud in the land, because the Twelve Tribes of Israel were born of Sarah's womb and Sarah was born a soul before she was born a Jew.

Both Sarah and Hagar had borne children of Abraham: the tribes of the desert who have called Palestine their home for 4,000 years, long before the 1948 War of Independence began. Perhaps Hagar's spirit wanted me to know something of the mother of us all. That was one of the revelations that lived like a dove of peace in Sarah's garden of promise when she passed me the treasure of the sacred as I sat among the bones of great souls.

So why did Sarah send me an Arab grandmother to open the gates of revelation that pointed to her own presence? Or why did the Arab grandmother send me to Sarah? Perhaps peace has been made between Sarah and Hagar beyond what is assumed as common knowledge, beyond the veils of the soul, where bonds of love exist even in moments of betrayal. Why did the lemonade-bearing grandmother open the memory of my soul to the matriarch Sarah, mother of a nation of Jews?

We never exchanged a single word, the grandmother and I, and yet so much passed between us. Sometimes even betrayal winds its way to love; this was the lesson of the day and the unfolding of the ages. Perhaps it will be women who first refuse to hate, who refuse to betray and who choose love above all else.

Later, I came to understand far more deeply what "passing the sacred" truly means. What I experienced on the hillside overlooking Jerusalem that day, about the sisterhood that endures all earthly burdens, I would not soon forget. I will always carry with me the intensity of the shimmering light that reverberated off the gravestones and the old woman's wise and simple and earthy presence.

It is meaningful to me to pass my story on, to repeat it to myself, to "pass the sacred" just as it has always been passed throughout the ages, from one heart to another, from mother to daughter, from grandmothers to new nations. The love of the passing is as unlimited as is the wisdom.

I will also remember that the nectar of the Gods can be held for all eternity in a simple glass of lemonade, to be passed on and on and on. Yes, I will never be the same. A sonic boom has issued forth out of nowhere. The Golden Gate has opened. The grandmothers are preparing the way.

I arrive at my planning meeting in the late afternoon, having missed most of the reports and discussions, but having gained deserts and oceans and skies of life. A new shroud of unseen light and wisdom became the swaddling cloth that graces my shoulders, and hopefully I will pass the wisdom that overcomes betrayal and will find instead the bond of souls who discover love even in the aftermath of forgetting. Centuries later, remembrance is revealed.

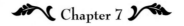

Chapter 7

The Wealth

Values of Money, Values of Life

Later that night, I shared a supper of grilled St. John's fish, a regional specialty from the Sea of Galilee, with the ambassador of a neighboring Arab country. I wanted to tell him my story of lemons and betrayal turned to love and forgiveness from the gravesite of the 144,000.

I wanted to tell him that the matriarchal Mothers of the Jewish and Arab worlds were at peace, that the souls of Sarah and Hagar had found union through their hardships, that they saw the errors of the past as the lessons that would shape the future.

I wanted to tell him of my love for Israel and the Hebrew people. I wanted to offer my story of hope and the wisdom of women, but of course I swallowed hard and obeyed all necessary protocol. I was, after all, an American woman meeting with an Arab ambassador.

Out of courtesy and my own sense of diplomacy I will not mention his name or his country, only to say we saw eye to eye on the futility of conflict and the devastating economic repercussions for the everyday people on all sides, even those who try not to take sides at all. He voiced and demonstrated through his demeanor a true regret for the suffering of the Israeli people. He also voiced his inability to accept the politics of perpetual domination. The

115

leaders of his country were more than concerned about the out of control terrorist problem, saying it was their problem, too, that no one was safe, not even him. My intuitive radar was on high, and I believed what he said.

We agreed that, despite the nobility of soldiers who love their country and fight for its cause, war is an economic luxury that lines the pockets of the very, very few and empties the pockets of the many. This was a line of thought that we emphasized. Maintaining diplomacy, he sighed, nodded and expressed regret at the slowdown in foreign investment, especially the kind of true enterprise that improved life for everyone, rather than those that merely exploit vulnerable conditions.

Instead of sharing my story of ancient grandmothers, I told a different kind of story and watched closely to see where the words fell. I told the ambassador of a meeting that I had had with a member of the Israeli Knesset, a good man who for the past term served as the Deputy Minister of Finance.

During our time together, some two hours, the Israeli politician had poured his heart out on a hectic day full of pressure and last minute decisions as we sat in his office, a stone's throw from the antiquities of faith that one could see in full view just beyond the window that framed his ambitions.

He offered me a detailed accounting of the adverse effects of conflict and war on the Israeli economy. He laid out the figures and charts and spreadsheets. I think I became all of Israel in that moment, the Israel that he longed to serve, because I was a willing sounding block that wanted to hear of his dream and his brilliance of thinking.

He lamented that soon the country would come to a crossroads of no return. Money and war would be the death of Israel, as we now know it. It tormented him to have to witness the downfall that he foresaw, and that had indeed already begun.

"It all starts with attitude," he lamented. "One way maintains civility, eases differences and soothes temperaments. One way invests in coexistence and seeks to mutually benefit. The other way invests in division and bloodshed and fans the flames of seething hatred, and takes pride in refusing to compromise and throws explosives onto the bonfire. So unnecessary, such a waste, so destructive, so much is lost," he muttered, shuffling the papers on his desk.

He lamented further of his struggles to get elected to his present position and that staying alive in the Israeli Knesset was a feat not many could endure. Not only was surviving financially an issue, but also the pressure to please, pander and prostrate before power.

He talked of the stranglehold of war hawks and the futility of moderates. He talked of the difficulties of getting anyone to listen, that each party member was lost in his own agenda, and the whole game of getting elected and staying in power threw reason to the wind. With some parties vying for prominence, the Knesset often resembled a fierce family feud among competing brothers at the bedside of a dying father, rather than a parliament of wise statesmen.

He talked of his frustration of not being able to deliver what he had promised, due to the backbiting and deal making common to politics. "I really thought I could make a difference," he said, as drops of perspiration began to gather on the expression of his stress, even though the air conditioning was turned up full throttle and I, sitting across from him, shivered because the room was like an icebox. "I've worked so hard. I've worked so hard," he continued.

He sat up tall and turned his head toward the Old City. He had the answers. He felt sure his financial plan for the country would lift his beloved Israel to a new light in world view. His policies of high thinking would bring investors back to Israel and sanity back to the region.

His plan would create bridges with Jordan for joint water programs and environmental projects that would provide jobs to Arabs. His heart was in his work and on his sleeve. "Let us change the world economically, and war will be obsolete," he affirmed. "Invest in our country, our land, our people, and Israel would be a shining example instead of a war zone."

This Knesset member, who in a short three days would either stay or go depending on the vote, was clearly in an Armageddon of his own. He was longing to do the right thing and yet feared the worst. His nerves had already begun to break and his heart was close behind. He was up for re-election and today, the day that I was sitting in front of him, was a day of reckoning and soul searching. More than anything, he longed to do the right thing.

I, the woman who was listening, gave him the space to empty everything, and as he did, I saw through the eyes of the future that he was ahead of his time. I also saw that although the visions for Israel may not be accepted now, they were indeed visionary, and would be the choice of new generations.

As I peered more deeply into unformed but probable possibility, I saw that his daughter, a law student with high

118

honors, would one day rise to power and that he would have another chance to make a difference down the road. Through her, he would continue his fight for a new economy, and his love of his country would thrive and flourish on a new vine.

I shared my insight, and he was inspired and visibly relieved. Taking several sighs of resignation, his center of thought turned to his young daughter, which turned on a new light in the room and warmed the air around us. "Maybe so," he pondered.

Soon his smile was broad across his face, as his fatherly pride opened new doors in his hope. He spoke of her brilliance and that he knew she was special from the moment when she was first born. And he spoke of his promise to her when her first breath was taken, when her little eyes first opened, when he had first held her in his arms; to make a difference, to create a better world, to be the kind of father that she would be proud of.

Now she was graduating from law school, already making her mark on the world and my shared insight only confirmed what he had known all along. He sighed and sighed again and seemed lost in the gilded gold photo of the beautiful dark-haired girl that sat on his desk, lost in his thoughts and yet suddenly wiser than before. Acceptance bowed to disappointment and found grace.

It was a strange and exquisite moment of intimacy that passed between us, like time was standing still and we were just two people telling the truth, despite all the pressures to do otherwise, despite the walls of the Israeli Parliament that surrounded us and the fate of a nation and perhaps the whole world.

Several minutes went by and neither of us said anything. All that we had discussed was just too perfect to be disturbed. Nothing could be added and nothing could be taken away to make our meeting any better. Hand shakes, thank yous, and good-byes brought us back to the normal convention typical of politicians.

But what we shared from eye to eye and from heart to heart would not be forgotten. Later I got the news that he had lost his election and I, too, sighed with deep regret, but remembered his daughter and allowed acceptance to light the future.

I shared my story highlights with the Arab ambassador who was now leaning decidedly in my direction, across the table and across the gap of age, race, culture and politics, that I had not expected such a conversation to ensue, especially not between an American truth seeker and an Israeli politician. Hearing of the Knesset member who wanted to share water with Jordan and give jobs to Arabs may have turned the tide of his thinking, although many promises and deals, treaties and accords lay scattered in the path of trust.

Having a war general as the prime minister of Israel did not offer much hope from his point of view. But then again, having dictators for leaders in the Arab world that he loved, was no less reason to worry. He was clearly a very polished and civilized man, not keen on the crude ways of cruel regimes. But he felt surrounded on all sides and pushed like a chess piece on a game board by the West, and dangled like bait by Arab sentiment.

A thick dark eyebrow was lifted, wrinkling his forehead in a perusal of new consideration, as he otherwise held his gaze steady in thought. Perhaps the idea of a young woman coming into power in Israel in the foreseeable future, a leader, a statesman, a lawmaker, gave him, an Arab man, a politician himself, something to ponder.

As the lights of the Old City shined into the deep night that held our words in safekeeping, his previous expression of pomp and protocol softened, as I too leaned toward him and closed all the gaps that I could think of between my world and his. Outside the tall glass windows where we sat was the jewel of the ancient world, Jerusalem, that all sides lay claim to.

The spotlights on the rampart wall cast long streams of color across the smooth surface of the patio pool out on the terrace of the restaurant. More spotlights highlighted the large fountain that trailed off and cascaded beyond what we could see. New ground had been tilled; the water of life began to flow.

Now we would talk. Now our conversation entered new territory, the rough ground of reality and the need to make sense of a world given over to an empty wasteland hunted bare of the kind of leadership that truly can make a difference. A meeting of minds made a new choice and took the first steps toward the truth.

Tonight world tragedy would bring out the frankness that might otherwise continue to hide the only good side of suffering and disappointment I could think of, given the direction that things were taking in neighboring Arab countries, the same land from which Sarah and Abraham once set out in quest of the known within the unknown.

We discussed with mutual regret the hard fact of the Western world's hunger for oil and economic advantage, that gives way to wolves panting in the shadows and vultures circling above the carnage of victims for the spoils of war. Making money is a driving force that stands behind the strategy of war thinking. This includes the type of money that comes from war and postwar related infrastructure and companies with the ulterior motivation of oil somewhere in their scheme of things.

"Outright greed will never be true commerce," I said.

"Yes, and foreign companies need to be sensitive to the needs and culture of the people," he said.

"Commerce should be an exchange that causes the global Tree of Life to flourish," I said to myself.

"The balance of power and the fuel that feeds it is the real issue," he offered the context of the obvious.

The rumors of conspiracy were touched upon, although the Palestinian issue remained in prominent emphasis as a symbolic and factual crux of human mismanagement. The Arab world would never be at rest until the people of Palestine also came to rest in the homeland of their ancestors.

We agreed that despite the shady deals of war-inspired greed, and the domino effect of the war that began with Iraq, we would one day have to come back to the Palestinian problem, all the way back to wherever it began.

As he said this, I thought to myself, for all the money spent on war and conflict, we could have built a new Holy Land many times over, the crown jewel nirvana of all travel destinations. We could have built luxury towers for the Palestinians and shining new settlements for the Israelis in places thought to be impossible, avoiding the places of dispute altogether. We could have changed seawater to the floodgates of milk and honey and more.

But instead, fingers are pointed at self-obsessed dictators as the evil of all evils. Meanwhile, it's hard to say which is worse, legal war or illegal war. Regardless of the legitimacy of a war that is declared by a slim alliance of world leaders and voted down by the United Nations and, in a different venue of justification, a war that is waged by terrorists. One thing is for sure, war gives a wide berth to too many ploys, not all of them legitimate and some of them profane.

There is a difference between vultures that feed upon the vulnerable and the eagles that keep a sharp eye on freedom. One in its wide spread essence will not violate the human condition. One will hunt the faintest smell of the wounded with a keen sense of when the weak will fall, or in some cases, of the weak that never had the strength to stand in the first place.

Some people have no conscience in preying upon the unsuspecting, or betting on weakness, or rigging the game altogether, or manipulating the world economy to suit and favor a tiny, tiny segment of the global population.

"Exploitation is exploitation," he said, head in hand. "It's a curse, I think, that is left over in the bowels of this place," he almost whispered.

"The despicable downside of perverted human nature loomed like a bloodthirsty dragon o'er the land," I added with a half smile of resignation. "Vultures are on every corner these days, in boardrooms and private jets, in dusty basements and hidden contracts, in covert meetings that exchange the forbidden, looking for loopholes of advantage, seeking to make their fortunes from the misfortune of the helpless. This vileness did not limit itself to any one race or culture or country," I continued.

"It was rampant across the board," he admitted, shaking his head and surmising the unspoken. What a shock it would be if we were ever to trace the long line of wheeling and dealing to its source.

"Who would we find standing knee-deep in the brackish waters of outright deception and the international cesspool of corruption?" I asked and let my question linger on the fragrance of jasmine and honeysuckle vines, to pay due to the paradox that hung on the night air.

With this thought we paused for a long while and said nothing, sipped wine and ordered dessert. Even though it was getting late, well past the hour of duty, we entered the dialog of deception head on. No one wanted to cut the meeting short. No one was ready to get up from the table where truth was finally being told.

The rampart wall just beyond where we sat leaned in closer. The spotlights that beamed into the shadows changed colors to affirm attention. The alabaster fountain surged sprays of water even higher into the night sky to declare acknowledgment.

We resumed on the note that the entire region had become a self-igniting tinderbox, with terrorists forming a global alliance all their own. Now, with our hands in open view on the dining table, the subject of illegal cartels was more than touched upon. The way that the cartels feed upon human weakness and hard times was the true evil, and this we both agreed upon vehemently.

The methods of international weapons cartels, narcotics cartels, diamond cartels and financial cartels that cause the appearance of one thing to hide the real thing, are common knowledge in the streets. Everyone seems to know it is going on, but somehow the travesty continues.

This was the crux of our discussion as the night wore on and our meeting went beyond the normal hours and normal topics of diplomacy, and ventured into the extremes of unbelievable circumstances spilled out into the open.

Weapons, drugs and diamonds, raw or otherwise fabricated, seem to be the favorite contraband. What is real, what is postured, and what is deliberately made to seem real even when it is not was the crux of our concern.

"I hear large volumes of raw diamonds continue to leave the ground throughout Africa and reputedly continue to end up in the hands of questionable characters and malevolent plans," I offered.

"This is common knowledge among Third World hopefuls, who would love to have a piece of the 'get rich quick' action," he said, swallowing down the last of his wine and pouring milk into his coffee.

Diamonds, being colorless, non-metallic, and impossible to detect, are easy to hide. Millions of dollars of the clean clear currency fit into a tiny little bag in the pocket of a jacket or pair of slacks, the more casual the attitude when smuggling, the better. When the raw wealth arrives in Antwerp or Amsterdam to be cut into polished gems, no questions are asked.

It's not the problem of gem cutters and dealers to dictate the mining laws of other countries. But it's an interesting mix of established businessmen in the diamond trade, the unknown go-betweens, and the buyers and sellers on all sides of the bargaining table.

Who's to say who ends up supplying contraband diamond wealth, huge wealth, into the hands of terrorists, whether they wear business suits or combat gear, the robe of Islam or the Star of David, or just US dollars plain and simple; so it is said, and much is surmised. Who's to say whether scientists from Russia and Afghanistan and the like have formed new clubs all their own.

Who's to say who ends up supplying nuclear secrets to oppressive governments or radical factions, and who is

125

really behind the money that buys global disruption? Who's to say who funds whom, or who profits and who gains from wealth that is moved around the globe like a rigged wheel of fortune?

This has been the word on the street for some time. Diamonds, clear and beautiful, small and priceless, the age-old symbol of love, are the new contraband.

Now the talk went back and forth in a rapid volley. The illicit link between diamonds and drugs, drugs and weapons, Antwerp and Amsterdam, and Tel Aviv and London has been the big word on the street for some time. This and the link between drugs, chemicals, money laundering and nuclear materials, is a round robin of corruption that goes well beyond the borders of any country. The cartels answer to no one but each other, and their allegiance is to fund each other, and thus feed the dragon of all dragons.

And here is where we left all of it up to a higher power. It was just too much, too much. What could anyone do? He shrugged his shoulders, closed his eyes, and with a deep breath of consideration told of his frustration and his dear wife's hope that he would resign altogether, find somewhere far away from here to retire, and enjoy their grandchildren. Maybe they could do all the things he had worked so hard for all of his life, but then again where could he go at a time like this?

Finally, and I think somewhat reluctantly, we ended our meal just before midnight as the waiters of the restaurant stood by politely, hoping we would bring the talking to a close. Once again, expectations had been surpassed and the choice was made for an intriguing feast of the truth, rather than the shallow empty bowl of superficial banter.

We went our ways, tired but not indifferent, having seen eye to eye and heart to heart, ending our meeting on the mutual tone of perseverance and the cause of peace, a new peace, free from humanity's violation of itself.

We walked into the night on separate paths and ideologies, but on the common ground that saw beyond the surface of things that only perpetuates the illusions that the spin-masters of the world's politicians invest in.

Since my talk with the ambassador and the Knesset member, more talks with both sides of the political circles of the region and around the world have shed light on what people really want, really care about, and what they value. In the midst of raging war and cruel conflict, politicians are willing to talk to spiritual leaders from faiths other than their own.

More people from different walks of life are reaching out to one another than ever before. More people are searching for answers. More people are listening. More people are calling out. More people are looking to the past, so as not to make the same mistakes. More of the world community are trying to do the right thing, even as governments are slow to take the high road. Change is nonetheless taking place.

My time spent as a visionary, as a humanitarian, as a fellow world citizen with leaders from various professions has made way for many eye to eye and heart to heart connections. One on one is the icebreaker of prejudice and outdated assumptions. It is from human connection that the roles and titles fall away, simple desires are voiced, and common bonds are established.

The hand extended, the meal shared, the differences seen as the richness of diversity is where we cross over from petty fears to the bounty of friendship, compassion and admiration.

What I hear as the "listener" is that home and family and children remain at the top of most everyone's list, along with a love of the homeland that has given them life. These are the values that we all value. In the midst of all the alleged and suspected corruption, there are indeed politicians and public leaders who are true servants, sincere public servants, who struggle to make sense of things.

There are many that I have met who have held their personal integrity intact, side by side with those who do not. There are those who are true statesmen, but sadly and regrettably, they are daunted by the hardships of political campaigns and the money game of getting elected.

But perhaps this unprecedented time of planetary decision will cause a rising up of a new leadership that will not be sold-out, a giving of wealth that sets a new example, and the holding of values worth holding, far, far from the battlegrounds and travesty of war, far, far from the unsound financial practices of existing election laws or corporate laws, and farther yet from the spoken and unspoken laws of war or the deception thereof.

As the planetary crisis heats up and threatens to boil over, more of the hidden is being unraveled and rolled out for the whole world to see. Recently released statistics from public news journals and magazines indicate the extent of American dominance in the world arena. With only 5% of the population, the US produces close to half of the world's economic output, and projections for defense spending are soaring to indicate that the US will spend as much as all the other 191 countries combined!

It should come as no great surprise that citizens in other countries are growing increasingly apprehensive of

America's role in the world. Who and what does America answer to? With whom and on what basis does America cooperate with other nations to secure a sustainable future for all world citizens?

The age-old rule is that power with no system of checks and balances is power that is prey to a loss of perspective. Our own country's constitution and democratic system is based on this principle. What principle governs our effect on the rest of the world?

The majority of nations are feeling far from trustful of a US government that boasts a cavalier top dog attitude toward military interventions. Hackles are up. Natural instincts are aroused that may very well fail to see the wisdom of American policy even if and when it is there.

Is the process of communication and consensus worth the time it takes? When we rush ahead, where angels fear to tread, are we really setting civilized examples? Would we want to be treated in a similar fashion? Would we passively allow another nation to barge into Canada or Mexico without regard for our opinion?

Some left-wing radicals in the US would very definitely claim that the citizens of America and the world have been hoodwinked, run over by a father and a son who have had their day, and that those days are numbered. An opposite claim would also be exclaimed that such persons should put up or shut up, love America or leave America, and the like. Both are the extreme, and most of us stand in the middle. And yet the questions remain, at the same time that the facts are what they are.

There is no doubt that the US has been the largest and most powerful economy in the world. But the US is also the world's largest debtor. Our lust for all things novel, wonderful and better, maintains a healthy consumer appetite that is fed with globally produced goods and services. Our "balance of trade" deficit has reached a staggering imbalance.

The hard fact is: the money must be repaid. Growing up as children we are all taught these basic financial matters as we watch our mothers and fathers balancing the family checkbook. The approach for our national debt has been to borrow from foreign investors through the sale of stocks and government bonds. This has worked for as long as it has because of the perceived strength of the American economy.

However we are now on the eve of a new story. We are self-creating a different perception. We are perhaps cutting off our nose to spite our face by acting as if we answer to no one. We are definitely in over our heads. We are closer to floating down the river, much closer, than American citizens in their insular presumption might comprehend.

Recently, both private investors and foreign governments have been looking to the euro as a more secure investment opportunity, and we have seen its value against the dollar climb dramatically, and also climb onto the high ground of old world wisdom and hard earned new world cooperation, which Europe can claim as the solid ground of legendary lessons learned.

These are the statistics of global economics, the economics of war. Is anyone listening to our imbalanced state of the union for a planet barely hanging onto its orbit? While I am not a financial expert, I am a tax paying citizen, an American citizen, and a very concerned global citizen.

I do not agree with the radical voice of peace activists that lay heaps of blame with played out rhetoric on everything that ever lived and breathed outside of themselves. I do not personally see the need to engage in mindless displays of rebellion and defiance.

I do see the need to be wide-awake and in full command of our intelligence. I see the need to responsibly discern truth from untruth, and to separate the wheat from the chaff. I do love my country, and I do appreciate that I have the freedom to also love a vision for a future that can only come from international laws that assure a sustainable environment and ethical corporate practices that are globally responsible.

I do not advocate war, and yet I know that the wide arm of human evolution may very well continue to choose war as a process that ultimately leads us to peace. And so I accept that I am part of this larger humanity.

Perhaps we need to experience a full-blown scenario of what does not work, in order to be compelled to get down to the brass tacks of what could work if the smokescreen of deception was removed from the equation altogether.

One can hope for a good earth as well as accept the process that brings bended knees to a new surrender. Even though a part of me is appalled at the mentality of war, and very well should be, I also see that war brings us, as do all extremes, to a sort of forced decision point. We are forced to face ourselves when extremes become the hour of reckoning.

Now in modern times our soldiers hand out relief supplies of food and water to sustain the lives of the people upon whose land the battle is being fought. New values are making history. This, although still a sad state of affairs, is more humane than ages past, when ruthless conquerors razed villages to the ground and raped and plundered with the vigor of pure animal aggression. We are indeed moving forward on the wheel of evolving human existence on this planet. Aren't we?

But is this enough and should we be satisfied with meager displays of generosity? How do we define generosity? As we watch our fellow human beings, the true victims of both war and dictatorship, push and shove with desperate grimaces on their faces, to catch the relief packages of minimal survival that are thrown to them off the back of army trucks, should we feel satisfied? Have we the privileged done our share?

Or instead, does the creeping thought speak in the shadows of our civilized minds, "My God, they are throwing these starving people almost nothing to rebuild their lives, like throwing bails of hay off the back of hay trucks to cattle that have just endured a bad winter blizzard."

Is this the face of our nobility? Is this our choice, our personal empowerment of choice? Is this the face of privilege? Is this the purpose of wealth?

It seems that no matter where we look, money and the misdirection of wealth lie behind every problem. Poverty remains our true enemy. Over half the world could become citizens with bright futures who contribute, who, through the spark of new dignity, could make a difference not only in their lives, but also to the benefit of the greater world.

Over half the world lives in a self-perpetuating squalor of poor health, poor education and no means to any end other than continued poverty. This breeds desperation, and desperation breeds anger, plain and simple. The polarity between lack and greed, too much and too little, is our greatest adversary. Can we not see the big picture beyond bullies, dictators and madmen?

What I see is that there is a screaming need for a new era of global economics that will move on the wings of great minds that are given the go ahead to sort out the distortions and dig out from under the deceptive thinking of the past. The premises of the survival of the fittest and gain at any cost are foolish approaches that are better suited for the chest-beating of the jungle. Our animal nature must evolve to a higher order of life and living, instead of eating its own species alive. We must become human beings, all of us.

The shortsighted ways of the past cannot sustain anything but the greed of those who benefit from such thinking and even that, I feel, is on the sharp edge of meeting its Waterloo. Poverty must become the focus of great minds and great hearts, the legacy of a new round table to which noble souls gather.

Poverty must be recognized as the single most important change that must be made. But this change must include not only the poverty of economics but also the poverty of spirit.

As humanitarian values become the new battle cry, human dignity will be restored, and from that uplifting the bright eyes of children will see beyond the shackles of the past and will rise up through their inherent nature to create a better future. Opportunity and cooperation is the mother that will heal the human spirit. Global guardianship is the legacy that future generations will remember.

Already, new and innovative education programs are being launched in the inner cities of America for underprivileged kids, and the results have been astounding, again proving that given positive environment and decent opportunity any child can quickly reach for the stars, learn and grow and succeed.

These charter schools and innovative alternatives are looking for the answers and creating the new methods that assure opportunity for one and all. The education of the world's children in an environment that fosters human values will turn the wheel of humanity's walk upon this earth to a truly higher order of life.

I listened to a lecture by a professor of economics from Harvard University recently on solutions to world poverty. This was not one on one or eye to eye; I was only a silent listener in the crowd. But I have to say the man was not only brilliant but also had his heart in what he was saying. He told the truth about the World Bank, Third World countries, war, famine and disease.

He offered all of the statistics that backed his contention that people who do not have health cannot repay loans. People who do not have access to loans or the stewardship of their own land cannot participate in the global economy. People who do not have education cannot develop the skill base from which to make a contribution.

This state of affairs was originally perpetuated through the imperialist activities that extracted natural resources from the countries that they subjugated many hundreds of years ago as strong empires sailed the high seas looking for wealth and booty. In most cases, the best was extracted from both land and humanity and very little was returned, if anything, other than the legacy of disease and the desecration of life as it had been before their arrival.

A wretched imbalance of the progression of human development and thus global economic relationships is now the compounding result. Sustainable corporate governance in all national, regional and global commerce and economics must be the hallmark of any new era that seeks to preserve and further life on earth.

In short, the professor's lecture produced many reams of statistics to present that we create enormous expense by not caring. The problems get so far out of control that we lose sight of what caused the problems at the root of the rot in the first place.

Like a marriage gone bad, a stitch in time saves nine, if only self-interest hadn't blinded everyone, creating the parody of opposing agendas and the disparity of haves and have-nots. Some day it's going to hit even the most "blinded by self-interest" people, that the planet we live on is but a tiny speck in the sky, with finite dimensions, resources and habitat.

The professor's statement was simple: by taking only 2%, a mere drop of the total world gross global product, and investing in education and healthcare, poverty could be ended. For 2%, we could change the world. For a mere 2% investment of our global wealth, peace on earth, good will to all, could indeed be the global legacy of the wealth of wisdom. War would no longer drain the creativity of humanity into its clutches, and instead, the bright minds of the young would be directed toward world good.

The Palestinian/Israeli conflict is a prime example of unjust economics, poor education and crippled opportunity that has brought a people to the cliff edge of desperation, even though all sides would thrive from the economics of peace.

The "no" to war, is also the "no" to social injustice, the culprit of economic imbalance. It is not a "no" to human life nor the lives of soldiers, many of whom are in the military for economic reasons. Some could not get an education or training in a trade any other way. The poor are the backbone of the military in almost every country; the kids have no other opportunity to get ahead, the nobility of patriotic sacrifice notwithstanding. Is there no other right of passage? Is there no other access to education? Must kids be willing to give their lives to get ahead?

Because of the circumstances in Israel and in any number of global hot spots, tensed-up soldiers assigned to get the job done, as it so often is referred to, run the gamut of human diversity. Some are nervous, some trigger-happy, scared and looking for a fight. Some are sullen, bored and looking for diversion. Some are noble protectors and soldiers of honor who take their duty to heart and are willing to give their lives. They are defenders of their country and their people and their mothers, and they do what they do with care and conscience. They are good souls and are loved by their families.

Like people everywhere, it's a mixed bag of the worst and best of humanity on all sides. The good and the ruthless stand side by side.

In Israel, serving in the armed forces is mandatory for all young men and women, and I will not argue the validity of this national defense policy. There are the usual "for and against" among Israeli citizens lined up in a face-off, that shifts like the desert sand depending on the peace time, war time mentality of the moment.

What I will say again and again is that our greatest wealth is humanity itself. It is not the oil in the ground or the stocks traded on Wall Street. Our greatest wealth is the potential of our young. This is a wealth that we should fall down on our knees to uphold, protect and invest in.

But here in Israel, the military is the law of the land. What I have witnessed is that there is a group mentality that comes with societies that govern from a centerpiece of military control, and what I see is that it often goes in the wrong direction. The over focus of a military based society is problematic, whether we look at countries in South America or Asia or Africa or the Middle East.

War can indeed bring out the best and the worst, but when the worst is running out of control, it is truly a horror of humanity and a thing of gut-wrenching regret. In order to be willing to kill breathing flesh, soldiers first have to annihilate their own humanity. They are trained to get the job done and are also trained to have no emotion about doing it. It's the trade school of terms of engagement, a value system all its own.

I can well appreciate that waking up each day with the possibility of losing their own lives or taking the life of another, is something that requires them to give up a part of their own souls. They don't have it easy: the soldiers, any soldier, the Israeli soldier.

And I felt tremendous, tremendous compassion for them, even the ones who scared me. I surmised that part of the Israeli collective humanity had already been lost during the holocaust, and this loss had been handed down to them from their parents and grandparents. It is hard to forget such tragedy. It is hard to go past the past.

My heart goes out to these kids in the Israeli army. It is especially heart-rending to see the ones who just aren't cut out for the military at all. The ones who are fragile by nature, boys and girls who carry their sensitivity deep inside but visibly tremble in their combat boots and look down at the ground, uncomfortable, when I ask them for directions and which way to turn, left or right, as they are posted on street corners throughout the Old City.

Paradoxically, one of the most holy cities in the world has soldiers posted on nearly every corner around the clock. This predicament is a planetary problem that they shouldn't have to bear in the first place.

I once had a young woman who was an Israeli soldier approach me after a lecture, break down and sob, asking if I could help her understand her life. Being in the military was torture for her. She was of a delicate nature better suited for a gentler vocation. Since then more and more young soldiers have spilled their hearts and guts out to me, in hopes of finding an answer to their anguish.

But in Israel the law is the law, and in the case of the fragile young woman, it is the law that she has to be a soldier and do her share. All youth must serve in the military, which means that all Israeli youth must first be trained to kill as a social, political and religious priority. College comes later, if at all these days. Bright minds are given as war-fuel to war councils of justified survival.

And then there are the kids who lose their souls completely, who become twisted with the power that comes from automatic weapons, like those who stand by jeering, while watching a fellow human being suffer or bleed or die. I've seen the extreme look in the eyes of these young souls, orphaned of their own consciousness. It is the look of utter meanness. I've seen it.

I have been a personal witness to the atrocity of hatred. It is not casual. It is not of duty or honor. It is of another world, the flip side of sanity, that same insanity that drives terrorism at its core. A hard and cold and cynical ruthlessness has taken over. The schizophrenia of the chosen or the unchosen, holy or unholy, Sarah or Hagar, Isaac or Ishmael, David or Goliath, Jihad or Zion, kill or be killed has taken its toll. We need to ask ourselves why.

In my view, among all the wounded in this conflict, they are truly the most wounded in this place of paradoxes. They are the casualties of a pristine promise that can't stop weeping. To lose one's humanity is to lose one's soul, a terrible frightful awful price to pay.

Youth with weapons cluster on the street corners throughout the Old City, as a necessary fact of life. This is their duty and their sacrifice. But often pride grows dangerously on dangerous soil. Meanwhile, I never forget that I am lucky that they are assigned to keep the peace.

It could very well be my life that they are protecting and, to be fair, this sharply cutting reality does not escape me. This is what they are trained to do, and this is how they are expected to be.

But I am told that some soldiers weep at night and collapse when they go home on leave to visit their mothers and fathers, because being tough comes with a lot of grief. Their parents weep for them, too, never knowing when a phone call will announce death or injury. So I feel compassion for soldiers and the parents of soldiers.

Meanwhile on all sides young men and women are asked to give their lives in the military and to do so with a sense of honor, an honor that grows strong from the bond that comes when you know your life is in the hands of the person who stands next to you.

But then again, couldn't the bond of mutual sacrifice come from a more constructive, productive circumstance than war? This being said, even though I feel that we as a planet are at a choice point and I choose peace, I also honor and respect the sacrifice of soldiers who give their lives for what they believe in.

This is just one more polarity in an age of polarity. Most people that I speak with don't want war but will concede to war as the only solution to keep home and hearth safe and free from aggression.

Most activists on the peace side of things don't want war, at the same time they feel compassion for soldiers, especially the soldier who by some twist of fate is in the right place at the right time to save the life of a peace worker. God works in mysterious ways indeed.

But what I have also witnessed is that humanitarians and relief workers also run the risk of soul loss through the loss of faith and hope and the seeming futility of their efforts to stem the tide of suffering.

There is a willingness now on the part of protectors of human values to make sacrifices for one's cause that run parallel to the willingness of soldiers to sacrifice for the cause of a nation. Peace workers and soldiers would get along well in the neighborhood of sacrificial ideology.

We are a unique lot, the self-assigned peacekeepers and hope-filled helpers of new education, the struggling environment, the cause of essential human values and much needed economic reform. We never cross paths with illegal diamonds, drugs or weapons and very little in the way of funding for the sanctity of human life and the birthright of opportunity and prosperity for one and all.

As insults are hurled between patriots and peacekeepers, let us not forget that we are all in the same backyard. We are not on opposite sides of the fence, not really. I feel that I have a lot in common with the patriot, that I myself am a patriot of the planet. Perhaps "planetary patriot" is another new term to be coined. Peace is a cause worth the nobility of sacrifice, whether one's ideology moves in the direction of soldiers at ground zero or relief workers who arrive as the bombs are falling to pass out rations and blankets to get through the nights that follow.

I am told that the number of people voicing the choice for peace is growing, but exactly how many world citizens are calling for peace is hotly disputed and discounted. At the same time all over the world sentiment is growing that terrorism must be stopped, but so must war be stopped. Wars do not solve underlying problems.

The worse it gets here in the Middle East and globally, the stronger the conviction and commitment being voiced on all sides. What will be next, will housewives in American suburbs take to the streets fighting one another in a pro-war versus anti-war massacre?

The paradox continues to become more and more absurd. Movie stars in America in full-hearted conviction are saying, "not in our name," to war, to all war, to this war. The ideal of a world at peace is held in sincere regard, even as more and more war movies are whetting the appetites of young boys and diehard patriots. Others in the entertainment business see war as the only realistic answer. I see an incredible power that lies in the hands of the infamous "Hollywood" to use such an almighty influence as media and movies to move the world onto high ground.

In wartime, everyone goes to the movies, it is said, and that business will be booming on movie sets and back lots of studios, even as missiles fill the skies and empty the world's treasuries everywhere. This is a place where a difference can truly be made and a legacy left behind. These are people who shine like stars and will be remembered for "not in our name." Not in our name, and then what? What will be the legacy? What films will be remembered from this time? What far-reaching eloquence will be expressed that inspires change and transformation?

Will the film industry continue to pump out more and more mediocre war movies just to turn a buck? Will this be yet another economic factor that plays out, affecting

141

the values of millions of people? Would there be an interest in something far more dynamic, movies that framed
the essence of the time and the true heroes that will in the
end turn the tide of our future?

What can filmmakers do to bring the vitality of human values, the wealth of our planetary potential, into the
bright lights and sweeping vistas of cinematic greatness?

Whatever transpires, we all can make a difference. We
all can take the high road to a new place of greater nobility no matter which side of issues we stand on. Wealth is
wealth; we as a planet are our own greatest investment.

Is not a more humane world worth investing in?
Should not our global thinking turn the corner in the direction of conscious evolution of human values? Should
not our UN programs for woman and children worldwide
represent more than a tiny tea cup when compared financially to the ocean of money that goes to fund the high-tech
demands of war?

The economic price of war is staggering and comes
with incomprehensible repercussions, the costs of which
are incalculable. The economy of human values is sustainable investing at its best and most noble.

It is here that I will leave my commentary on money
and wealth, peace and soldiers, and values and economics. I will leave this territory of the age-old issues and the
all new dramas that bring together Arab ambassadors and
American visionaries, who sit on the same side of the table
looking out over Old Jerusalem, as the wealth of the world
cascades through jasmine vines and the prayers of the
prophets.

Chapter 8

The Women

Mothers of Soldiers, Mothers of Souls

I am no one special. I am only a mother. I am one of many mothers who have come to the Middle East initially on the wings of idealism and the deep red promise of the blood of the sacrifice of even my own credibility. You cannot be here and not cross the line of convention, erring according to the opinions of someone about something. Political circles in the US call us a *special focus group*, and declare that serious decisions regarding war cannot be swayed by our advocacy of peace, due to the fact that we are considered an insignificant sector of American and global society.

But despite the opinions of the politics of the day, I am one of many who feel compelled to respond to an inner knowing that a balance to global governmental politics must be voiced. I consider this time in history to be a time of conscious evolution. However, as the name "conscious evolution" implies, my influence, whatever it may be, is intended to be offered in a consciously respectful manner in consideration of all the differing viewpoints that we as a diverse global humanity hold dear.

This said, there are those who feel a special call to arms to protect not only the sanctity of the region, of the Holy Land, but also the sanctity of human life globally, through non-violent humanitarian means. My work embraces the core of human conflict here in the dust of the prophets, but also in many places of causes globally. I do not consider myself a hothead, an extremist or a left-wing radical. I consider myself an intelligent world server, even though some would say that my nature leans in the direction of spiritual idealism or idealism of some kind.

In comparison, I'm sure that the slave owners in the South during the American Civil War, considered the anti-slavery Abolitionists to be the idealists and betrayers of their day. And yet they were compelled to be the voice for change, even though the need for change was not as yet recognized by the masses in the South. Likewise, I feel that the movement toward a more humane world and ultimately a world without war is an idea whose hour has come.

Hailing from diverse backgrounds, philosophies, religions and convictions, peace workers, humanitarians and what I sometimes more appropriately call world servers have converged in unprecedented numbers at the grass-roots level in the many places where human values are calling with a desperate but unshakable voice. We are the bridges between the east and the west. Many of us seldom if ever participate in a peace marches. For some of us, the demands of working in the trenches, executing practical social, educational, relief and aid programs leave us no time for peace marches.

We are a new global alliance without walls or formulated constructs. We are authorized by no one and yet are the largest philosophical collective of like-minded souls ever assembled in one place at one time, the place of the heart and the place of a different kind of survival.

We belong to non-governmental organizations (NGO's) and close-knit groups of vast diversity, and our

144

mission is largely global in scope, even though the Middle East is now the feature story, the drama that brings all factions of the human dilemma face to face. The curtains are drawn open. The stage is lit. A saga is unfolding with many players on all sides chiming in with no script and, I would guess, no real clue where it's all headed or what could possibly be the grand finale and curtain call.

Survival of a different, a more benevolent kind, is the goal of world service and those servers who are giving their all to the cause. Women in increasing numbers are filling the stage and are seated in the audience. They are the producers and the ticket vendors. They are everywhere in every capacity. The theater is full to capacity, and now women are spilling out into the streets.

Every day, I am told of someone new who has arrived in the region, a new group or agency or relief advocacy, who has joined in answering the call, the inner insistence to do something to make a difference, even if what can be done is nothing more for some than bearing witness to the atrocities. We also are joining in like-minded alliances all over the world, with hotel conference halls, town plazas, city avenues, community libraries and personal living rooms becoming our impromptu meeting places.

As women, we gather on the side of a new decision, and a new choice, one can understand the issue on all sides well enough. One can well understand the rationale that is put forth in favor of force and war, kill or be killed. But for many women, a gnawing internal awareness knows that this rationale can only perpetuate more of the same. And I think this is the point. A different kind of decision must be made, at the same time that missiles are being launched from either a well-meaning or misguided premise.

Regardless, I think it was well said that, "One cannot resolve a problem with the same mind that created it." The brilliant Einstein said this many times. Perhaps the mind of a woman is well worth exploring.

Foreigners, who really don't have much of knowledge of the situation, join locals who have lived here in the Middle East all their lives. Liberal young college women from America flock to Gaza and sit side by side with Arab mothers wearing the veil. Aging silver-haired women from European countries converge on the streets of Baghdad to give aid to the wounded and homeless. Housewives are fundraising for victims of terrorist attacks here in America.

Our common bonds are the desire for a peacefully sane world on the one hand and the inability to sit back and witness human suffering on the other. The foreign "helpers" listen and respond to the locals who just want to live a reasonable life and are fed up with all the fighting and the cruel reality of so much destruction. Because they are mothers, they are good at listening. The mothers are listening.

Being mothers, they must develop the intuitive side of listening with the birth of their first child. This intuitive wisdom is God's gift to the survival of the human race. Otherwise, how could the mother sustain the life of her infant who does not speak and cannot voice its own needs? The mother, all mothers begin the relationship with their child solely through intuitive listening.

This art of special listening is also an excruciating painful talent, when the need is known but the response that is needed cannot be given due to a lack of resources or the absence of an environment that can sustain human life. I can think of nothing worse than the experience of the mother who feels her child's pain but is helpless to remedy that pain, the mother who feels her child's hunger but cannot feed her child, or who longs to see her child shine but cannot assure her child the basic necessities of human life.

Long before the current round of turmoil, a group of mothers who call themselves the Border Watch stood day in and day out along the blockades surrounding refugee camps and occupied territories where Israeli soldiers stopped cars and inspected their occupants. The Palestine refugee camps have been an atrocity since the 1948 war, and remain a problem for the Israelis who feel they must control who comes and who goes.

Sometimes the drivers of the cars that are scrutinized by soldiers are known terrorists. Perhaps these terrorists are funded by the mysterious conveyer belt of diamonds, that become drugs on the streets, that become money for weapons and bombs... who knows?

When found, the drivers of these cars are arrested or even shot on the spot, depending on their previous violations against the general population of Israel. Westerners read about the border clashes in the newspapers while sipping coffee on their way to work, numb because it's an old story.

The women of the Border Watch post themselves as witnesses of humanity, not far from where the Israeli soldiers are called into account for the lives of the living and the deaths of either the unfortunate or the deserving. The women stand as mothers, most of them. They are grateful for the respectability of their gray hair. They are grateful that they have lived long enough to be mothers and grandmothers. Some of them have sons who are soldiers.

Most of the soldiers are still teenagers or in their early twenties, at best. A few are older and have their reasons for making a career out of the military. But most have, in fact, not been long away from their mother's supper tables. Some no doubt would prefer to be at home and find their dinners waiting for them, through the kindness of their mother's heart and her skillful ways in the kitchen.

And so the Border Watch women watch with the eyes of mothers, hoping to curtail unnecessary cruelty, hoping to bring the young soldiers into account for the sanctity of the life that mothers give to their children, be they Arab or be they Jew or be they anyone else.

A few years ago, I broke down in tears upon reading the account of one activist in particular, who had been organizing peaceful resistance to the increasing violence in Israel and Palestine long before the famed and fateful intifada insurgence even began. She's a real die-hard, who just kept doing what she's doing, year after year.

Over the years she quietly orchestrated sit-ins, stand-ins and marches in the name of peace and the wisdom of women. She had given her life to the cause of human rights, and she organized women in particular. Her story is relevant now. Her story has stayed with me. Her story is but one of so many.

When I first met her, my heart went out to her because she looked so tired. There was a hardness to her, the hardness of someone who cares deeply, but struggles with it. From my own experience, it's impossible to care and also survive the suffering without a bit of hardness to balance out the backlog of tears in the night. I doubt that she knew the extent to which I cared about her circumstances, or the depths of the very visceral compassion that had taken hold of my heart as she shared her experiences with me.

Not long ago, after all her years of unpaid work and sacrifice, she was invited to Washington, DC to share her activist insights. The thought came to me that she deserved some kind of peace grant for her quiet but significant efforts. But like Mother Teresa of Calcutta, the saint of the poor who toiled without recognition most of her years, the peace activist's heroics have gone largely unnoticed. No one is smuggling the peace activist diamonds to fund her efforts.

No one would even fill a tin cup, were she to beg on the street. I assure you, activists and peace workers like her don't have time to beg and don't have the advantage of clandestine circumstances. They just have to get by. There are no medals handed out and no guarantees of medical care or fringe benefits for their sacrifice.

In her case, considering the long run of the grueling years of volunteer peace work, and the pitifully short run of telling her story to politicians in the US for an hour or so, I consider my friend the activist to be an unsung heroine. It bothers me that the nobility of her humanity is not recognized as anything special most of the time. She, an Israeli, described her trip to America as difficult. She came back to her beloved Israel frustrated and poorer for the journey, no diamonds, no dollars, no grant or funding in hand. There was no award and no financial compensation for her travel expenses, let alone for so many years spent in the trenches of social activism. She looked even more tired than when I first met her, and yet she carries on.

If it were ever within my power, or if ever I could do something to make a difference in her life, I would make her life easier. I would shower her with what she needs to carry on. Perhaps having a secretary would lighten her load, perhaps money to put gasoline in the tank of her automobile, perhaps funding for women's peace, education and leadership programs. I don't know what she might see as her blessing. I just know that she deserves better.

People like her should be held up as role models for children to emulate during their formative years. If we look at western culture, what is the message that we give to our children when Barbie Dolls and G.I. Joes become the role models?

Her story still impacts me. She told of the time that she was the driver of a car, trying to get through a road-block at a border checkpoint marking the separation between the Palestinian and Israeli territories. These are the military checkpoints, the hot spots that are the constant subject of news reports. As an activist she is a member of the Border Watch women's group. She is a Jew.

Her passenger was an Arab and also a dear friend. Her friend, a pregnant mother-to-be, was obviously in great pain, writhing in the throes of labor as her as yet unborn child made its way down the birth canal. The Arab mother had been in labor for a long time, and there were complications. Despite the fact that moving her to a hospital would involve unusual risks, the risks of trying to travel through checkpoints in Israel, the decision was made to get her to medical care.

My friend, the activist, rose to the occasion of seeing her through the checkpoints to the hoped-for safety and attention of a hospital on the other side of the world between Arabs and Israelis. What she saw, however, broke her heart and damn near broke her spirit. She saw soldiers forcing the panting and trembling mother from her car, to be roughly treated and cruelly subjugated. She saw the soldiers jeer at the round-bellied Arab woman, as if she was the scourge of the Earth. She heard them make ridiculing remarks and vicious accusations.

They refused to allow the pregnant mother through the checkpoint. Instead they stood by in a cocky arrogance, laughing and smoking cigarettes as the pregnant mother broke down and dropped to her knees.

In an unbelievable worst-case scenario, the calculated risk quickly became a gross and tragic reality. What began as a risk worth taking now became life threatening. The poor woman had no choice but to lie down on the side of the road right where she was. She couldn't control the descent of her child or its fate to be born in such surrealistic conditions, conditions that could only be described as a nightmare of human defilement.

She was forced to give birth in the dirt. Her child was born to the welcome of machine gun-toting teenagers, posing as future fathers of a nation, sneering with the ignorance that comes from the depth of their own pain of forgetting.

It is unthinkable that mere youth can decide the fate of birthing mothers. Who gives the young and inexperienced the power over life and death? This thought truly haunted me long before my friend sent me a letter sharing her pain-filled story.

This same anguished thought struck me hard the very first time that I came to Israel and witnessed the predominance of so many young boys and girls in uniform carrying guns. Of course, strife and insanity always plays out this way with younger and younger gun-toting youth worldwide.

When I first came to Israel, I wasn't prepared to see large numbers of young women soldiers shouldering automatic weapons. It felt very uncomfortable I have to say. An automatic shiver went up my spine of not feeling safe because usually women could be trusted not to be annihilators. Not that I don't believe in non-sexist equality of opportunity, but what kind of equality is gun-toting for future mothers?

Of course survival shapes all rationale. But I wondered as I read the horror-filled gut-wrenching border check story, what if a female soldier had been present, would the cruel treatment of the pregnant woman have scarred the humanity of every single soul present to such an atrocity. As it was, the soldiers were standing in clusters like snarling wolves, armed with menacing weapons, all but spitting on the newborn infant who gasped for air in the dust on the side of the road. Would a woman allow a woman to give birth in defilement? I cried for a long time when I was told this story.

I was in America when I read the activist's letter. The paper upon which the words were written bore not only her heartbreak, but also her anger. Who could blame her? What happened was unthinkable. What she had witnessed over the years was far more than her letter could ever hope to put into words on a page.

You could see a different kind of craziness in her eyes. The track marks of hope and futility lived side by side. The commitment to take a stand, to say "no" to the loss of souls, to say "no" to the degradation of the helpless. To say "no" had taken all of her strength for a long, long time.

My heart went out to her, too. Her letter was one of the turning points in my work as a visionary, as a peacemaker, as a spiritually motivated humanitarian, as a human being. I don't know if she knows that. Probably not.

There are so many stories to be told from the side of the fence where peace workers and humanitarians hold their torch, and with much sacrifice become the torch, as the cause for love and truth, the inherent good will within the human spirit continues to call us to it's rescue. I've had to be selective, staying true to my own life-changing turning points, taking care not to become a fanatic myself, to know my convictions, but also practice tolerance and compassion for all of the roles being played out, from presidents to peacemakers, from soldiers to rock-throwing Arab youth.

This is a war of human insanity, of losing our way. We can blame no one but ourselves because this is a collective planetary problem. From the intelligent placement of responsibility upon ourselves first and foremost, we must find our way. My own quest has been to find our way in the midst of the unfound and still lost.

Here in the Holy Land, not all peace makers are social or peace activists. Some are spiritualists of varying faiths and dedicate themselves to prayers and patiently, quietly occupy the Old City's plazas and sanctuaries. They bear witness to places like the site of the Last Supper, the birthplace of Mother Mary, the Western Wall, the Rabin Square, the Holocaust Memorial, and the Shrine of the Book which displays the Dead Sea Scrolls.

A large percentage of these light-bearers pray for peace and benevolence around the clock. Young rabbis join old Catholic priests, monks from Tibet join the women, nuns from many traditions join the hippies and activists because praying is praying. They choose an inward path to peace.

Instead of attending peace marches and sit-ins, they bear testimony to a higher wisdom and maintain the lament for divine mercy. The circles of women are everywhere. There are rabbis and sheikhs who sit together in interfaith dialog, that understanding might come from bloodshed, as the women listen with the ears of the heart.

This is one of the areas that I have facilitated through our seminars. Understanding is always the bridge to the heart that creates new pathways of possibility. We must all seek to be bridges of one kind or another for a new kind of survival, one that breaks away from the cruel exclusion and prejudice of the past and comes to rest in the sovereignty of the human heart.

Women take food, clothing and medical supplies out to the Bedouin camps in the desert, to families whose lineages reach back before anyone was a Jew or a Muslim. Several hundred thousand Bedouins have been cut off from basic necessities because the roads are blocked and supplies aren't getting through. Their suffering has become heart wrenching, and they indeed remain a lost tribe of Israel, at the tail end of all consideration, a people left in another century, but with something intrinsic to offer through their ways and wisdom in the desert.

The Bedouin women very much want to rise above the archaic conditions that have been compounded by small-minded tribal chieftain power, to find their own power to feed and nurture and educate their children. Women, who are helping women, form the bulk of the effort. Women use the wisdom of listening to respond to what is needed.

The Bedouin bridge is a bridge that must be built. They are a people who must be included in the aftermath of war fervor and frenzy. Women will build the bridges with their bare hands, if necessary, to see that their children have a better life.

All of this has driven me to find answers and to serve as a bridge myself between the visionary realms and the hard concrete of practical on the ground in-the-dirt remedy. It was impactful for me to watch these women of many organizations, like Border Watch, go about the business of showing up every day on the lines of peace making and humanitarian activism, as if they were reporting for a nine to five job anywhere, anyplace.

But Israel, Iraq, Afghanistan and the entire Middle East are not just anywhere and anyplace. It is the hot bed, the burning bush, and the flash point that could change life on this planet for every soul who lives and breaths and hopes to continue to do so.

It is rare that there is any mention, any attention, any credit given to the grassroots, behind the scenes, true backbone of everyday people actively making a commitment to the intelligence of the peace process on the evening news or in any newspaper that I've ever seen. Zilch.

Awards to women are few and far between. Funding to women is likewise scarce or non-existent in many countries, and I have to say, far from adequate and even farther from admirable in the US.

For many years women have struggled to get good and viable programs off the ground, programs that help people to overcome the pitfalls that lead to war and the trauma that is the face of war. Maybe as we eat a steady diet of war and more war, continued terrorist attacks and the like, we will eventually come back to what really needs to be done to stop war and terror altogether.

Meanwhile, women, like the mothers of the Border Watch, go to work in the salt mines of the peace effort, not knowing if they themselves will be the next targets. These women see it as their "life's work" to do what they are doing. Although profound in every possible way, and anything but routine or ordinary, they simply accept the hardship and the challenges of volunteering for a peace movement that, in its collective context, has so little recognition in the world arena of men who choose war and terror.

Today women remain either a special interest or fringe group. Tomorrow they may very well be remembered as the heart that went out to all the world, when we as a human race teetered on the hard edge of cold, cold annihilation.

Has anyone in the US Senate ever heard of the Fifth Mother, or the Global Peace Initiative of Women's Spiritual Leaders, or the Women of Vision and Action organization, or my organization the Peace Promise Initiative, or any of a host of other women's organizations and leaders dedicated to promoting practical programs for people in need and peace in the world? In some circles peace is an unpatriotic dirty word. In other circles, peace talk is the steady diet of proactive, positive social thinking.

I speak with a passion of the intelligent efforts of great minds, because the lenses of news cameras would have the world believe that peace activists are only "whackos" from the leftist fringe, with pink hair and tie-dyed tee shirts. It is maddening for a spiritually motivated humanitarian like me, to witness the uncanny way that the camera selectively seeks and falls upon extremists, and interviews lean heavily on the side of emotionally wrought college kids.

Why don't news reporters more often interview the intelligently constructive, socially contributing mature women who form the majority of the humanitarian, peace and social change advocacy? Why is the public not shown more of the intelligent solutions being voiced and practical programs being launched? There are indeed conventional people who are taking radical measures for the first time in their lives, many of whom are ordinary women who would never think of painting their faces or wearing their hair in pink dreadlocks.

But they too, even pink haired activists, play a role. Desperate measures are indeed being sought, precisely because we have fallen upon what most people would consider to be desperate times.

Perhaps it is also time for a new era of global guardians to create a few new media alternatives that are not controlled by politics. From my point of view, when public media loses its soul to the money game, what we have in the end is a one sided imbalance that saturates the public mind with its own self-serving agenda until it all comes tumbling down.

Perhaps women will rise worldwide to rock the cradle of new enterprise, new finances, new media, and new leadership. Perhaps a young Israeli law student, daughter of Knesset politician will find her way to the top but will also remember why she is there.

As the Israeli army moved into Ramallah in the spring of 2002 to flush out Arafat and his stronghold, a stronghold of women marched for peace, silent and wordless in the face of lumbering military tanks, soldiers and terrorists alike hell-bent on a confrontation; the women marched sure-footed straight into the lair of the lion. They did not gather in support of Arafat, the entrenched ruler. They gathered to protect the innocent that were in harm's way, as ruthless men on all sides began their assault.

The women, some of whom knew their own sons were the soldiers on the other side of the fence, marched into Ramallah to protect the people who had no protection, no advocacy, no voice. They were Arab and Jew. They were women.

And they were over 4,000 in number, back before demonstrations and peace marches had become commonplace. They came from every direction, from every economic and social background. Many wore white as a statement of the purity of peace and human values.

They were willing to be killed for their cause. Again, they were willing to be killed for their cause. 4,000 women stood together willing to be killed for their cause. And being killed or wounded was a very real possibility. The bullets of soldiers and terrorists don't discriminate, and sometimes the finger that pulls the trigger does not care.

They are among the self-regulated, self-organized, self-motivated and self-financed, as they set about the business of bringing an end to the suffering that they live in the midst of.

If only the nations of the world, the powerful nations, the wealthy nations could have some comprehension of the people who are holding the frayed edges of the Middle East together: the ones the politicians don't see and don't even know exist; the ones who gather together and sit for peace every Friday at the Wailing Wall; the ones who take food and clothing out to the Bedouin tribes and build medical facilities out of straw bales; and the ones who try everything possible to continue monumental projects in the fragile land of rock and desert, and they do so on next to nothing financially. And then there are the ones who convene in public forum throughout the world now, as a growing sense of global guardianship is taking hold.

And then there are the women who have joined the ranks of the unrecognized, women who have literally collapsed in my arms, crying like babies, worn-out and frustrated, seeking refuge from their exhaustion, but more than exhaustion, seeking relief from the pain that they can't somehow be doing more. These are the ones who go door to door to gather blankets for refugees. There are the ones who empty their pockets and personal bank accounts for their fellow humanity.

These are the people who do it all for free, with no campaign whatsoever on their minds, other than the commitment to stop the suffering, in the bold-gutted center of it. These are women who, from their own human dignity, are simply responding to a crisis of human depravation in every way possible, as war chests are filling with the guns and weapons of dictatorship.

Despite all the obstacles and setbacks, despite the lack of funding, despite a lack of fair access to the media game, something important is swelling and coming alive within the hearts of women worldwide. When I received the word that a group called Women of Vision and Action were calling for an International Women's Day of Peace, called "Gather the Women," I was elated.

Millions of women rose to the occasion and continue to do so by holding gatherings, meetings, circles and NGO board meetings all over the world, millions of women all voicing a single call for world peace in the midst of the rattle of sabers and military action that kills innocent women and children and elderly and young men in their prime in unprecedented numbers.

But more than this, a literal revolution is taking place in the world of non-governmental organizations with well-planned solutions being launched every hour as a positive response to global crisis. My own dreams and visions and around-the-clock efforts run along parallel lines, coinciding with the global effort that is sweeping through the lives of women in their offices and homes and workplaces with the same response, an immediate and instantaneous response to stand and be counted, and moreover to roll up one's sleeves to improve the quality of life for everyone.

Perhaps if the people who sit in the boardrooms and command rooms of power could witness the gunfire that broke out between terrorists and soldiers, that took aim, triggers pulled hard and hateful into the peace-seeking feminine humanity that had amassed in the name of peace at Ramallah, one of many new congregations of women that stood strong, as death bullets shot whizzing over their heads…

Perhaps if politicians had witnessed the dignity and courage of housewives, students, professionals and activists, young and old all marching together, something would be ignited and the flame fanned to do something radical like legislate for human values.

Idealism dies hard when everything else has failed. Perhaps the diehard Palestinian problem could become the living resolution that changes the world for the better and sets an example for conflict resolution for future generations.

Perhaps we, as women, will no longer be called a fringe group or a special interest group not deserving of due. Can the women of the world, over half of the total population, be called a fringe group? I think our day, our era of leadership is coming, leadership that embraces politics, finance, medicine, education, science and most of all human welfare. We are the ones who listen.

Moving on the grass-rooted wisdom of gatherings, meetings and conferences that have gained momentum in so many countries, I have gained insight from these women, the salt of the earth and the wombs of new generations. They come to my seminars and peace conferences with their strength as their wealth, and I go to theirs, offering what I can. They are educators, doctors, lawyers, housewives and students. They come wearing high heels and beach flip-flops, business suits and hippie dresses. They are not willing to sit idle and silent. They are not willing to repeat the tragedies of history, like when all of Europe sat in passive blindness to the schemes of a madman. They can't, and they won't.

Even the young Queen of Jordan has been known to march in the streets in protest of human suffering and the cause of improved lives for women and children. I applaud her for her passion and caring, and also for her personal respect for her religion. I thought to myself, a prominent person who lives in the public eye, who is willing to be seen and be heard for the cause of peace, for the welfare of her people, and for the integrity of her culture; this is rare indeed.

Good for her, may her example inspire women around the world. But may we all remember that we are the advocates of all people everywhere, all souls and the birthright of a true humanity; one that will rise up after the ashes of war horror, of stubborn struggle, of madness and greed have fallen silent and are no longer the choice of world citizens.

And so my own work and thinking and inspiration move on the momentum of those who have gone to the gut of things. I only hope that the love in my efforts does these women justice. Maybe there is the force or the hand or the heart of something that is greater than all of us, greater than all the conflict that humanity ever heaped upon itself, moving through the days and nights of all of this.

Maybe I am not the only woman who feels called to do something to turn the tides, in this "burning out of control," senseless fight called the Middle East conflict that rages now in every country around the world, in some way or another, the war of human values, the war of conscience, the war of religions and politics and economics and oil.

Several years ago after a day of hitting hard brick walls and doors slamming in my face and backs turning in refusal, I retired in the evening with a troubled heart, and the mental condition of hope fading into despair. But I prayed for a vision, a message or some form of direction. I awoke the following morning from a crystal clear dream. I was given a vision that is simple and yet all-powerful in its message and its result. This dream has shaken me to my core, as if the power of God descended upon my being.

Although I do not compare myself to great souls, I could no more ignore it than Moses could ignore the directive to bring the Ten Commandments down from Mount Sinai, or than Gandhi could ignore his inner passion to take a stand on the political oppression of the people of his Indian homeland, or than the Dalai Lama could ignore the destruction of Tibet and his people's way of life, or than Mother Teresa of Calcutta could ignore the destitute; an inner fire that couldn't be compromised or sold-out burned within her giving her strength and guts and compassion.

This is the fire of true leadership. This is the fire dream that is burning holes in my doubts. It is a living light and a living power that is quite simply beyond me. It moves me beyond my own fear and sense of inadequacy in being able to make a difference.

It came in the form of a revelation like watching a movie of the future in Technicolor. In my dream, I watched in amazement as women of every race and culture began to gather together in the call for world peace, for social change, for human dignity. The joy and the energy and the power that was shared among us all was overwhelming. To be a witness to the unity of women made my heart swell, heave in my chest and crack open to a greatness of love and purpose. Jerusalem became one of the primary focal points of the gatherings. I could feel my body in full response although I was dreaming.

Even though the struggles of Israel and Palestine served as a catalyst, and the devastation of Iraq and Afghanistan fueled the flame, and the grim results of terrorism on US and Western soil ignited a new demand, the unified message was world peace. To love and to protect and to nurture the world's children was the single motivation. We sang for peace, prayed for peace, marched for peace, spoke of peace, taught the virtues of peace and called for peace as one voice.

The women embraced even the soldiers who fought, as they, too, deserved the sweet peace that rewards their sacrifice. And so the women even sang songs for soldiers, and from the songs came vision and from vision, the call to action poured into new efforts, as the reality of compassion began to flow out to those in need.

The simplicity of this demand for human dignity crossed all boundaries of religious, national or political affiliation. Even though it began with a single call to gather, I saw the gatherings becoming larger and larger over a period of time. I saw them becoming more and more frequent.

Soon our numbers were so great that we held the gatherings in large tents and then in a series of large tents, large white tents that looked like whitecaps in the sun, and we carried all the times we had sat under the billows of the white tents of ancient times together in our hearts. And then there were no tents large enough to hold the swelling numbers of women who gathered for peace.

Soon we simply filled the Old City and the New City and cities all over the world with not only the call for peace, but active solutions and personal involvement. We were everywhere, standing side by side, fearless and filled with a common power that belonged to us all. I saw women coming into Jerusalem from all over the world, even though it meant tremendous personal sacrifice on the part of many just to make the journey.

They poured into Jerusalem in great numbers. In time, the women were joined by countless men and children. All shared the universal belief in human dignity and human values, fostering the right to live a life free from the fear of world destruction. In my dream vision, the gatherings took place even as the bombs of conflict fell from the skies.

The gatherings continued to grow in size and global significance, until all the world watched the "Women's Call for Peace." Because the gatherings were by some miracle finally televised in their true content, our call for peace reached the living rooms of people in every part of the world, from every religion, from every economic background, from every nation.

The numbers were too huge to ignore any longer. And the call was heard; and the women were seen; and the leaders of nations were moved to think and act differently. Hearts were opened worldwide in the desire for peace, but more important, the fertile ground for new ways of living around the world, was seeded with the choice for cooperation and coexistence.

A new vision for media and television was given birth with power programming that showcased people who cared and dared to make a difference. The power of this dream was awakened within the minds of the multitudes. And it became a living thing. A new life was born to all the human family. Peace on earth became the treasured child of all families, and the human spirit shared by us all became its rightful guardian and caretaker.

From this common desire our hearts beat in unison. We became the vast majority. The world became weary of war. And then a global decision for peace was made. Peace became the global choice. The prophecies of the ages for a great and golden age of peace were made manifest.

And the children of the world rejoiced, and all the world's citizens were of glad hearts, inspired by the promise of human dignity for all. The dream then lived on, with every soul on earth making a noble contribution to a sustainable future of global good will, prosperity and abundance as our human birthright and inheritance of life.

When I awoke from this dream of women remembering their internal promise to uphold and nurture life, I knew I would never be the same. I knew that what I received through that dream was a miracle, a miracle of love and power.

Perhaps this dream is voicing the plea of the children of the world who have no voice. What I will share with you is that this dream is an absolute mandate. It is a call from the heavens, from our Creator, and I knew when I woke up that I was not the only one who was given this dream. I was asked, as many were also asked, to call women, all women from everywhere, to come together for world peace and a new era of global guardianship.

No other agenda is present within this utter simplicity, this moving mandate to stand and be counted, to be seen and to be heard. When peace and the proactive choice to make a difference is the absolute desire and the noble choice, the resolution to world conflict will turn the corner and head in a new direction.

It's a matter of choice. The message to be broadcast and the purpose of our coming together is simple. Our coming together is a living, breathing statement of choice. The simplicity of choice is its power. Making a promise to peace will make it a reality.

I was in Tel Aviv in the fall of 2002, when I was told of the 'Gather of Women' movement and that many women had received the same or similar vision that I had received. I was in the thick of things, with everything escalating on all sides and the eve of the war of confusion fast coming to everyone's backyard. I received this call from the women that I had met at the women's spiritual leader's conference at the UN in Geneva.

It was an affirmation that positive forces are indeed working behind the appearance of things, and this was reason to count our blessings. Perhaps the peace between Sarah and Hagar, that I envisioned while sitting in front of the Golden Gate of the Old City wall, among the sunlit grave markers of past prophets, was moving through the mass consciousness of the women of the world.

Yes, this is what came to me; this is what came and found itself on the pages of my efforts. It is here that the spiritual seeker becomes the humanitarian and the humanitarian becomes the builder of a new era, and dreams become the inspiration that open the heart and cause us to engage. It is here that a human being becomes a human being.

From this dream the ongoing project and commitment to the Peace Promise Initiative and the concept of global guardianship was born, and with its wet-faced emergence came the daunting work of bringing dreams to the holy ground of how we live and what we do, and practicing peace and world service knowing that our lives depended on it.

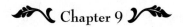

Chapter 9

The Journey

Lessons of Blindness, Lessons of Sight

Everything happens for a reason. Count your blessings. My mother used to always say that. She said it
a lot as if it kept her alive. Sometimes just by repeating
this simple phrase, my mother's wisdom helped me to
accept the self-imposed mishaps that lay strewn in my
path, when I still dramatized the tediously mundane, as
if it were a priceless piece of art in the Louvre. And sometimes that particular combination of words seemed like
nothing more than an excuse to ignore what was mine to
carry. But then again, my mother died with a smile on her
face. Not many people do.

It's been an overly long day, filled with extremes. It's
not easy to go from the holy ground of gravesites and
disappearing grandmothers to the arguments of peace
workers who can't even agree on the pecking order of
personal philosophies.

I have plunked myself down at a little outdoor cafe
that seems like an island in the midst of worlds that don't
meet in the middle. I am sitting in the Muslim Quarter of
the Old City because I like coming here. The faces of the
shopkeepers in this little corner of the Arab sector have
become familiar to me and I have become familiar to them.
I've come here often enough over the past few years that

I receive nods and smiles as I walk through the narrow passages that wind through the neighborhood. There's something about the tangible humanity of this part of Jerusalem that reflects back a simple richness and my body all but drinks it in, the smells, the colors and the hum of life.

I need to go over my notes, collect myself and consider some new proposals before calling my secretary about tomorrow's schedule of meetings and tasks. We will need to check out a new conference center that is located between Jerusalem and Tel Aviv that is mutually owned by Arabs and Israelis. The only problem is that they might not have sound and audio equipment, which means we'll have to rent it and also operate it. This has to be factored along with the security issues. Our security advisor has vehemently warned that just because the center is partially owned by Arabs, this won't stop terrorists.

I order my favorite, fresh-squeezed pomegranate juice, while perusing the short menu of regional cuisine. A broad-cheeked man, whom I haven't seen here before, graciously takes my order, eying me with a combination of kindness, curiosity and uncertainty. He's not quite sure of our status of male, female, Arab, American, server and customer.

He chooses to be charming. He chooses to open his heart. He chooses to return with a glass of fruit juice, offering a genuine politeness that is much appreciated on my part and common to the Arab culture on his part. I am comforted by his warmth, his flashing white smile, and his sincere manner.

To be the guest of an Arab is a demonstration of the reverence of friendship that is extended by culture and tradition to the guest. A weary traveler will be welcomed, embraced, fed and honored. This has always been my experience in Egypt and Israel and Palestine and Jordan and Lebanon. His gesture of kindness is embracing, giving a loveliness to the simple experience of taking a midday break.

The clear pink-red of the pomegranate juice, a local delight, reminds me of the Kool-Aid drink my mother used to give us as kids for a backyard treat in the summertime. It is tangy tart on my tongue and sends a shiver through my body, and I notice it kind of gives an interesting alertness to the mind. And over 50 years later, I feel my mother's broad smile that always came with the pitcher of Kool-Aid back in the 1950's, when the American Dream was taking root in the US after the war. It is a bright sunny day with a clear sky; the cafe is peaceful; so far, perfect for collecting my thoughts, organizing details and pausing just to sit and be still.

Feeling safe and taking a deep breath, I remember something about the color of the dawn this morning as it melted darkness and turned things around to give me hope, hope enough to count my blessings, and I drank it in. Yes, counting blessings was one of my mother's better habits. When I was young and drowning in my own foolishness, I thought both she and her comments were just old-fashioned, idle, outdated words falling stern and ridiculous from her mouth when my frivolous antics caused her to grieve with worry.

Now that she is gone, my memory is awash with all the things that were good about her, and her now wise and enlightened counsel. I am close to building a shrine in her most holy name, as an offering to the angels for the consideration of her sainthood, counting my blessings for all the times she counted mine on my behalf.

The angels surely sang their full-throated best when my mother passed on from this world into the next, walking willingly, like an arrow of grace and certainty straight into the arms of death. She had called me at seven in the evening to politely inform me that she had decided to move on, that she had had enough of her weary body. She had lived her life. She had spent her lot. She had found her treasure.

Five hours later she claimed her self-chosen gateway and was gone. Just like that. She died with a smile on her face. She went into the arms of creator without so much as a fleeting flicker of a struggle and I need to say it again; by her own hand of surrender and by her own decision, she slipped away in utter bliss with a smile on her face, no less.

At her funeral she looked like she was already keeping company with the highest of the heavenly host. The look on her face transcended her death and transcended her life and transcended all the times that she had to say to herself, "Everything happens for a reason. Count your blessings," just to keep on going.

Lying there in her casket, her hands were folded across her chest in peaceful supplication, with fingers gracefully turned at the tips, as if she had practiced this special mudra her entire life and had mastered the ability to change the fabric of reality with the gesture of her hand. Her hands and the way they expressed her grace told her life's story of sacrifice and surrender. Hand postures of benevolence, mudras of blessing, mudras of benediction, followed her into the afterlife, like I imagined the Christ with hands uplifted while he blessed the multitudes, fingers outstretched as he anointed the faithful from the Mount.

I had all but filled the entire chapel where her funeral was held with yellow roses, hundreds upon hundreds of perfect yellow roses, the day I said good-bye to her. Their delicate sun-hued petals paved her ascent to the starry realms, I hoped. Even the steps that led up to the carved chapel door were blessed with yellow roses. Each rose was in memory of all the times she had said, "Count your blessings." The petals, which were scattered from the stone steps outside all the way down the aisle to where she lay at rest, had a memory all their own.

My mother died with a smile on her face, like an enlightened saffron-robed master from the Himalayas. From what I understand, monks and holy men in faraway places like Tibet and India spend their entire lifetimes trying to achieve that kind of command over the flesh. It's all a matter of surrender, I think, and the willingness to turn your mind over to a higher power for remaking, to gain the ability to see things differently, to see beyond what something appears to be on the surface. Death for most souls is a struggle of paramount proportions, a shocking finality, and the presumption of a terrifying darkness and the silent silence of nothingness. For my mother it was grace and relief, living and dying, joined side by side without struggle or complaint.

Like her enduring spirit the thought is still with me, to see beyond circumstances without struggle or complaint. Actually it is more than a thought, it is whispered benevolence that calls out to me in my hour of need from across the galaxy, or farther yet, "Look little one, see with the eyes of the heart." It is the kind of thing that the mothers of saviors and messiahs would say, or maybe my mother.

As this thought trails into the next, I set my intention to see beyond what seems to be real or ordinary or perceived. I cast my eyes into the deep well of my waiting heart and search for new visions or old visions, any kind of vision that endures and transcends. I close my eyes and swill down the last swish of pomegranate juice, setting my glass down on the little round tiled table.

The narrow shaded streets beyond where I sit are quiet. The surrounding Old City is oddly peaceful, as tourists are few and far between these days and most folks don't go out anymore. People stay inside, as if dusty old walls can prevent the blindness of world leaders from pushing the button of a slow moving holocaust that will not stop this time with a single race or culture.

People are inside, which makes it quiet and empty outside, but I feel profoundly at ease and relaxed. It is an emptiness that is full. I feel surrounded by my mother's love, as if she wants to show me something, one last gift from mother to daughter. I give in to the tranquil sense of letting go, and allow myself to drift off as if in a daydream.

Through my mother's memory she lets me know that she wants to show me something. I am shown a room full of blind people. Their eyes are closed. The eyes of my heart are wide-awake. It is as if I can see through the windows of love to unfaltering, unwavering, crystal clear perception. My mother's presence is floating like a faint silvery reflection of how I remembered her, welcoming me to her world of wisdom and she is softly, ever so softly saying, "Everything happens for a reason."

Strangely, as I stand among what I have presumed to be blind people, I am aware that I am the one who has been blind, blind as a bat, blind as a vacant lot of blank dark-eyed emptiness. I can see now that the blind people in the room are not really blind. They use their blindness as a doorway into true seeing.

The doorway, like the beautifully carved chapel doors that welcomed my yellow roses, is flung open. Each rose petal is like an eye that can see the face of God and the reason behind truths and secrets and revelations. Yellow roses are filling the air, drifting like suspended halos all around my mother's gestures of beckoning. A pathway, a celestial carpet, a yellow brick road is strewn before the footsteps of free souls who have gone to God in the bliss of a trusting heart. Yellow roses leading wayward souls like me to the illumination of angels and their hearts of golden mercy.

Allowing this excursion into my mother's wisdom, I am overcome with gratitude, like the cripple who has been made to walk, or the cancer victim who has been cured, or the mother who has just breathed life into her dying child, or the blind person who has just been given sight for the first time.

All the feats of Jesus rush past on my inner mind screen, as if Lazarus had not only been raised from the dead, but had also been granted the Herculean strength to become a champion Olympic runner, bearing the torch of the eternal flame for all of humanity. Everywhere, Jesus is healing the sick and lifting up the dead and causing the blind to see. Jesus is gesturing skyward and with barely so much as a touch, ignites my eyes with light, blinding, awakening light, as my upturned eyelids tremble and flutter and well up with the wetness of awe-struck overwhelm.

My mother was a Christian, although I, who have traveled the world as a seeker, consider myself a universalist, a humanitarian, a lover of life, a spiritually inspired guardian. But through my mother's love and faith I am seeing and feeling the spirit that moved through Jesus from a new perspective, wide-eyed light-filled benevolence. It is the same spirit that moves through every soul when the soul is awakened to its goodness.

My mother's grace is parting the veils from my world to a new world of possibilities. My mind is reeling. I feel as though I have been blinded by a centuries-long blindness and then in a single moment, in a flash of lightening blazing across the velvet void of the night sky, all is illumined with the brilliance of a thousand suns. I can see color, shape, texture and movement for the first time, transposed upon itself in multidimensional wonder of undulating creation.

But more than this, I can see meaning. I can see purpose. I can see the great sweeping hand of fate and its abiding wisdom, the hand that gestures stars and great solar bodies into their right time of birth. The eyes of my heart have opened, like deep pools of never-ending perception, born with the birthright to an innocent unity with the eternal procession of life, to receive understanding and to make sense of it.

With an acute shudder to viscerally register such good fortune, I can now see beyond a shadow of a doubt that the surface of things in the world of men and women is not as it appears to be. Walking into the light, I can see with the vision of bliss and am absorbed by my surroundings.

Glancing around the room, I can clearly register that the blind people are not saddened by their blindness. They are in appreciation of what their blindness has enabled them to see. It is almost like I am witnessing an elite club of special people who, through their refusal to accept their physical blindness as an adversity, have used their condition to design a new future.

Like my mother who left this world, and all of her worry and suffering, smiling, they have transcended their condition with effortless triumph. They share a special bond of fellowship, and that bond has broken the tenacious web of illusion that holds the world of earthly souls in its suffocating grasp.

The "blind that are not blind" have overcome all illusion of blindness, like the day I drank lemonade on the hillside of the 144,000 with the Grandmother of the Tribes. Seeing with faith, the opening of the archives of the past, showered me with the songs of Sarah, the matriarch of the Tribes of Israel, and the strength of Hagar, the womb that bore a new generation that filled the desert. In the end both returned to love one another as sisters and daughters of the same God.

If only women everywhere could see that Sarah and Hagar have made peace after 4,000 years, perhaps new holy books could be written for a new age of sisterhood. Perhaps women worldwide could see what needs to be seen, rising up into the promise that feeds all souls and all nations alike. Perhaps yellow roses would grow in every garden and bring the fragrance of truth to the living.

I can feel the sense of ease among them, Sarah and Hagar and the far-seeing blind people, their ability to see the most important thing of all: their own essential unity, their natural commonality as a single living breathing reality. As I continue to observe, I witness a serene confidence among them and an encouraged creativity that is being passed from one person to another. Their unity is a wonderfully contagious miracle.

The room is saturated with the excitement of the unlimited prospect of boundless creation as the catalyst for giving and receiving. The atmosphere is saturated with the wealth of the communion between souls. Blessing and good cheer and the expectation of the new and as yet inconceivable splendor is the jeweled and rose-covered ground upon which they stand.

They are seeing with the eyes of the heart, so much more than was ever conceivable or imagined, and for this they are grateful. They are living in the spirit of counting their blessings and celebrating the blindness that enabled them to have knowledge of their true sight. The glow of their hearts is infectiously inspiring, as I myself am taken in by the radiance that is dancing in every direction.

I notice that there are large golden altars placed in a circle of luminous alcoves around the room. Upon the altars are monolithic volumes of what I am immediately aware are sacred scriptures, living holy books of light-filled fiery letters, letters of origin, letters like the breath from the first of all beginnings.

I just know, like a mother knows her own child, that these are not just holy books written by human minds, they are the Great Books of Time. Like the seeing blind, I see with love eyes. And the heart vision that the pages are radiating is the purest of light, gossamer, subtle, yet piercingly bright as a stargate. The Word Is.

One by one, the people approach the altars in reverence, slowly making their way around the circle. It's as if they are receiving a vast and universal education by engaging in a precise and spontaneous ceremony of wisdom seeking. Each step that they take is a devotional offering.

Each foot forward touches the tender velvet of yellow roses. Each altar that they approach is alive, receptive and forthcoming, like a beloved parent who beckons and embraces the approach of a cherished child, coming home from an eternity of wandering upon the cosmic high seas. The Word Is. And the Word Was.

As each one bows down before the altars of wisdom, their hands are outstretched in supplication, in the mudra of holy making. Hands held in prayer-filled reverence, the gestures of blessed gratitude, cause the books to open, and the translucent pages to turn. Placing their fingertips tenderly upon the holy books, just a wisp of a touch is needed, just the barest skimming of a feather's touch, simple with the caress of love, the volumes of eternal wisdom are turned on.

It is as if even the altars begin to hum a celestial intonation, a vibration of promise and heart. Sacred letters of fire seek the hands and fingertips of these awakened souls. The holy books are literally singing with a living intelligence as the blind people absorb the wisdom therein. The Word Is. And the Word Was. And the Word Will Always Be.

With rapt attention and eager concentration, each person spends the allotted time flying over the pages, like soaring golden eagles and pure white doves, with a wholeness of body, mind and spirit, which reminds me of the totality that is engaged when a surfer rides incoming waves that mysteriously rise from the ocean's depths. The touch of devotion and the offering of the heart lift into visibility what looks like ancient symbols that pour like streams of fiery liquid light as the living pages are steadily turned and their contents gathered in. The Word Is. The Word Is. The Word Is.

My mind flashes to realize that they are reading something that could be compared to Braille, but it is much more. They are reading a form of spiritual vibration, it seems, and by receiving a language of symbols, the Great Word, through the heart and fingertips, they are registering information on a combined sensory and intuitive wavelength. They are reading not just information and not even just wisdom; they are reading the experience of the quality, nuance and character within the symbols. They are gathering in the essence of meaning, the fiery ignition of lettered thought, before the fall into form takes place. They are reading the omnipresent life within the ALL of Wisdom. They are reading the timeless intelligence within the symbols, The Word that has ever been the great life of Agni that turns the wheels of time.

The all-seeing congregation is inspired to the point of being transported to some exalted altered state, because the experience of such a vast and spontaneous continuum of information is so liberating. They seem as though they are in utter bliss, but at the same time they are very intent. There is a definite purpose to all of this, which they clearly take seriously. Even though they are working together in a state of union, wonder and creativity, each one seems to know their specific duty. They are servants of the Word. They are guardians of the Word. They are messengers of the Word. And the Word Was in the beginning. And the Word Is.

Even though I am aware that I am sitting in a chair in a cafe with the sun in my face, in the late afternoon of a breezy day, I can feel tremors and quakes of profound understanding moving though my body. The energy of the room of people that I am witnessing in my dream-vision state is absolutely electrifying. I am crisply aware that I am watching pure genius reveling in its own joy. Just to witness this is a miraculous gift.

Then it hits me. Had I not, in trust, stopped to sit down in this cafe in the Arab sector; had I not drunk deeply of the nectar of pomegranate juice; had I not trusted that I could be truly safe in the embrace of Arab hospitality; had I not paused to look more closely at this room full of seemingly blind people; had I not remem-

180

bered to see with the eyes of my heart; had I not remembered my mother's quiet breath when she said countless times, "Count your blessings. Everything happens for a reason;" I may have missed the true perfection that was unfolding. I might have missed the whole thing and been able to see only with blinded sight, the limitation that my ordinary thinking would likely have imposed upon this reality of infinite wonder. Instead, I would have hurried on my way, and never for a second have been willing to sit alone, an American woman in the Arab sector.

O God, the now-apparent sin of my thinking, "They are blind and see nothing but darkness," has come full circle, the same blindness that once built golden calves and atom bombs, is wide awake with new insight. All the world is fighting all around me and no nation is safe anymore. How we shut the door, we humans, to what could really be! How we close our eyes to what would set us free!

Finally, I am in the fullness of a life-changing understanding. Each pathway of perception opens a very different door of possibility. Yellow roses are everywhere. Yellow roses are filling my heart with the eyes of angels and the single eye of God. As a result of the dream vision of blind people and the common bond of Sarah and Hagar returned to the sisterhood of their humanity, the hand of God reached through time and space to put a stamp of remembrance on the contents of my personal history.

Like a letter taken to the post office and stamped with an imprint of destiny, I too was imprinted to look beyond the surface of things, to the hidden but real, and to the deeper meaning of the lives of the living and the possibilities that await our discovery.

With the words of whispering angels who said to me, "See with the eyes of the heart," taking hold and integrating into every fiber of my being, I sense how this experience will inspire my work as a peace maker, as a soul who seeks to serve the supreme possibility.

But even these trailing thoughts are swept away, like the ocean's undertow pulling nameless grains of sand from the edges of the shoreline. Gradually, stillness takes hold, smoothing the surface of residual thoughts, and I am able to drop down beneath any remaining ripples of soul searching, as I leave my journey to the realm of the blind, but spiritually awakened, and the union of the mothers of future generations behind and gradually return to rest and mellow in the secrets of my heart.

With a newfound understanding, I open my eyes. The gentle hand of the Arab waiter is taking my empty glass and wanting to know if I'd like to try his mother's specialty, a dish that's sure to please. "Yes," I respond. I'll take his mother's special fare. Pile my plate high. The rest of the day can wait. With mouthfuls of savory stew, onions and spices and plump raisins and the tastiest of warm soft bread, I continue to give thought to the day ahead, feeling safe and fed and grateful.

My thoughts flow easily and gather in the smells and sights that surround me. This brings order and new ideas to my schedule of possibilities for tomorrow. Already everything looks different and hope-filled, empty of blindness and full of seeing. As I leave the little cafe behind, I notice that my footsteps seem cushioned with light, as if each step is being guided. Once again I remember the spirit that is behind everything. It's been a good day in Jerusalem, and I am glad for the wide white smiling of the souls and great hearts that live here.

Chapter 10

The Messengers
Wings of Nations, Wings of Flight

Sitting across from me, hands folded on the table, are two gentlemen both dark-haired, both dark-eyed, both native sons. They have come to discuss their role in next week's conference. There is still enough hope to continue to meet. Would discussion panels on assigned topics be better than separate discourses?

One wears a suit and is running for a Labor party seat in the Knesset, the Israeli parliament. One wears his hair long and organizes sit-ins for peace every Friday in the plaza in front of the Western Wall. Both want peace. One tells me new candidates are needed, maybe even a new party; something has to change. One tells me even the soldiers who patrol the Western Wall say that they hope all the prayers of the sitting peace-crusaders will bring peace; even the soldiers want peace.

After meeting with the two men from opposite sides of society, we decide on panel discussions, and we choose three other speakers to join together on the topic of shared land use, environmental issues and reconciliation. We decide on multi-speaker panels because the men, the politician and the hippie, were able to work through their differences and see a common goal, eye to eye.

I sigh with relief that the matter is settled. Sometimes there is an edge even between peace makers, especially when we seat an Arab and a Jew next to each other at the same table. Grief and the loss of loved ones strains even the most noble of intentions. This morning's meeting was smooth, like the mahogany tabletop that reflected back the effort to coexist, cooperate and forgive. Hands were folded peaceably for most of the talking. I was grateful. This makes my job of interviewing and planning and organizing a lot easier.

They decided on their own to coexist, to sit together, to share the limelight, to speak as a unified group. I didn't need to point out that sitting on the panel together shows solidarity, sets a good example, and shows that coexistence is possible. They decided the same thing on their own, the politician and the activist. The first meetings of the day are off to a good start. We shake hands, pat backs, and agree to meet again next week after the conference is over, to address the more immediate issues of keeping the peace programs funded.

They leave the room shoulder to shoulder still sharing viewpoints. I'm pleased to see open dialog bridging the gulf of differing life styles, cultures and ideologies. In this precious moment, peace is more important than social or religious or political polarities. The keynote of unity and cooperation is following them down the hall and making their steps lighter and more hopeful. The thought, "keynote of unity and cooperation" continued to reverberate into new ground upon which an acceptable future might be possible.

Then I'm the only one left at the table. Empty coffee cups remain as I reflect on the larger matter of planetary coexistence, the shining surface of the conference table mirroring back my state of aloneness and relief, a coexistence I am slowly getting used to.

Thinking back to a few months ago, when I was talking to a group of a hundred or so during a lecture that I was offering at a hotel just down the street, I remembered one of those profound moments that helps me not only to get through the day, but to also do so with a conviction of purpose that helps me to stay the course. I remembered sensing that something more was waiting to be touched upon. I was the keynote speaker at the conference and somehow the "keynote of nations" began to speak through me, as if the concept of a keynote woke up and started ringing.

This surprised me as much as anyone. It surprised me because it was as if the living power of God-given goodness within the origin of things wanted to be understood, wanted to be spoken, wanted to be heard, wanted to be given life in the place where it was most needed.

A keynote is the true original premise, the purpose or motivation that brings something to life. A keynote is a primary theme or thought or idea that gives shape, context and content to our existence, or the manifesting effect of the essence of a thing.

The concept of keynotes in general was revealed to me on a trip through the Sinai Desert a few years ago. It was there, stripped down and surrendered, in bewilderment and humility, that something broke open revealing the divine idea that each soul is propelled into life with the sounding forth of a great purpose. Like a cymbal being clanged, like a kettle drum being struck, like a tuning fork ringing true, each soul is set forth on a course of divine destiny.

A keynote strikes the tone of a clear potential. I guess this is where the celestial chorus of angels comes in, with the trilling of trumpets and the harps of heaven, which first filled the sea of nothing with the life of everything.

It's hard to put into words something that is as abstract as a keynote of divine origin and yet this fact of resonance is at the core of the finite in its infinite reflection. But the best way I could describe it is that the clear tone of a keynote sets us all straight. Every soul has a quality that will be its gift to the whole of life, in fact to all of creation and everything in it.

Personal fulfillment and our quest for identity and meaning will always be fleeting and full of angst until that original keynote, quality or sound is set free to ring like the mother of all church bells across the landscapes and seascapes of souls. A soul, every soul must be what it was created to be in order to reach fulfillment, otherwise it suffers the torture of unfulfilled purpose, denied self-realization and the punishment which we inflict on ourselves and innocent bystanders when we fail to ring true. Every soul must be what it is.

Imagine what it would mean to a child if its soul was intimately known and nurtured. How would a child feel if society saw it as their responsibility to know and foster and develop a child's keynote of existence? A child's greatest potential would be set free to fulfill itself, if the adults who cared for him truly understood his deepest intrinsic nature. Rather than being shut down according to social dictates, a child's authentic essence could be valued; a child would be known and understood.

Qualities like courage, truth, justice, purity, compassion, love, mercy, wisdom, strength, balance, intelligence, gentleness, beauty and power would have a chance to reverberate through the child's life according to the divine design of each little soul who comes into this world.

Not only would the children shine with the self-confidence of knowing who and what they are beyond race, culture and religion, but children would know each other at a deeper level beyond the trappings of their flesh, its color or the social attire that so sadly often veils the beauty of a soul, the face of a child and the future of an adult. I say this because we all long to be and feel understood. This is where the emergence of fulfillment and meaning begin.

Instead of raising an entire society of children, here in the Middle East and around the world, to either cringe or strike out, they could be raised to feel the strength of their own inherent possibility. An entire generation of youth is being raised to reflect the worst of outer circumstances, rather than reflect the beauty and strength of who they really are.

And so, serious questions about the future of children must be asked. What will Palestinian children grow up to know of themselves if the hardship and conflict continues? Will inner desperation perpetuate an outer seething revenge? What will Israeli children, who carry gas masks to school, grow up to embrace as their individual and societal ideology? Will it be an ideology that snuffs out the clear ring of their soul's natural essence and replaces it with a national vendetta? Could this tragedy be reversed through a healing campaign to mend souls to make them whole again?

In the aftermath of the fight between war and peace, the real work will begin. Broken hearts, shattered souls and damaged minds will need a major resurrection. A new era in peace education must be brought to bear. To return a lost soul to its origin is indeed a work of compassion. Perhaps what lies ahead will be called the "Era of Great Compassion." I call it the "Great Work."

And just like people, nations have souls. A nation has a sound of greatness and a note of individuality to ring true. A nation has a purpose to strike, a chord of being to fulfill and a chorus to be showcased. Otherwise, nations end up frustrated and hell-bent on taking the wrong fork in the road, just like people.

The fall of a soul into the sadness of an unfulfilled life is indeed the ultimate reason a soul's true nature should be upheld. Unfulfilled potential is a sadness of lost opportunity that so often twists itself into contortions in such an onslaught of opposites, reactions, and priorities that original premise is lost, and like a fallen soul it too grieves its own demise.

Along the same line of thinking, the fall of nations can take hundreds of years. But when they do fall, the death of dreams haunts the land and the people. It's usually a slow process, but sometimes it happens quickly. With that thought, the round robin of nations rising and nations falling comes to mind, with the endless procession of great empires that have been reduced to decay and rubble, the demise following the glory days when their footsteps were at the head of the pack.

Is this because the founding keynote for its birth has been squelched by the sour sound of human stench, the kind of stench that masquerades in lofty pretense, as an excuse for the hard cold truth of the survival of the fittest and the desire to dominate, make money, sell weapons, pedal drugs, smuggle diamonds, etc. at any cost to the collective human dignity?

Well, the thought that each nation is mandated with a higher purpose, that each nation is set into motion from a universal archetype or divine quality or principle characteristic, gives an idealist like myself a shred of hope. It gives me a willingness to keep saying what must be said as all the world moves toward the edge of irreversible consequences. To say it in a thousand different ways in every possible nuance and language and utterance, from casual remarks over coffee to profound moments of passion that explode in a room full of people to sculpt a soul's future and sometimes sculpt the future of an entire nation.

As an American I have taken to using Canadian maple leaf ID tags on my luggage for international travel, because I feel safer being identified by strangers as anything but American, given the sentiment of most other nations. I would be so honored if America would get on with the mandated business of striking the resounding purity of its actual God-given purpose, rather than getting side tracked by some of the presumptuous hyperbole that is so despised by the rest of the world.

Most Americans don't have a clue why other cultures and nations don't like us. I wonder if we as a nation will look back at our own glory days and ask why we didn't see the message on the walls, or listen to the wisdom of our forefathers or respect the opinions of our neighboring nations. Or if by some miracle of human spirit and inspiration, will we rise above the plight of our own arrogance to see that this, and all of the ignorance that goes along with it, has been our primary enemy all along?

Perhaps we will shine as the land of the free after all, and become a true leader of a free and prosperous future for all souls. I believe it is possible, but I also watch for signs that might whisper the inevitable.

And so, along with everything else today, amidst stale cold coffee and overflowing files of speaker profiles, and long, long hours that began before daybreak, I remind myself of the audience who listened to my lecture and was moved to tears at the thought of the nation of Israel having a keynote that will be its crowning glory, maybe, just maybe, at some distant bend in the road or possibility of circumstance.

It seems that everyone knew what I was talking about, even if it wasn't through ordinary reasoning, as if a chord of remembrance had been struck by King David himself. As lovers of the Holy Land, of Israel, of Zion, of even the occupied territories and refugee camps and of Palestine, a silence fell upon the room that opened wide for the sound of a nation's soul to be struck in full-throttled comprehension.

We can understand the quality of a nation in terms of a keynote that embodies a specific theme of purpose, if we can conjure the comparison of a pure sound like the unique tone that vibrates when a string on a harp is pulled back with a mighty purpose, plucked hard and set free, like a warrior pulling the string of a bow taut enough to unleash the force of intention, straight as an arrow into the heart of a matter. It is the tone of resonance from which a thing is born. It is its natural and God-given state of original creation, the only power that there is, and in my humble estimation, the only hope for any kind of survival anyway.

I don't have conventional knowledge about the kabbala, but I do understand its essence. I think there is a correspondence of philosophy here, especially if we were to see all nations as a Tree of Life that is the basis of earthly well-being at planetary levels. If every nation fulfilled its God-given purpose of original premise, intention and inspiration, then we would indeed witness a sustainable future for our children and maybe even something close to a promised land. I hope there is a new power to that Tree of Life concept of the kabbala that showers the ground beneath it with bright red apples of knowledge. I hope all the mystics and prophets have their way in the end, and that it takes root like an almighty force of divine qualities, sounds, letters, thoughts and keynotes that inform our future.

Somehow, the thought of a nation having a soul stirs my heart and lifts up something noble inside. It really speaks to me. But I will tell you that my trip through the Sinai was not an easy one. I didn't think I would survive it actually, keynote or not. I felt confounded and flung to my knees, as if my legs were broken and my bones were scattered among the countless, nameless, lifeless sand dunes, buried for all eternity without purpose or memory, flesh stripped away by an angry sun that burns into everything including keynotes.

For most of the two week trip, I felt assaulted by the blast furnace heat and beaten senseless by the glaring intensity of mere daylight reflected off of what can only be described as oceans of sand; that and the onslaught of my own angst. But there in the midst of near heat exhaustion, sweat and tears, was a remarkable break in the clouds of struggle that I have never forgotten, a special life-changing suspended moment that has stayed with me like the merciful drink of sweet water from an emerald green oasis.

To weave it all together, there was the coolness of sunrise and the rock monoliths laden with the blood-cries of past history, places that rise up from the desert floor like the Masada and Mount Moab and Mount Horeb and Mount Sinai, which gave rise to something in my heart I hadn't expected.

The culmination of my Sinai journey was the climb to the top of the revered site once traversed by the prophet Moses. Although from what I've heard, exactly which mountain was actually made famous with his footsteps is one of those endless historical debates.

In general, no one agrees on anything here in the Holy Land, which seems to be a prevailing out-of-tune keynote, the off-key, fallen kind. I began the ascent up to the pinnacle of Mount Sinai in the cold black between midnight and pre-dawn, to avoid the unbearable heat and gather in the miracle of a sunrise in such a place of power and legend and lore.

Having managed the exhausting climb, I sat perched among the rock outcroppings, expecting the spectacular light show of watching the sunrise common to the mountaintops, but nothing otherworldly had crossed my mind. I assure you my mind had been fully engrossed with the complaints of my body and highly attentive to the swelling response of my arthritic knees to the uphill climb.

Sitting for some time in a winded effort to recuperate, a stillness came to pass as if divinely guided, and I was given a wide berth by the other climbers and tourists who had also joined in the long wait for night to end and dawn to begin her majesty, which left me alone to fully take in the summit.

Perhaps I was hyperventilating from the climb; perhaps it was just my day to have a vision; perhaps the presence of Moses still lives and hovers among the rocks making extraordinary things happen; I only know what I felt and saw and witnessed internally.

In an absolute certainty, like the phoenix rising from the pyramids of ancient Egypt, a revelation spoke or rather exclaimed in a decidedly trumpeting kind of grandiosity, as mere speaking does not do justice to what was conveyed to me of the destiny of souls and nations and the dark side of struggle and ignorance that beset the twosome and challenged each in mysterious ways. Well actually, it was a winged phoenix that appeared in all of its radiant and golden glory, or at least the vision or image or essence of such a thing. Regardless of the debate about what a vision or a revelation is or could be, I hold dear and carry with me what happened to this very day.

Spreading its wings in the sky of my mind's eye, this bird of might and magnificence took flight, rising up through the ashes of an apocalypse in the triumph of making it to the other side: the other side of ignorance and conflict and struggle and sorrow. Like the dawn it knew its own majesty, this bird of the pharaohs and pyramids. It knew its place in the "halls of wisdom" that the ancients whispered about.

Shooting upwards, heaven-bound like a rocket, the phoenix of cosmic skies became the bird of paradise, swooping and soaring in winged testimony, leaving visions of new creation in the wake of its wingspan, the creation of all things promised. Pyramids were only the beginning glimmers of what this bird of paradise had in mind. A future world was revealed, cities of wonder appeared across the horizon like great bio-spheres of human fertility and accomplishment.

As if it were a messenger from deity, as if it were born of solar fire, as if it were dipped in the golden breath of angels, the bird imprinted with each flap of its shimmering, sun-tipped wings, the signs of sacredness in the sky. Above the desert floor and the mount of Moses and the Chapel of Elijah the bird bore the signs of things to come, stretching across the great expanse of vivid blue.

By then I was on my knees and then some, when words in a mystic language of light and sound billowed and raced like a tidal wave across the horizon, proclaiming the promise of a great nation, a nation of good will, a nation of ascended souls, a nation that would crack open the barriers of time, like a supersonic jet, to usher in a thousand years of peace and prosperity for every soul on earth.

The phoenix of the ages proclaimed a sacred new Israel as the destined gatekeeper of a new era of promise on earth. Could this be possible, given all the bickering debate and swords raised high in mortal conflict that is so much a part of the Israeli, Palestinian, Iraqi and Middle Eastern life thus far?

I was stunned and had to rub my eyes and shake my head to be sure that I wasn't hallucinating. But there it was before my wide-awake, sitting-straight-up reality. There it was in hi-fidelity audio effects, the screeching and cawing sound, of wings cutting the air, and sounding forth the sound of the soul of a nation. The phoenix was painting the sky with the story of a great nation's destiny, dipping its wings in the sacred letters of origin and the Supreme Will that became the vision of goodness manifest.

And then, as if this wasn't enough to boggle the mind, there was more. Out of the dawn that was unfurling an orchestration of pink and amber came another bird, a bird of keen sight and sharp senses, a bird of proud purpose. Before me, above me, and all around me, a great falcon soared and circled, winging its way into full view on a ray of light that had no beginning and no end. It had its own story of greatness and wisdom, calling and cawing in a clean clear piercing of earth-shaking, canyon-rumbling, flying high above all the clamor down on the ground screeches, where mere mortals struggled to survive throughout the ages.

The falcon was regal in its dipping and circling, a messenger that told of a great nation, a desert nation, a new people, who would rise from the ashes of the unexpected and soar to greatness and promise. In its wake was a procession of children; children born of desert sand, yet filled with the essence of ancient suns, suns that radiated the fiery world beyond time itself.

The falcon's screech pierced some kind of time barrier. This is the best I can do to understand it, thinking back and looking back to the vision I had in the Sinai. The screeching shook the ground and made me tremble where I sat. The screeching was filled with the cries of the collective human soul, the cry of cries, the cry of angst and desperation that blended with the cry of knowledge, the cry of a soul's birthright and the cry of a soul's demand for redemption.

The screeching was like a sonic boom, in the way that the sound of it went beyond the wavelength of what my ears could hear, and reached instead into the domain of the heart, and then I knew the falcon was truly a harbinger, a protector, a messenger from the highest places.

It foretold of a new nation of golden children, who will rise up from the fate of being the world's unwanted orphans, transcended through fate to become the world's cherished reminder of the value of every human being. No longer were the children of Palestine pushed out of where they belonged, not in Egypt, not in Jordan, not in Syria and not in Israel. No longer were these children forgotten and left behind to eat dust, as fast paced Mercedes raced through deserts from oil well to oil well passing them by.

A new day proclaimed their birthright and the sound of truth proclaimed it. Billowing from behind the falcon's winded wake was a purity of sunlit proclamation, "All are children of One God. All are children of Abraham. All are the tribes from the Beginning."

And then yet another bird, of no less grace and majesty, swooped into view. Out of the dry desert dawn came a winter-white dove, bringing the grace of benevolence with each flap of its wings. Coming in on the new day's first whisper of a cloud and the whisper of things to come, it joined the others. It too called and cawed and cooed, painting the sky with its essence of God-given goodness, so full of grace and good that even angels might weep with awe.

The dove fluttered and danced her dance of peace and redemption, and flew from the falcon to the phoenix, circling and swooping around them. Then it became apparent that the dove was weaving the two together in a figure eight, the symbol of infinity. Circling and circling, as it were, creating a biosphere to which the three birds would each bring their unique nature and keynote of being, keynote of thought and purpose.

The dove flew straight into the rising sun like a rocket bird with white, white wings, headed straight for the center of a fiery presence, returning again in a brilliance that the eyes of mere mortals could not bear.

From the peace dove of future suns rose a new world of nations, a new global citizenry of people, a new prodigy of human life that bridged oceans and ages, the past and the future. Many thousands of souls from around the world and children from every land were gathering into the wingspan and promise of the dove of peace.

The sun followed the dove across the horizon, with a shining that gave light and radiance to one and all. Great was the light that shown upon all three birds of destiny, which gave life to the heartbeat of each winged messenger to resound a keynote of hope and promise and birthright for every soul on earth and the divine destiny of peace among nations.

By then I was past skepticism and was fully far-flung in awe, and of course I was weeping, too. I was a witness that watched the platinum-winged phoenix beckon the white-winged dove and the golden-winged falcon to follow. "Hear us, hear each song of destiny," they cawed, cooed, sang and soared.

Together they danced and spun and wove and braided tail winds and images of the future in mid-air, mid-flight, mid-winged wonder, of the promise of things to come. The image of flight, the kind of fancy dancing in the sky that the world's best-trained pilots try to emulate, was at its best here.

"We have always been one," they cawed and screeched and screamed into the dawning red glory of the sunrise, "We have always been one: one family, one nation, one kingdom, one future. The desert of the past and the desert of the present and the desert of the future belong to all of us. We each have our purpose and our day and our measure; we each have our place. But as surely as we live, as surely as we have mastered flight, we will fly together and we will fly as one, unified before the great ones that first made wings to fly and birds to soar as messengers of things to come. We are the callers of remembrance; we are the keepers of a nation's soul. Together we are the harbingers of a triple nation that will be home to the family of man, the collective spirit of humanity in all of its diversity, a diversity that bellows the resounding splendor of all the keynotes of every soul in full harmonic perfection."

I cried and heaved for a long time after the birds of promise flew off into the center of the sun that came spiking up like a sphere of fiery testament, casting a new light on the same Mount Sinai that had manifested stone tablets some 3,500 years ago. I couldn't help myself. I was rendered helpless, humble, hopeful and grateful all at once.

I sat on the mountaintop, until the scorching heat demanded that I seek the shelter of lower ground and the shade of palm trees. I made my way down the path to the bottom, humbled and speechless, but renewed and sure-footed. I understood why the Chapel of the Prophet Elijah had been built on the side of Mount Sinai. This was indeed a holy mountain of vision and promise.

I know what I saw, and I know what I heard, but I never put any of it into words, until the day that I spoke to that group in Jerusalem and the concept of keynote fell upon my heart and soul. There in the telling, the keynote of nations rang true, emerged, inspired and informed a room full of people with the living reverberation of the truth of origin and beginning, despite my rational mind's belief that visions were fleeting things that have nothing to do with real life.

I can call the writing in the sky in the wake of winged messengers, the Word of God, if I want to see it from a spiritual viewpoint. I can even call it a mere figment of my imagination. It doesn't matter what I call it; it only matters how it impacted everything that I did, years later. What was made clear in essence about the "sound of souls" and the "sound of nations" has stayed with me and has given me hope, even as the worst of things is still very likely to play out here in the Holy Land, in the aftermath of adding Iraq and the whole burning region to the fray and the destruction being rent around the world.

This vision of purpose gave promise of things to come, no matter the hardship or sacrifice. It proclaimed a future of goodness for all of humankind. It told of the phoenix and the falcon and the dove flying side by side, no doubt some kind of symbology for the superpowers or super religious. It fed my heart and tumbled over in my existence like the refreshing gurgle of a lifesaving spring whose precious waters anointed the heads of kings and sages.

It promised that a great alliance of nations would rise from ashes. It promised that the falcon and the dove and the phoenix would fly as one, each under the power of their own wings, but each in the beauty of a six-winged miracle. It promised that the Red Sea had not parted before Moses in vain.

It promised that the sounds of souls could change a nation and lift it up and cause the angels to sing the way that they did in the beginning when Abraham first left Ur for Canaan with Sarah, when the promise of a new nation was still to be born on the horizon of time. Perhaps the Savior and the Messiah and the messengers of keynotes and visions and nations were all on the same side after all.

And so I spoke of these things with the audience, who sat on folding chairs in an air-conditioned ballroom, in a polished, modern, glass and marble hotel that overlooked the Citadel of David. The keynote of a nation is like its higher purpose, its destiny fulfilled, its divine mandate born from the throne of creation, wedded to the hope of a people.

It is like a cry for life when a nation is coming down the birth canal of its forefathers' thoughts, as the longing of the human soul calls out its noble desire, pacing at midnight, pacing at dawn, waiting and praying for a new life of possibility and exacting extraordinary measures to bring that new life to a legacy of people and their prayers.

I spoke to the now raptly attentive audience about how the gifts and talents and qualities of a nation exist, even if they are buried beneath the quagmire of the past. Just as all human souls are created in the image of God, even if that light is often hidden from view, also buried under centuries-old ignorance and illusion. The "sound of a nation" is not so different. Its light of goodness longs to become a living reality, despite how ignorant we humans can be.

I shared that through divine providence each nation has something essential to offer the whole of the world. And just like when a quarreling family learns to get along, all are benefited in the long run if cooperation rather than conflict is the song of the day that warms home and hearth and gathers everyone into its embrace.

Peeling loud and clear on that day in an ordinary lecture of extraordinary meaning, was the resounding understanding that the United States was born on the keynote of "The Law of Justice" As I absorbed this keynote, I knew that most Americans felt this keynote and resonated with it, whether they were consciously aware of it or not.

The rapt listeners, mostly Israeli residents, mused at the keynote that inspired the United States, and some laughed at the irony of it. If only "justice and freedom for all" could be extended beyond its own interests and beyond its own borders. Some couldn't help but sneer at the hypocrisy of it. Some quietly contemplated the matter, and some got to their feet so as not to miss a thing, to listen even closer, to take in what was being said.

I shared with them that more than once, as an American, I have felt a reverent knowing come upon me when reading the Declaration of Independence for the United States, nobly penned by the great statesman, Thomas Jefferson and our founding fathers. I said that as an American, the Declaration of Independence is a deeply meaningful, almost spiritual document that voices a collective intention. It simply must become true here in my country and true with regard to the way in which the United States influences the greater world.

In America our keynote as a country is "The Law of Justice." Our Declaration of Independence is the mission statement of this premise. And so I invited the audience to feel the power of truth in excerpts of the Declaration of Independence:

"We hold these truths to be self-evident, that all men are created equal, that they are endowed by their Creator with certain unalienable Rights, that among these are Life, Liberty and the pursuit of Happiness. That to secure these rights Governments are instituted among Men. We... solemnly publish and declare, that these United Colonies are, and of Right ought to be, Free and Independent States... And for the support of this

Declaration, with a firm reliance on the protection of divine Providence, we mutually pledge to each other our Lives, our Fortunes and our sacred Honor."

To pledge one's life and fortune and honor is indeed a most noble thing, a profound thing that gave birth to a nation.

And then it also came to me that Israel was born on the keynote of "The Law of Life." It was as if the spirit or memory of Moses or Abraham was speaking through me. My voice boomed. And as I spoke about it, the air could have crackled in the room. These were Israeli Jews sitting in the chairs. Nobody was laughing. Some were openly weeping.

Cooks and waiters were coming out of the hotel kitchen to peek in on what was going on, drawn as if by a magnet to the peeling remembrance of truth. The rabbi in charge of the religious effects of the hotel appeared at the doorway of the conference room with a keen newfound interest in what was transpiring.

The keynote of Israel had risen to life like the phoenix of my vision in the Sinai and revealed unto itself the remembrance of what it always had been. A combination of relief and gratitude for something lost and then found swept the crowd. Everyone was moved, some profoundly so. I felt as though Abraham, the obedient father of the tribes was standing among us.

The keynote was not merely words plucked from the mind of mortals. The keynote was a thing of divine creation and it radiated throughout the room. We all felt its presence. It was dear to the heart of every Israeli present in the room.

And then as if divine providence didn't want to leave anything essential out of the recipe of truth and things eternal, the keynote of the Palestinians rang out, "The Law of Purity." Next thing I knew the sound of it just fell out of my mouth, like the loudspeakers that broadcast the Muslim Call to Prayer five times a day.

Through this revelation the nature of the Palestinian cause became more understandable. Purity, living a life of purity, even in the onslaught of the glamour of modern day life; there is a nobility to this law, this intention. There is a beauty to the way it lives through a people, who are struggling to find their true identity in the midst of the impurity of purity. Fanatical vengeance is not a true and God-given purity, and yet is among the distortions that we as a human race continue to play out. Purity does endure in the silence of the secret heart.

Of course it didn't take long to come down to earth and reconnect with the fact that we seem to be living the opposite of any and all divine keynotes. We live at a time of the utmost, crazy, black and white polarity. We seem to be caught in a "fun house" with mirrors that turn everything upside down and inside out.

We seem to be doing the opposite of what we should, all around the table of convening nations. The positive side of races, religions, cultures and nations gets lost in misinterpretation, small-mindedness and reaction. More could be said on this note, much more, but it is for each of us to remember the good, the true good, and to change the negative.

The realization that came to me and the audience and came to bear like plump grapes hanging from vines, is that both souls and nations have a choice: to embody the keynote that gave birth to life or instead, and sadly so, to embody its opposite. The flip side of our God-given glory is where we will find our greatest distortions. I remember in that moment someone saying, "within our weakness we will find our strength."

In a natural wave of minds and hearts uplifted, understandings began to move around the room, as people spontaneously began to voice metaphors, quotes and analogies of the dilemma and the divine premise of unveiling our own true purpose as nations, as souls.

As this profound moment swept through the audience, I came to realize that the keynote for our beloved earth was "The Law of Unity," and more specifically, "Diversity within the Unity." A keynote is like the light of God guiding us to what we are in divine concept, and that what we are and what we will one day come to realize, is what we have always been.

If only America remembered the "for all" part. If only Israel obeyed an all-inclusive Law of Life that is more vital than convoluted doctrines and involuted intellect. If only suicide bombers could take their zeal for purity to the core of things and set themselves free from the self-aggrandizing quest for spiritual heroism and the desperation that loses its own soul.

Of course these "if onlys" are mere idealist ponderings, but as ponderings there is merit to be discovered if one ponders deeply enough and gets past the crusty edges of convention, religiously or otherwise imposed, to the essence that matters to the sustainability of life on earth.

If only all sides would love the land that they live on enough to make peace a priority. Since the intifada began, the fragile, sandy, arid environment of the Holy Land has taken a beating, a hard and brutal beating. If any keynotes are ringing, they are out of time, out of sync, painful to the human ear, painful to the land and painful to life.

Ecological projects that were desperately needed have come to a standstill. Global environmentalists would gasp in shock if they knew what was taking place here. The groundwater and aquifers are being contaminated by opposing sides that don't care anymore. They place revenge and retaliation on the list of essential expenditures, rather than cleaning up the water that is becoming undrinkable.

If only they would join forces before it's too late; before the desert in its own retaliation turns on itself, swallowing up everything with dry sand, because the water has gone bad and as a result has gone into hiding. What then of mothers and wombs and children and life?

If only the Palestinians were not driven to the desperation of taking apart old car batteries in their homes, to get the lead out of them, to sell on the black market to feed their hungry children. Lead, a heavy toxic metal, is lethal to humans. Battery acid and lead spill on the floor that babies crawl upon. Battery acid and lead are on the hands that offer breast milk to infants. Battery acid and lead find their way to the dinner table and to the groundwater below buildings. The water that runs beneath refugee camps is cringing, as all manner of the effects of war is dumped thoughtlessly into the hope of the land. Palestinian children are showing signs of retardation because of lead poisoning.

If only the sound of Justice and Life and Purity could turn this nightmare around. Can the world of original creation endure such a painful demise of its premise? We live in a time of Sodom and Gomorrah, where environmentalists work long and hard to get a shred of attention to their cause, while pop stars are put on thrones of fortune, whether they like it or not. And the world's greatest user and polluter of the world's resources, the US, refuses to attend global environmental summits.

The question that faces the human family and the Justice of America, the Life of Israel, and the Purity of Palestine, only a few keynotes of what so many nations could be, is: can we be redeemed when we are caught in the nightmare of such distortion?

Well, as with all revelations and profundities, it doesn't take long to come back to the existing reality of a world that might not survive itself, and yet the truth of truth persists like a blazing fire. All nations just have to remember the true essence of their soul to retrieve and fulfill their higher purpose on this planet. Then each will add its resonant sound to the noble chorus of nations, fine-tuned like a philharmonic orchestra to the heart-rending, mind-expanding pleasure of world citizens.

Before finishing my lecture, I invited everyone present to again feel and know and speak the beauty and power of the keynote of Israel, as well as the keynote of Palestine. Those in the audience were moved to full-on tears as the personal resonance with the keynotes moved through every heart. The keynotes of Life and Purity were indeed compatible, and not only compatible but also essential companions of existence.

There was not a dry eye among them. It was one of those moments when The Word and the Sound were upon us, and The Word and the Sound were perfection, and The Word Was. Israel is a great guardian. Palestine bears a promise. The greatness of new nations is a possibility, the promise of this is real even as I am a witness to the shame of nations in the eye of God, and I pray, in the hand of God as well.

So, is the keynote of the nation's soul, "The Law of Life," an eye for an eye ideology, or is the keynote something far more noble, compassionate, and evolved?

Everyone present knew the answer. This is the thought that we left the room with, based in the truth, if only for a few precious moments, we experienced the greatness of nations and the understanding that nations are born of a noble premise, convened from a higher purpose. The hopes and dreams and sacrifices of its people have a greatness, a gift, a purpose. The light of nations burns in our collective dreams and memory. It burns and it cannot be drowned out, not by war or ignorance or hatred.

And so I find myself sitting alone at an empty table, and with this morsel of remembrance, I too weep to realize there is more here than meets the eye, more than what we see on the surface of things, and as a result I am better able to keep my sights on the road ahead, to review the next possibilities for fundraising, how best to finish out the day and finish out the next series of meetings, some of which will be difficult, to look ahead for the straight and narrow of it, to stretch my vision to the bends and turns that will come years from now.

Like the squeaky notes of a violin played by a child, the perfection of the virtuoso plucks and slides the bow across the strings unseen, but yet with the promise of possibility and newfound adeptship. With the symbology of desert birds of peace as a reminder, I can accept that something in me goes unanswered, so I can bear the quest of seeking and remember the flame of unity and the greatness of nations, all nations.

To remember is a noble duty, and as I sit in the space where this meeting ended and the next one will begin, I feel a strange expectation. Angst in the Holy Land. Hope on the horizon of my heart. Angst in the minds of mothers of soldiers. Promise on the substance of visions for a better future. Polarities, opposites, the good and the bad, to turn left or to turn right, to see, to know, to remember and to make the choice for the path that endures and feeds life to all who seek the way. Has it ever been any other way?

Yes, it is another day in Jerusalem. Early this morning I woke up feeling already exhausted. I longed to go back to my dreams and sleep for another ten thousand eons. A full day of obligations followed hard on my first sips of coffee, but remembrance soon transformed a weary spirit into a determined will and the love of doing what's right.

My day began with worry as I watched the television showing the face of my American President. He expressed regret for the loss of American lives. He does not express regret for the loss of peace makers who have stood in harm's way and have themselves become targets of bullets and bulldozers, bombs and battles. The lines on his face spoke of the clues of cluelessness, despite his assumptions of righteousness and his own well-meaning effort to lead the American people out of harm's way.

Leaders of nations would do better if they held the keynote in mind of the land that they lead throughout their day. We all know that dealing with the terrorist issue is a grave and difficult matter. But we also know that dealing with political mistreatment of the disadvantaged is also a grave and difficult matter. I, too, carried the worry of nations into my day, but then it all turned on a dime with the recall of a revelation, when I remembered the unity of highflying birds of spacious skies and the keynotes of noble nations of a good and gracious earth.

Perhaps I should add the American Eagle to jet streams of visionary falcons and doves who followed a golden phoenix into the unknown of a greater light, and the greatness of nations who remembered their forefathers' true intentions, and perhaps nations that would even remember the love of founding foremothers, the good hearts that gestated the birthright of our shared existence.

I will stay the course, and I will return again and again to Jerusalem to navigate the raw intensity of bombs and tempers, hopes and disappointments. I will grow strong in the scorching heat of this place, in the relentlessness of it.

Perhaps there is nowhere in the world where the past, present and future are so intertwined, hopelessly inseparable, married by a timeless unquestioning fate, stubbornly defiant in the refusal to merge into a natural rhythm of coexistence, and yet does coexist in its own bizarre way, even now. Perhaps polarities and opposites dance in the night when no one is looking, partners that seek the magnetic pull of irrational companionship.

If I were to wake up one hundred years from now, what would be the story of this land and its people? What would follow on the heels of morning coffee on any given day? Would turmoil, unrest, fighting and bloodshed still be the curse of the Promised Land? Or would the prayers of the legions of souls who have held the vision of a land of milk and honey have taken flight, and finally call down a merciful blessing from above?

Would the phoenix and falcon and the dove fly side by side, screaming with daredevil delight as they dive earthward in fearless abandon? Would the keynote of "The Law of Life" ring true throughout the land, inspiring all nations by example? Would "The Law of Purity" be the promise of the Promised Land and be realized at long last? Would the "Law of Justice" ring true for one and all?

Would a new temple be built in the name of peace, home to a truly United Nations? Would peace have spread its golden wings of wisdom over a new generation, freeing humanity from the bloodletting of past ages, opening the gates of mercy to a benevolent future?

Yes, what would Jerusalem, crown jewel of both Israel and Palestine look like, feel like? What would she be? Would we see doves winging in peaceful coexistence with falcons, flying together over the spires and towers and gem-topped domes, as the phoenix soars on ahead, higher and higher and higher with a crystal clear eye to what lies beyond? Perhaps we would see the eagle crossing the Atlantic Ocean on occasion, bearing gifts of amber wheat in its claws and sweet cherries in its beak. Idealistic? Perhaps. Possible? That is up to each of us.

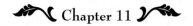

Chapter 11

The Desert

Seeds of Survival, Seeds of Life

A young woman obviously out of breath and thirty minutes late came to me at the end of the day, wanting to be included on one of our symposium dialogue panels. The day that she came for her appointment was the last day that interviews could be accepted. She was also seeking funding for her relief efforts with the Bedouin desert tribes who had become lost in the strife of the region.

She sat down on the sofa in my meeting area, barely introduced herself, and proceeded to pour her heart out. At first she spoke like a conveyor belt on high speed, in exasperated run-on sentences that made my head ache and my heart wince. It was like she had love and panic all rolled up into a single altruistic emergency. Her hair kept flopping in her face as she gestured with long-waving arms to accentuate what she was saying.

Her inner sense of things had begun to ring with a desperate alarm as she told of the terrible conditions among the Bedouin villages and camel camps out in the remote areas of the desert, as a result of all the clampdowns throughout Israel. Because of what has literally become the war on humanity, basic necessities like food, clothing and medical supplies weren't able to get through. Little children were suffering.

The young girl with smooth child-like skin was in her late twenties or perhaps early thirties, the age of my own children or even younger, and was leading a relief effort on her own for the needy who have been badly battered by all the violence, bomb attacks and political bickering.

What was immediately clear to me was how badly she needed relief herself. She was near to breaking. She was traumatized by all that she had witnessed; when human dignity is run over and left in the dust. Life was hard in the desert even in the best of times. Nights were cold, the sandstorms brutal. She was exhausted, depleted down to the bone marrow and in need of a long rest.

When her pleas got to the point of a high-pitched whine, I demanded that she stop. She had begun to shake with her grief and her cause and her fight and her worry. The staring empty eyes and open sores and wounded souls of the poor and helpless had gotten to her and were eating alive whatever she had left of herself.

I put my arms around her and gathered her in, rocking her and stroking her hair. How could I as a mother do otherwise? Her desperation had called to me and had won me over. I rocked her for a long time and got her to promise to take better care of herself. Since then I have continued to offer a protective wing to her.

After giving her a good long talk about pacing herself, filling her cup before filling the cup of others and other tricks of the trade and rules of survival that humanitarians, peace workers, and relief crews swear by, at least those who are in it as a livelihood, she left in a little better shape and I felt confident she could hold her own on the panel of women speakers at the conference. The panel's topic would be collaboration between women's leadership alliances and relief workers.

Now this young woman lives in my heart, and makes my searching even more crucial. Her stress, burnout and empathetic condition made me think hard about everything that I wished could be different. If only the ultimate answer of all answers would ring clear, audible and articulate. The tension is building; the demand is building; how can we respond to so much human need and suffering?

I am aware of a new sense of urgency, as if time is running out and all will be lost unless the missing pieces are retrieved. I think in some ways the whole of the human race feels that something must be revealed, made clear, like a lightening bolt flashing across the darkness announcing some kind of 12 step plan for planetary survival.

I understood more than ever how she felt, but being older and more experienced with pain in general, I had learned to accept and manage, at least somewhat, the suffering of humanity. But she got to me. Her inability to accept the suffering of the Bedouin tribes, numbering some 250,000 souls that had been included in the project proposal, had gotten to me, and in truth needless human suffering should be unacceptable to us all.

I went to bed that night with the young crusader on my mind, and woke up the next morning, wishing I could do more. As I was going through the usual routine of brushing my hair and getting ready for the day, I can't help but wonder. And then, a massive wave of sadness and grief rolls through where the young relief worker had left off with her clawing desperation. What I have always managed to keep at bay in the past comes crashing down all around me.

Pictures of malnourished desert children fill the spaces between mouthfuls of the eggs and tomatoes I am having for breakfast, a luxurious repast by their standards. Meanwhile I am feeling cranky about so much time cooped up in hotels, having yet another hotel breakfast, and long for the simplicity of cooking something simple like oatmeal for myself in my own kitchen. I even get a crumb of toast caught in my throat as a sudden surge of pain pierces outward through my flesh from deep inside.

Like an imbedded heart thorn of old pain that had a hidden history, my entire chest begins to wince and heave. Momentarily, I feel lost and too small to survive. I feel terrified of failing, as if I would be skinned alive and eaten to the bone, far worse than the young woman I had cuddled in my arms. But failure has no time and no place. The fear of failure is faceless and without mercy. This is what makes it such a frightening adversary.

I get up from the table piled high with papers and files, books and reports, plans and proposals and lie down on the bed, closing my eyes as taut as a weathered drum; tears begin to brim and spill over in an unstoppable avalanche. This time I am too tired to hold the swells back, and giving in, I allow myself the satisfaction of emptying out the caverns of palpable loss.

After having consulted and advised the young relief worker, there I am sobbing in a morass of unnamed regret and futility until the wetness of my pillow brings me back to myself.

As I lie there mopping my face with tissues, out of nowhere, out of old hope, the image of a prickly pear cactus comes into view. Worse yet, I begin to see starving children struggling to eat the thorn-covered fruit with thin mouths that thirst and scavenge. Thin hands and faces are being torn and scarred.

Stretched out as far as the eye can see, I am shown the prickly pear cactus poking its head up above heat waves of shimmering sand. Miles and miles into the distance, the pink-fruited cactus plants are struggling to hold onto their meager due from the desert, dotting the landscape like survivors washed ashore after a shipwreck. The entire expanse of the Sinai wasteland is scattered with prickly pear cactus and empty-eyed children searching for sustenance. Survival is at a high noon hour of relentless reckoning.

This gruesome image is symbolic of the suffering of the forgotten Bedouin, our forgotten humanitarian, and everyone else caught in the grip of such horrid circumstances. Here in the Middle East, all odds are against anything green or innocent in this stronghold of severity where the merciless assault from the scorching sun is in full command. Roots dig deep and limbs scavenge only to be suffocated, snuffed out in dark finality by empty sand dunes that shift and creep with the wind, burying everything in their wayward path.

In this undertow of emotion I feel the severity of the barren mountains that gave no shelter to the wandering tribes of the past, and little to the Bedouin of the present, jutting proudly against cloudless skies as if to say, "We remain; all else comes and goes."

Even camels are known to die in this heat-locked waterless sea of sand, where Moses fell to his knees, begging for mercy, begging for water, and begging for bread. In angst, in desperation, in the visioning of the prophet that he was, he climbed to the mountaintop to stand in submission before the memory of the burning bush that guided him out of Egypt, to find himself standing again on another mountaintop that overlooked cactus and displaced orphans. There he quenched his forty-year thirst and hardship with the fire of remembrance and the ashes of the laws of heaven. He fed stone tablets to the hungry in the heat of his wrath and the power of his ecstasy.

Looking on, over his shoulder and poking out of the rocks where he stood, were the prickly pear cactus that awaited him and witnessed his descent from his lofty heights, lined up like soldiers along the trail of his ascent, worship and fear. The prickly pears, tough-skinned spiny fruit of the formidable, were the thorns of faith that survived all odds and prevailed. Here in the desert the prickly pear cactus is everywhere. The terror of survival and the joy of life are at opposite ends of the spectrum and yet never take their eyes off one another.

This image is given to me, perhaps by benevolence itself. Perhaps there is mercy in small measures after all, to show me that the thorns of this desert plant protect and sustain the tender fruit beneath the surface of the sun-weathered, wrinkled, and parched exterior. Starving children only need to learn how to go past the thorny shell to reach the sweet nectar held inside.

A thorn is a thorn, however, and it is sharp with the ability to cut, prick and penetrate by nature. A thorn is something to respect. I remember a few words of wisdom once offered to me, "You know the Jews are like the prickly pear fruit. They are tough and tenacious on the outside and tender and succulent on the inside. They are protected by a thorny tree of life, one that is destined to become the eternal lotus of the oasis." That is why they are sometimes called the "Sabra," the Hebrew word for prickly pear cactus.

Sweet fruit surrounded by thorns; this is a paradoxical characteristic, a seemingly incompatible fluke of nature like the terror and the joy of survival that coexist with the coming and going of violent storms and gentle breezes.

How often are we grateful for life when we fear we may lose it? How grateful we become for the dearness of life when we are whisked or plucked or saved from the cliff edge of annihilation.

But the desert does bear fruit and so does the prickly pear cactus, thorns notwithstanding. And when you are hungry and thirsty, the sweetness is all the better for the absence of all else. Thorns of faith protect the essence of what's beneath the tough exterior. Thorns of faith protect the essence of the soul of a people, a nation, and a future.

The Hebrew people won my heart a long time ago, even if I get lost trying to understand the intricacies of their religion or where the line in the sand is drawn between religion and cultural nuance, or religion and politics, or cultural nuance and politics, or the line between the skyscrapers of Tel Aviv and the domes and towers of Jerusalem and the tombs of the prophets and the desert tents of the Bedouin that stand in clusters on the outskirts of the conventional population. It's like trying to separate the thorns from the thorn bush, the roots from the ground or the fruit from its sweetness.

Sometimes love and divine favor are beyond all logic. I shake my head at the senselessness of the battle here amongst the rocks and the mounts and crowns of thorns, but I know without a doubt that I love the Jewish heritage and the noble and warm-hearted souls whom I have met throughout the region.

I love the sound of their deep-throated, guttural language and their tenacious and often stubborn adherence to a divine mandate from thousands of years ago. I love their ingenuity and fine art sensibility that sculpts futuristic, sky-reaching architecture, astounding visions through finely-tuned hands that paint, carve or chisel wisdom into stone and canvas and gold, and cultivate miles of prolific vegetable fields, where only rock piles and thorn-covered cactus existed before.

Yes, Israel is sweet to my ears and dear to my heart, and I pray for her survival and for the joy of her transformation that she might survive and indeed have everlasting life. May the blessing of the House of David that foretold of eternal favor be revealed in its truest light, that we, who wander the desert of terror searching for the joy, might come to understand such a blessing and such a proclamation, what it means and how it will come to pass as we face the future.

King David was surrounded by the terror of betrayal that became the saga of his life, and yet the psalms poured from his heart in a sweetness that found the mysteries of divine favor descending from on high. Now the psalms are still being played out thousands of years later and maybe thousands of years to come through a divine plan that only the ancient ones could grasp, even as they reach through time to pass the knowledge to the pure of heart.

Who will find the miracle that joins terror and joy in such a way that the memory of loss becomes the fertile soil for a new Tree of Life that bears the fruit, not only of coexistence, but a supreme coexistence that upholds the sovereignty of souls and nations, and yet gathers every life and every contribution of differences into an alchemy of greater abundance, a tree that becomes a forest of promise, the promise given to kings and prophets bestowed at last to the children of the world?

I pray to receive the sweet promise from one generation to another, that lives like a holy book within the Sabra, to ease the demands of the future and the burdens of the past. I pray for the integrity of the Jewish people to shine in its entire anointed destiny as David and Solomon and Abraham and Sarah look on, smiling as they peel back the tough skin of cactus fruit and suck the sweet nectar to the very last, luscious drop. I pray that there will be flukes of nature forever on this earth, especially sweet ones, like an oasis that spreads the fruit of wisdom and the living waters that quench the soul.

I pray to understand the Sabra and to learn from its mystical symbology. I pray that my platter will be piled high with the enduring fruit that is surrounded by thorns and the psalms of David that have lingered through the generations that called down mercy and blessing even in the dark hours of betrayal and defeat. One simply has to peel away the tough skin of appearances to uncover the essence of fruity flesh, the nature of a nation still to be born.

If I were to see the Jews as the fruit of the cactus; and I offer this comparison as a loving ode to true essence; then I would see the Arab people as the pomegranate. With the dewy taste of the prickly pear on my palate, comes the natural desire to balance sweetness with the zing and tartness of the pomegranate, another desert fruit of long-standing favor and flavor and, I have to say, a fruit that is quite new to me but quickly gaining ground as a favorite.

I would embrace its shining red pumpkin roundness with new respect, even though its exterior is hard and seals inside itself a treasure. But the value of the treasure is hard to see if one only sees the hard outer skin of the pomegranate and the hard-seeded interior. It is here that survival causes us to look deeply to find what we might not see otherwise.

To appreciate this abode of hard-seeded succulence is to appreciate the Arab people, to look beyond the struggle of the human drama to the seed of God that lives through a people. To look inside and outside is to learn something of the natural and God-given attribute of the Arab people and the uniqueness of Islamic faith. It's a stretch to see a similarity between the pomegranate and Muhammad, but I invite the exploration.

When I think of the multitude of shiny seeds joined in a firm sea of translucent pink, what comes to mind is the story of Muhammad's first vision of Archangel Gabriel in the cave of Hira' on Jabal an-Nur, the Mountain of Light. There he stood. There he prayed. There he called forth. The veils between the worlds of man and the abode of the Gods were parted, enabling Muhammad to see the image of Gabriel formed from light alone. There he was told to "Read in the name of the Lord who created man from matter."

The revelation was so powerful and otherworldly that Muhammad ran from the cave in panic, half fearing that he had lost his sanity. When the profound answers the call and pours itself into the ordinary, it is difficult to deny, but also difficult to believe, even for the prophets who visioned the impossible becoming possible. On his way back to Mecca he looked up only to see the image again splayed across the entire sky.

"I am Archangel Gabriel," he said, "and you, Muhammad, are the Messenger from God."

His fear was quelled in no small part through the love and reassurance of his beloved wife Khadijah, a simple woman who loved him and bridged the tendency to doubt with faith.

Just as the inner fruit of the pomegranate swells with seeds, so was Muhammad swelling with gratitude for the miracle he had witnessed, the love that showered down upon him and the blessing that he received. The calling of a prophet was upon him and was changing the world. The messages he received from the Angel Gabriel over the next twenty years became the Qur'an. When the love claims you as its own, one can only be that love no matter what it asks of you. It was the least he could do, given what he had been given.

In the company of nothing but the empty stone walls of a desert cave, he had seen the face of the Beloved. He had seen the heavens and he had seen its holy inhabitants. He had seen all things and all places. He had seen God's love for humankind and his heart exploded just to see it. And he saw it all alone in a cave where he had sought refuge from the ills of his day and the ignorance of forgetting, with the future domes and skyscrapers of Mecca and New Mecca waiting to be awakened, to rise up from the desert dust nearby, as future witnesses to the greatness of the heavens that had opened and the prophet that became God's messenger.

Full of passion for the phenomenon that had turned his mind to gold, he felt it his calling to pass the sacred on to his wife, his children and all those whom he would soon influence, and to remember each facet of the jewel that he had been shown. His heart could not bear the thought of forgetting the grace of God ever again. Being prone to visions myself, I can truly resonate, even passionately, with his point of view. Remembrance on a planet of forgetting is surely, sorely, sadly and supremely needed.

The treatment that gave birth to Islam moved from Muhammad's desire to always remember God. During his

Night Journey when he ascended from the sacred rock on Temple Mount through the seven heavens to the tree beyond which was the Throne of God, God's commandment to observe ritual prayer 50 times a day seemed quite sensible.

But on his way back down, the prophet Moses convinced him to go back and ask for a reduction in this number, upon which God cut the required number of prayers in half. But when Muhammad passed by the prophet Moses again, Moses told him that this was still too many. So Muhammad returned to the Throne of God one more time. This time God reduced the requirement to five prayers each day in the embrace of the remembrance.

For the world of women who feed hungry families and the world of men who work among the fields and flocks of grazing camels and sheep, this devotion set into motion a new nation, one that knelt down in prostrating prayerfulness five times a day. Woven rugs became sacred. Prayer rugs were woven especially for bended knees. The remembrance took hold of the desert and spread like a wild fire to become a population of a billion modern day followers of Islam and the Qur'an of his visions. The melodic and heart-opening Call to Prayer, the Adhan, is sounded five times a day throughout the Middle East, continuing the remembrance in the midst of the hard-shelled reality of a contemporary world gone mad.

Many westerners see the Muslim faith as being behind the times. But I can't help but wonder what essential piece is being held and cherished and protected that perhaps the rest of us can't see, that lies within the purity of a seed of life that can be given to the whole of humanity.

The abundant seeds of the pomegranate remind me of Muhammad's desire to kneel down and pray fifty times a day, in his weeping joy and singing desire to remember his creator. For me, there is a teaching here, a remembrance, an example. How often are we called to pray in the western world? So many offer prayer only during times of crisis. Perhaps if prayers were more bountiful, crisis would be less so. Pomegranates and prayers, remembrance and reverence are qualities of Islam and qualities of the human heart. May the seeds of remembrance always be abundantly remembered.

I wonder if he were alive today what he would say to the terrorists who bomb the innocent and to the Mossad soldiers who shoot to kill. What would he say to both sides of the war? What would he say to each way of thinking and the justifications that cross the line, trample it, and leave remembrance up for grabs and interpretation, like a ghost that was once given life through the vision of a prophet and the angel that came to earth in radiant blessing?

I say that there is a supreme wisdom in the essence of all faiths. It is only the ignorance within a human mind that shadows the beauty of truth with the squelching dogma that masquerades as the terror of survival.

I hold out my platter for good measure and ask whoever will listen to pile the pomegranates high on my plate of life and to pile on all that the seeds of life can teach me. They, too, are the fruit of the desert and the taste of remembrance with their multitudinous seeds of life glistening beneath the surface. I learned a long time ago to look beyond the surface of things, even though to do so is a little maddening. It always leaves me wondering and poised on the verge of the next question.

I want to go all the way back to the anointing of Muhammad, and even further to the crashing, cruel and grief-filled moment when Ishmael was cast out of the family of Abraham into the sands of an unknown future with his mother, Hagar. What path did they take; what ravines and gaps in time did they cross; what leaps of faith did they strive for; what trial and tribulation did they suffer; what did they carry in their hearts to their graves; and what did they pass on to their children? Hagar, the mother who once bore Ishmael, bore the seeds of a family line all the way to Muhammad.

If we were to trace the lineage that strikes out bravely across the desert, what would we find between the life of Ishmael and the life of Muhammad? Muhammad was a descendant of the family tree of the Father of fathers, Abraham. Their lives were like a bridge of blood from the parting with the father, to the ascension to the throne. What seeds of faith and seeds of bewilderment followed the days of Ishmael's journey from his father's side to find their way home through the angel's touch upon Muhammad's brow?

The Arab word for pomegranate is "rumanah." Rumanah is sweet on my mind, glistening red in its beauty, character, passion and unique qualities, like the Arab people. They too are a jewel of the desert land, a surviving people, and a great branch of the Eternal Tree of Life.

And in my idealist analogies, if I were to add one more treasure to my basket of desert bounty, it would definitely be the olive. It would be the olive, plain and simple, growing on the barren hillsides despite the obvious odds against its survival. Not to leave the Christian faith out of the fold in the scheme of my thinking, I would find the olive as a very pleasing and proper fruit to assign to followers of Jesus, the small green lumps that are born from the scorching sun of the fiery Word.

So much life springs from the tough-skinned olive, made soft and edible only through the steeping in brine. But after the brine, is not the olive pleasing to the tongue? Does it not grace the table at breakfast, lunch and dinner in all parts of the world? Does it not ooze forth with the oil of anointing, from the flesh that surrounds a single hard brown seed of the One God? Does not the olive deserve due consideration in this comparison of the fruits of the desert and the characteristics of cultures?

Inwardly I nod in agreement, still marveling at the ongoing display of morning beyond my rumpled sheets and breakfast tray. Another day is beginning, as time whittles itself to nothing and our seminar for inner and outer peace creeps a day closer. I have invited olives and pomegranates and cactus fruit to coexist for three days in the same basket of bounty.

My shy but sure secretary suggested that we open the event with prayers, prayers from a priest and prayers from a Rabbi and prayers from a Sheikh. I nodded and gave her the go-ahead to make the arrangements, and hopefully the invited spiritual leaders will accept the offer. Hopefully they will put their hearts into it, hopefully they will remember all of God's beloved people and do us all some good with the power of their prayers times three. God knows we need all the help we can get for the peace conference to smile back at us with its success.

I doubt I could share my insight and musing about desert fruit. It would be too much for such a serious place and such serious times. They might think the woman from America has gone too far, too idealistic, too romantic, too out of touch with the harsh reality that they face every day. The kind of analogies that reduce the Arab/Israeli crisis to a basket of fruit are, well, just too much. But it stays with me, this thought, this musing and it feeds my heart.

Outside my window is the Mount of Olives, and so olives factor perfectly. The hillsides all around the Old City are blessed with their pale silvery green and knowing ability to give whatever is needed. Yes, the olive is important. Its characteristics have much to teach anyone who will listen to the wonder of its flesh. There is a great symbology in the fact that they are inedible if they are eaten before going through the transformation of salt and brine and vinegar. This is the alchemy between God's original creation and the surrendering of the inner fruit of humanity to its own metamorphosis.

Comforted by this analogy, I do well to remember that my own fruit of wisdom has often been sun-kissed and plumped up, resurrected and permeated with the presence of great souls each time that I have answered the call to return to Jerusalem, to enter her heart and her bowels and her ramparts, to return and to remember the intensely tangible mix of the colors, textures, sounds and smells of spiritual life. The air is thickly laden with esoteric nuance and the richness of human passage, and to breathe it makes me a part of a grand scheme of planetary import.

As a peace worker, as a teacher of essence, as a self-assigned global guardian and as a daughter of the divine, I am happy to hold exhausted young women in my arms and offer motherly advice. I am also in reverence of the deeds of these same young women who grit their teeth and swallow their sensitivity so they can put their arms around a hungry war-ravaged child and a desperate dying mother.

It makes me sad that pilgrims and tourists and busloads of the faithful don't come here anymore. It makes me shake my head to see the flow of money of tourists and pilgrims, who once came here full of wonder and childlike appreciation for the spirit of this place all but non-existent, and how this flow of giving and receiving has dried up, with everything going to the cost of bombs and so little going to the future of children!

One taxicab driver, who said he used to make five trips a day from the airport in Tel Aviv to the Jaffa Gate of the old city, hasn't seen anyone who wanted to come to Jerusalem in over five months. For the last five months he has sat drumming his fingertips on his dashboard, losing hope minute-by-minute, hour-by-hour at the curb outside the airport.

He said I was his first passenger in all this time, and he was joyously friendly. But one sorry customer needing a one-hour ride wasn't reason enough not to sell his cab and leave. "The only problem with selling my taxi," he lamented, "is that taxi cabs are now a dime a dozen, selling for nothing, because no one has anywhere to go. And nobody cares. With roadblocks every few miles, and bombs in the skies our future, why bother?"

This man, who once made a living driving a taxi five times a day, was also an Arab who shook his head in dismay and disbelief at where all the terrorism was headed. Sighing in a combination of pitiful resignation and childlike need, he talked about the fear with which he went to bed at night, and the grief of his wife, whose elderly father was killed last week by a fifteen year old neighbor boy from his village. Seeking the glory of God (Allah) and the virgins of Heaven with such passion that it snuffed out his own young life, which had barely begun, and snapped the necks of mere onlookers, among them the elderly and beloved father of the taxi driver's wife.

Arabs sometimes kill Arabs because the bombs don't care who is on the receiving end of the destruction. Only people can care about that.

Side by side with the brief but potent hour that I sat shoulder to shoulder with the taxicab driver dressed in western blue jeans, live all the times I have brushed shoulders with Priests, Rabbis, Sheikhs and Mullahs, all dressed in their full regalia. These regal contenders of the Old City who once congregated at every turn of the winding cobblestone passageways that became a single maze of multi-tiered ancestry now lay low, a shadow of their previous visibility when times were good.

During the time of peace and tourism the wisdom of coexistence and "live and let live" kept the shopkeepers busy and smiling and children fat with full bellies. How often I was moved again and again to stare without shame, as if I were a two-year old child myself, at the spectacle of black-caped priests and white-robed sheikhs and long-bearded, ringlet-haired rabbis when I first came to Jerusalem.

Do they know how it touched me, how it ignited my imagination, how it set something free in my small world of western relativity, to see them and smell them and listen to the reassuring hum of their fatherly banter? Do they know? Could they ever guess?

Do the politicians know the cornucopia of grace that visitors from around the world receive when they come to Jerusalem? Do they understand the cultural deprivation when the Holy Land is not safe for visitors and pilgrims? Travel warnings have been issued, and all the tours have stopped, and the tour busses have been repossessed by banks and loan companies and are parked empty and lonely in vacant lots with nowhere to go, like the hoards of taxis with no eager passengers.

Do they know how important a basket of desert fruit is to the rest of the world? I delighted in the old Arab men, who clustered in small groups of cultural devotion, wearing flowing robes of desert descent, and deep weathered faces that tell of hidden creviced canyons that give shelter to sheep and camels, and wrinkled mouths that wrap around the hookah, as they smoke tobacco in the pipe with passionate dedication.

The narrow passages that wind their way from gate to gate are made sacred by the big-bellied laughter, as the pipe is passed around the circle of initiates who have known the pipe since their grandfathers first gestured to them as young boys to join the men and pass the sweet smoke from heart to heart and malehood to malehood.

It is a tradition with time on its side, to think and talk and play cards on rickety card tables and drink thick black espresso coffee, so thick and so black as to define the men who swill it down. They sit like kings outside of small shops and cafes, as if they owned the streets. And I have grown fond of and familiar with the blending of aromas, the coffee and sweet tobacco, as it wafts around the corners.

Large jars of olives stare out from shop shelves and the pomegranate juice-stands stacked high with paper cups keep the old men company who bask in the sun nearby, and quench the pallet of curious onlookers from far-away places like me. Pomegranate juice, prickly pear jam and olives wet with oil and vinegar are part of the great scheme of things. I don't want to have to choose one over the other; the diversity is what gives value and richness to life. This is what I treasured before the war closed the gates to the many and gave refuge to the few.

I love the diversity of Jerusalem; the diversity itself is the greatest treasure of all. I love how the pungent aroma of hookah pipes drifts up through the deep-throated melodic call to prayer that is sweet to the ears, as it is broadcast from loudspeakers five times a day without fail throughout the entire city. Well-worn rugs come out of nowhere to welcome the knees of the faithful, who stop dead in their tracks, withdraw from the bustle of the city and prostrate themselves in the quietude of divine remembrance. To experience this is nothing short of awe-inspiring. To see it touches something that needs touching.

I cannot count the times I was moved to tears, just to bear witness to the beauty of Old Jerusalem. There, in the very midst of centuries old factioning is the continual commingling of these three faiths. From my perspective as an unbiased and undoubtedly simple-minded visitor, I didn't care which prayer or which faith was echoing off the great encompassing walls that encircle the ancient city to be distributed unto all eternity, or which fruit would taste better; I fell in love with them all. I had no investments, political or religious, that favored any one of the traditions over the other. I simply learned to be glad for diversity, for the way that choice expands our human thoughts and feeds the mind with greater possibility.

If the mind is open; if the mind can crack open the door; it can see beyond its own small world to the rest of existence, to savor the taste and the smell and the touch of all that is given life and all that grows on the Great Tree of Life, laden with the delectable promise of many shapes and colors and sizes and flavors of the harvest of humanity's bearing.

Rather than succumb to the poison of judgment and its cold grip on promising minds, I found passion for the divine presence within all the cultures that found a place to live within myself. This is what makes Jerusalem what it is. I am often brought to my knees in captivated reverence, wishing I had a rug to break the hard surface beneath my kneecaps, as I sit with Jewish women who hold toddlers on their knees at the Wailing Wall, or follow Catholic priests holding candles in their hands to light the way down the steps to the lower chambers of the Church of the Holy Sepulcher.

So many prayers have been brought to the altar of faith. The endurance of the human heart amazes me. My own prayers are often added to those already lingering in the air, the same air that breathes in the essence of cactus fruit and rusty red pomegranates and oil-laden olives, then exhales the blended fragrance of all three without knowing that there is any conflict whatsoever over the matter of differences.

The richness of faith as Jews from around the world gather at the Western Wall of prayer and divine favor, the power of the Bar Mitzvah, and the nodding as if to drink in the Torah have deeply touched me, a foreigner with a greater desire to seek and serve our creator of all things. Chills run down my spine at the sounding of the ram's horn blown by old men in full regalia in the call of divine blessing upon young boys whose destiny is soon to begin.

Chapter 12

The Road

Journey of Dreams, Journey of Choice

While peace makers gather throughout the world to fight for peace, the fight over who will reign over these stone walls and holy vestiges rages throughout the Middle East in a measured pace, a clamor of late-breaking around the clock news reports. A major peace gathering was held in the center of Old Jerusalem with tens of thousands arriving from around the world.

Headlines announced that over two million protested around the world, joining the wave of "massed intent" to choose higher ground, the high road of peace and global responsibility, rather than the wave of irresponsibility that has so often been allowed socially, environmentally and economically to be passed off as global progress or western interests. Sentiments run high. People are fed up. The demand for the high road of human values and a new planetary balance is starting to ring.

Perhaps our planetary keynote is finding itself. Perhaps it is a keynote born of our collective human dignity. Perhaps the benefit of "diversity within the unity of nations" has begun to break upon the shores of intelligent thinking at a mass level of consciousness.

Perhaps it is possible to be a peace activist and at the same time love one's country and also care about the young women and men in the armed forces who are willing to give their lives for the "security" of the people of their nation. But then again isn't true security the point, security that assures a sustainable existence for the human race? We stand as a race before a fork in the road, a threshold of choice.

Even though the question of high roads and low roads, peace and war are enough to suck the sap out of the Tree of Life, I can feel that I'm reaching my own sucked-out limits. A pleasant evening would do a lot to regain my own humanity. There's a certain point where deep breaths and resignation absolutely must cling to self-created calm. A flash of mind, of full presence, makes the decision to enjoy the evening, to take it in, to be normal, to live in my skin and savor the simple things.

Heading back to my hotel at a slow leisurely saunter, I look forward to a quiet supper with a few members of our staff. I can hear the echoing of TV and radio news reports drifting from doorways into the early evening air, as I wind my way from the Western Wall to the Jaffa Gate. The familiarity of cobblestone that never changes gives me a sense of comfort.

Nothing extreme is being announced, but everyone is on a continual state of alert. I am grateful for a low-keyed newscast. Nothing horrendous seems to be lurking in the air for the moment, and for a moment there is a reprieve, a welcome reprieve, as if the whole of the Old City can take a break from the wretchedness of war and the questing for peace.

And yet there is an eerie stillness to the sunset that reflects a soft amber on stone walls and walkways, as if the narrow streets and arched gates know that this day of calm precedes the storm that is creeping in from the horizon of future fate. I can feel both sides of reality, but this temporary calm is no less a blessing, the gold light moving across stone walls no less serene.

But still there is a quiet and severe knowing in the air that the storm is coming. It has been a long, long time since an entire day has gone by without headline bulletins announcing the latest siege, insurgence, bombing or standoff into living rooms around the world, but this still day is like the quiet harbor that awaits the inevitable. Everyone knows the terrible crush of a tsunami wave will soon be headed to shore.

Turning the bend in front of the Jaffa Gate I pass through and under its archway and cross over to the right hand side of the road. I could have gone left. Both directions will take me home. One road moves along the Old City wall. One road wraps around and becomes a busy commercial street. I choose the quiet comfort of the rampart wall walkway.

I pass by three school children who are walking fast, obviously in a hurry to get home, backpacks filled with schoolbooks on their shoulders, and more than likely also gas masks. The easy joy common to kids on their way home from the school day is gone from their eyes. Their faces are set, as if they haven't smiled or laughed in a long time. They must not be over nine or ten years old, but the weight of the seriousness of their plight has taken its toll. I wonder why they are walking alone in the first place.

As I pass them on the walkway, I offer a smile in their direction. I hope to offer something more than a smile, perhaps the simplicity of someone who cares. A moment of decision and indecision causes a pause, a gap, a frozen interlude. They hesitate, and then cast their eyes to the cement under their feet. But then they tilt their heads in my direction and for a moment a humanity that crosses the boundaries of age, race and religion is passed between us. Small tentative smiles reach out and spread light; even a flicker of hope is understood. And then they reach the corner of the intersection, pause and turn to the right, continuing on their way home to their mothers.

My thoughts turn to the plight of all the innocent children who must still be sent to school each day. Their mothers must, with wrenching hearts, deeply troubled hearts grapple with the stark reality that their beloved little ones might not live until the end of the day to return home to the family dinner table.

Arab mothers and Israeli mothers alike feed their children breakfast with the same daunting horror that spins like a hurricane in the back of their minds, spoon in hand, biscuits coming out of the oven, not knowing what they will witness on the news or hear when they answer the telephone. Fathers do their best to protect and love, those they protect. Some carry guns; some carry bombs; some pray; some fight, and a few just run away.

Another Arab summit last week in Jordan did not bring the warring nations that sprang from the loins of the prophet Abraham any closer to peace. The lines of opposition seem drawn in the sand and the dust and the dirt more vehemently than ever. On some days, more recently on most days, hope is dying on the vine like withered fruit, sucked dry of its innate God-given vitality by the constant failure to find the way out of this self-perpetuating, confounded, convoluted conflict.

A pall of deep psychological depression is gripping most people that I have met. Even the Old City wall seems to be weeping. Friends that I've known for years seem locked in a glum numbness that hasn't hit bottom quite yet, but is well on its way. Rage and revenge spike the ball into the other side of the court, and you can see pain and desperation in the eyes of the few people you rub shoulders with on the street. It seems that the road to peace is a long one, a long, long road that becomes the teacher of the unexpected and the inevitable.

This is the atmosphere that the peace maker lives in, works in, and must come to terms with. It is the nature of things, the nature of the work. I have another day of meetings scheduled to interview potential speakers for the meeting at Neve Shalom, a cooperative village of Jews and Arab Israelis. Somehow they've been able to hold onto at least a shred of their dreams and visions of coexistence, peace and remembrance.

The people who live and work at the center have worked hard, fought hard for a mutual future. Perched on a hilltop and holding the vision of coexistence, they have tried to carve a road to peace out of hardscrabble and the battles of the past.

During my meetings, feeling somewhere in-between being a fool and a mediator, I do my best to keep the playing field balanced and fairly representative. My job is to offer an opportunity, a stage and a platform for all the voices of all the sides of possibility to be heard, and I hear plenty from everyone, including the soldiers and ex-Mossad who are assigned to guard the welfare of lives wherever it is that my work, meetings, gatherings or conferences are taking place.

There seems to be a left and right to everything, radical and orthodox, moderate and passionate, Likud and Labor. The polarities are impossible not to trip over. I seem to fall on my face daily. I feel like a fool because it is impossible not to step on the toes of cultural convention, or through my ignorance of the political and religious protocol that is so important here, rub somebody the wrong way. Religious sensitivity runs high, traditions run deep and political mindsets are sometimes like steel traps.

I feel hopelessly lost, trying to navigate the religious end of things, as so much of my prayers are given over to asking for forgiveness ahead of time for crossing the lines on long-held beliefs that I'm not even remotely aware of. It's like walking a tightrope, or tiptoeing on the razor's edge not to offend anyone unknowingly. Feathers get ruffled, hackles raised and scorn is amply heaped for the most innocent infraction, from my point of view.

Of course, being an American with a cultural talent of my own for a natural, inbred blind arrogance, I am often a target. We Americans are so very, very blind to how the rest of the world sees us. Our tendency of bold and brassy individuality is often viewed as crude and presumptuous by other cultures and countries. So, being an American and a humanitarian is a challenging mix, because even if I unwittingly seem overbearing without realizing it, I am also compelled to be true to myself and to speak my mind when I must.

It is a thing close to torture to be a "sensitive person," let alone a peace maker in the midst of a blood-soaked holy war over things which belong first and foremost to our Creator, especially in a place where the covenant between Creator and creation is held as sacred above all things. It's a thing to weep about, the getting used to blood-soaked holiness. We sink into resignation going in both directions. The covenants of the past are bountiful in this land, but they are faint shadows on the horizon that no one knows how to bring into the reality of present day practicality.

We have the promise on one end of the spectrum and trouble on the other. The Ark of the Covenant glistens golden in the middle, adorned with arched-winged angels stretching as far as they can; ready to topple over if they stretch any further excusing the raw side of things, when human beings use God and religion to justify brutality. Please note that I have already apologized for my remark about such holy things as arks and angels, and I hope that any offense taken can recognize my good intentions.

Domination and abuse in the name of religion is an old story that sends crusaders marching in every direction, banners held high. Wars over God are the ultimate paradox and may be the ultimate crime as well. Will the war over religions ever end? The angels that look on must shake their heads as they do their best to bless all the souls who give their lives, soaking the ground with the blood of their bodies on account of religious fervor.

Yes, it's a paradox of the very highest order, as the angels reach across the sea of human suffering to protect the sacred law that is at the heart of all things, and presumably at the heart of this conflict in some mysterious way that unfolds the Divine Plan.

Here it's all a matter of interpretation, and this is where we all get into big trouble, deep trouble, tormented trouble, and the kind of trouble that we live to regret. And, more often than not, not only do we become owners of troubled regrets, but we also leave a troubled aftermath as the legacy that we bestow upon our children and their children. I can't help but drop my head onto my knees, unable to even so much as shift my countenance to show either condemnation or dismay.

Every so often it all just drops to the bottom of a bottomless pit, with trouble, trouble everywhere, sinking like a lead weight, sinking like heavy stones to the bottomless bottom. The depression that hangs in the sullen air, on the streets, in closed restaurants and empty shopping centers is virulent. Normal life has all but screeched to a halting non-existence. Most people have withdrawn and stay at home behind locked and bolted doors, and in some cases barricades. And yet I have made a firm commitment to enjoy a good and restful evening with friends and colleagues. It would be so good to talk about something besides war and peace.

But for the most part everyone would want an update. So much is happening so quickly, coordinating our work here with our work in the US. Perhaps we could at least talk about the up side of the road to peace. Almost every day I hear of a new initiative or alliance. My own passion is the Global Guardianship Initiative, which brings peace work to peace living and actively works with international groups on major projects of global benefit. Many good and intelligent people have brought every possible resource and contribution into a cohesive focus.

The Global Guardianship movement emerged from a conference for Women Spiritual Leaders at the United Nations in Geneva that brought together women leaders to search hard for what can be done. It was a truly spiritual gathering of feminine wisdom and power. Many of us were meeting for the first time and little did we know that so much would come from a few short days.

Everyone went home on the high road as architects of a new movement, a movement to actively, personally, immediately set about creating a better world. Women leaders from foreign countries from all walks of life and cultures and traditions became my friends and colleagues.

The Global Guardianship Initiative took all our years of service in the spiritual, humanitarian, peace and environmental arenas and brought them together in a new intention, to create a cohesive plan and to engage more effective and integrated efforts. Something very, very sacred and essential was seeded among us and we walked away from the United Nations inspired and excited.

We had chosen a new road, one that we would build ourselves, the road to becoming stewards and guardians of our planet, far beyond the well-wishing of good intentions to concrete plans of practical vision and tangible action. So many women were carving out new territory by engaging the politics of the heart, of humility and caring. A new premise was under construction.

One of the speakers at the conference was a Jewish mother from up north of Haifa who had lost her son. His head and that of another school-aged boy had been crushed in by several angry rock-wielding Arab youths. Neither of the little boys came home ever again. They had been walking home from grade school on a fine spring day along a dirt road at the bottom of an isolated canyon. Suddenly, in a thrash of rage, they were ripped from their mothers' hearts.

This mother told her story about the strength she had found not to hate. She told us that there were days she couldn't lift herself out of bed, so deep was the grief that possessed her. To have her young son meet with such a violent senseless death over-loaded her senses and short-circuited her heart. But in the end she chose the high road. She chose not to blame and condemn. With so much talk about the sacrifice of soldiers and the hardships of battle, we would do well to remember a mother's hardship of losing her child and the sacrifice of choosing love over hate.

Instead of seeking revenge as an antidote to her pain, she started a group for grieving parents, for both Palestinians and Jews who had lost their precious children. I hope that her choice for peace, which arose from unbearable pain, sees her through to the other side of despair and blesses her each step of the way. Her talk moved over 500 souls to tears and gave me strength. And I needed it.

I am grateful that Palestinian and Jewish parents grieve together and find a way to coexist in their pain. Some continue to walk the road of peace no matter what. Because both Jews and Palestinians have shown me their goodness and grace, I cannot cast more favor in the direction of the legendary chosen ones or less favor to the supposedly less worthy, less chosen, less anointed.

I have made dear, dear friends on both sides of the fence, and on both sides of the checkpoints. I have supped from the cup of such humanity, such generosity, and such nobility. The Middle East is laden with much fruit, sweet fruit, juicy fruit of the human kind.

Almost without exception my personal exchanges with both Jew and Arab, have been filled with grace and good humor and no trouble of any kind. I have grown to admire the beauty of each of their cultures, the music, the gestures, and the flavor that makes life worth living for the rest of us.

Such wisdom, such hearts these people have, generous hearts that go the extra mile for a friend and would spread the kitchen table with the last crumbs of food in the house to feed a weary traveler. Such bright minds that seek a better future for their children. For me, as a naive outsider, very naive I admit, it is hard to fully grasp why we cannot live and let live, here and everywhere else. When we meet the human side of their lives it's hard to envision the stark reality of soldiers and terrorists.

Throughout history, we have witnessed the phenomena of nations being enemies one day and allies the next, as the laws of survival dictate the final judgment that bends the wills of mice and men. Military commanders of mighty legions would turn over in their graves if they saw yesterday's enemies being invited with cordial pomp to today's champagne brunches.

The beast of survival is happy to lick the wounds of adversaries, if it means a better deal down the road. A mere hundred years can alter the landscape of culture, color, creed and criteria. A flip of the coin can turn everything upside down, inside out and backward. The long road of world affairs has an undulating way of slithering along in a collective winding snake dance, taking surprising turns around the twist of the bend.

One can turn right or one can turn left it seems. I turned right this evening and received the smiles of three school children. They turned right and hopefully made it all the way home. I remembered one woman's story, one who chose love and sat together with the parents of the youths who had taken her son's life. She sat with them in peace.

In America, in the great Old West, the cowboys and Indians are a good example of flipped coins, snaky deals, twisted turns and a long, long road to peace and coexistence. Perhaps it is impolite even incorrect to extrapolate my own sense of things out of the context of accepted convention, as the European settlement of America was a very complex unfolding that took hundreds of years, involved immigrants from nearly every country and cultural group on the planet, and in the process met nearly as many tribal groups and nations. But I think this analogy bears attention.

As the waves of settlers rolled across the continent engulfing everything in their paths, an attitude, a tone, was set that played itself out in varying degrees depending on the circumstance. But in this push across America, the tales of the cultural icons of the "cowboys and Indians" were created, which endure to this day and have become favorite themes for television and cinema. Turn on any channel, any time of the day, and sooner or later you will see a saga of cowboys and Indians being retold with cinematic flair.

The white settlers, and the Indians were once mortal enemies, but now the Indians claim "coup" in the Supreme Court, and cowboys roll the dice in Indian-owned, white-man-financed casinos, a paradox indeed. On the backside of history when America was first moving west, the US government backed the then 'big business' side of things. Isn't this always the story? The road to opportunity had money written all over it; every sign on the wayside, every intersection of new opportunity, every billboard of progress had the almighty dollar claiming the right of way.

In short, all the tax advantages, all the water rights, mineral rights, railroad rights, road rights, almost all of the land rights and any other kind of rights that could be raped and pillaged, scraped or plowed into even the most absurd rationale went to the cowboys, the white settlers and the corporate intruders of the day. The outnumbered Indians, after a long hard fight, were forced into submission and forced to give in, in order to survive.

True to our Anglo roots of imperialistic nobility, we had our white God on our side, and that God was a "just" God, a God that gave us full license to kill anything that stood in the way of grabbing whatever we wanted. It was a convenient religion, a convenient philosophy and convenient politics. The white God nodded or at least looked the other way when the white man pushed whatever stood in the line of progress off to the side like road kill.

The Native Americans wanted no part of it and wept at the demise of everything that mattered. They wept oceans of tears, weeping all the way to their imprisonment on the "reservations," a politically conjured American word for refugee camp.

The forced march of the Cherokee from their homeland in the southern Appalachian Mountains to the reservation in Oklahoma was particularly severe, and even the textbooks of public schools in America can't hide this brutality. The historic march took place in the dead of winter; gun-toting soldiers rode high on horses, while half-starved women and children trudged in the snow beneath them. Many did not live to see past the stinging of their tears, dying on the way. The old and young dropped nameless into snowy graves, but were grieved for by those who loved them and held them dear. It came to be called the "Trail of Tears," as nearly one in four died en route.

To me this was an unspeakable travesty and a violation of humanity. There have been many small holocausts that add even more grief to the great holocaust of World War II. The treatment of the indigenous tribes of America was indeed a holocaust from their perspective.

It was also a holocaust of a way of life, that way of life being the "religion" of the Indian people, the beliefs that they held dear and lived by. The tribal elders were revered for their wisdom rather than their cunning, their guardianship of all life rather than their dominion over it. Chief Seattle, one of the leaders of the Suquamish tribe in the northwestern United States, cared for his people and the land. He knew his place upon the earth and in the universe, and his thoughts traveled the stars.

His words, which remain with us today, have gone down in history. And even though he never so much as had a pen in his hand, his words have been written for all thinking caring people as his legacy. And legacy is a good thought to consider. Legacy... What is our legacy some 150 years after Chief Seattle's words were spoken? What is our legacy? What will it be? What will our grandchildren remember us for here in America or wherever we call home?

As Chief Seattle was faced with the inevitable treaty forcing him to hand over all that he cherished for a "reservation" far from the white settlers, out of their way, out of sight, out of mind, he said:

The Great Chief in Washington sends word that he wishes to buy our land. But how can you buy or sell the sky? the land? The idea is strange to us. If we do not own the freshness of the air and the sparkle of the water, how can you buy them? Every part of the earth is sacred to my people. Every shining pine needle, every sandy shore, every mist in the dark woods, every meadow, every humming insect is holy in the memory and experience of my people. The shining water that moves in the streams and rivers is not just water, but the blood of our ancestors. Each glossy reflection in the clear waters of the lakes tells of events and memories in the life of my people. The water's murmur is the voice of my father's father.

We know that the white man does not understand our ways. One portion of land is the same to him as the next, for he is a stranger who comes in the night and takes from the land whatever he needs. The earth is not his brother, but his enemy, and when he has conquered it, he moves on. He leaves his father's grave behind, and he does not care. He kidnaps the earth from his children, and he does not care. His father's grave, and his children's birthright are forgotten. He treats his mother, the earth, and his brother, the sky, as things to be bought, plundered, sold like sheep or bright beads. His appetite will devour the earth and leave behind only a desert.

This we know: the earth does not belong to man, man belongs to the earth. All things are connected like the blood that unites us all. Man did not weave the web of life; he is merely a strand in it. Whatever he does to the web, he does to himself.

Before the white man came, their lives revolved around harmony with nature, with the plants and animals, seasons and cycles that surrounded them. They prayed and danced and whooped and hollered and walked and rode their proud ponies in step with the green grass and the brown prairies. They had no roads. Their religion was a faith that worshipped the goodness of Mother Earth's bounty and the spirit of all creatures.

They watched in mind-boggling horror the blood-lusting slaughter of vast herds of buffalo, the very thing that the tribes depended on. They watched as the buffalo were gunned down for mere sport to the point of near extinction. The buffalo that fed and clothed the people were cruelly wiped out, wiped away, and nearly wiped off the face of the earth. And their way of life was wiped out too.

They were a people who humbly prayed before taking the life of a buffalo or any other animal, who communed on bended knee before, during and after the sacrifice of one life given to sustain another. To them pompous trophy shooting, any kind of trophy shooting or killing for pleasure, was the epitome of shameful bar-

barism. To kill the sacred buffalo, shamelessly and without purpose, was an unspeakable horror.

On the other end of the spectrum, in complete disrespect of their long-held beliefs, the whites called the Indians "savages." To fulfill that imposed imagery, the Indians became a self-fulfilling prophecy. They got damned good at taking coup and scalping the white man, taking direct aim with a tomahawk at the broadside of his overgrown head, and burning down anything that the white man built. They learned how to take advantage of all the roads the white men built too, and hid in the bushes for surprise attacks. They were the terrorists of their day and proud of it. Who could really blame them? Who could say?

In the wake of buffalo-less prairies and mountain meadows, the Indians crashed hard on the white man's concept of progress and headed to near extinction along with their buffalo. They walked a road that was red with the blood of their children, and bitter with the loss of freedom and the taste of the white man's bit in their mouths. They were treated like animals, sometimes even worse, prisoners in the land of their grandfathers, and broken as a people from too many broken promises.

Now in the modern Wild West of America, the situation continues to improve. Many of the tribal reservations are strongholds of beauty and natural wealth. Some of their children are graduating from college as lawyers, and doctors and leaders in their own right. Many are walking the high road, dedicating their lives to pursuing the Red Road of their forefathers and are making every effort to retain the keynotes and nuances of their culture. But they are also becoming an integral part of America, helping to define who we are as Americans.

They fought hard side by side with the white man in World War II. Who would have guessed that cowboys and Indians would fight side by side to subdue a common enemy? Some say the use of the Navajo language as a code to convey military information was a major factor in winning the war. They paid their dues and earned their pride. They even built roads to their reservations. Who could have guessed? Who could have known?

Of course everything is not yet perfect. Alcoholism is the sad antidote to the loss of cultural identity. The economic picture remains dim on many of the reservations. There are many social ills that are in tremendous need of retribution, but the healing continues. And at least the children go to sleep at night without the fear of bombs and bulldozers destroying their worlds.

Meanwhile, it is a new day for America as young whites from good families flock to the reservations to pray with the tribal elders and smoke the peace pipe. The Sun Dance draws big crowds of devoted souls who preserve the tradition of personal sacrifice and wisdom seeking.

White people and red people sit side by side at Pow Wow Gatherings drinking Coke and Pepsi. White people wear Indian jewelry. Indian people wear cowboy boots. Indian music, art and culture is sought after, collected, bought and sold, even worshipped. The "Santa Fe look" has become a classic fashion statement. The white men proudly display Indian artifacts on their fireplace mantels and drape hand-woven Indian blankets costing a small fortune on their sofas. The whites have taken to Indian pride as their own heritage, a paradox in and of itself, and get teary eyed at the sight of buffalo and cry during award-winning movies like "Dances with Wolves."

Meanwhile, the cowboys are now the ones who are crashing hard on hard times. Their numbers are down to nothing, outnumbered by a different fate, an organic fate, a fate that is hard to see unless you look back over your shoulder to errors of ages past. Cowboys only know that cattle prices are way down, hope is down, land prices are way up and taxes are up.

So now, the cowboys that are left, the remaining few, the very few, can barely afford to buy hay. They can't let their cattle starve and they can't afford to feed them either. Ironically, some cowboys have even decided to raise buffalo. There's money in it, better money than cattle, and the buffalo are a whole lot smarter than cows.

Now they pay a dear price for their lack of foresight a mere hundred years or so from the days when they ran the Indians off the "God-given" land of their native grandfathers; pushed them, with a hard heart filled with ambition and future guilt onto land which even the Anglo land-grabbers didn't much want; and called it a reservation.

And then a twist of fate reared up out of nowhere. Glory be and glory behold, if those reservation lands didn't have a heck of a lot of oil and coal and uranium in "them thar' hills," a "Who could have known?" twist of fate, and a sharp bend in the road that no one considered. The Cherokees who walked the terrible Trail of Tears ended up with oil fields under their feet.

Also on the positive side of healing, there are many new land stewards, self-educated and self-designed environmentalists who see it as their life mission to buy land and return it to its natural state, who respect the Native American tradition of preserving the earth and its sacred web of life. They are buying land and treating their land with reverence and employing sound ecological principles.

Many are taking care to return the land to its pristine state and are becoming environmental guardians of the land that was once stewarded by America's own indigenous peoples, who lived on the land for thousands of years without disturbing it. And so the native grandfathers of the past are no doubt smiling upon the new breed of land barons who take it upon themselves to be stewards rather than mindless exploiters of our good earth. This is indeed a turn in the road that can be applauded.

Along these lines and from somewhere out of my childhood memory, side by side with the choice for love and the refusal to hate, the cowboys and Indians and dramatic reversals of fate and fortune, comes the story of the apostle Paul of Tarsus, and the road that he walked upon the day that the revelation of Jesus of Nazareth was upon him, and his life changed on a dime. Within these wide-ranging changes, the doors can open to heaven or hell, depending upon which way we turn our hearts... depending upon which way we turn our hearts.

In his case, it didn't take two hundred years of organic twists and turns; it only took perhaps two minutes or two hours. He made a choice immediately and never turned back. There he was on the road to Damascus, quite absorbed in perpetrating havoc on the pesky Christians, who honored the ideology of the shepherd boy Jesus, rather than the Emperor of Rome, when out of nowhere an unexpected twist in the road became a twist of a very personal kind.

With dust and donkeys as his witness, he fell to his knees as the Heavenly Host opened the white Pearly Gates to the higher realms and the vision of Jesus himself descended to ground level, bringing him to his senses. Who would have guessed that a Roman, who hated Christians and the phenomenon of Jesus, would become a disciple who shed tears at the thought of "the Savior?" Even his mother could never have guessed that he would change his name from Saul to Paul, so that the Christians could love him and receive the gospel from his previously Pharisaical Jewish lips.

And so I think to myself, this too seems like another befitting example of the life-changing events that no one could have expected. Blinded for three days thereafter, the famous Paul of Tarsus was made to see. Yes, from a miraculous bend in the road, the Roman Saul became the Christian Paul.

Like the revered prophets before him, he spread the Word. He had never even met Jesus in the flesh, and yet he became a founder of the Christian Church. Who would have guessed during the years he meted out the worst of his wrath to any Christian who crossed his path, that he would live out his life praising the glory of the one his fellow Romans had crucified? Who would have guessed? How could he have known that his life would change so drastically, to the point where he found himself on the other side of the road by choice and the power of revelation?

Could there be a lesson here? Might there possibly be a shred of wisdom that could be applied? The revelations among the spiritual elders of the Native American tribes are legendary. Might revelation descend upon certain chosen ones of Arab and Israeli concern?

Here in Israel, in the continuing aftermath of the Holocaust, it seems that the ability to see down the road would be a Godsend. When we dig in our heels, we sometimes lose the very thing we most want and aspire to. When we fail to see the big picture beyond ourselves, when we fail to look down the road at all, we then live with our own ignorance and bear the brunt of our own doing. But if we can stretch to see ourselves, our eyes open to more than just our own opinions, especially when we have lost the way, then perhaps the dove of peace can point the way.

The choice here in the Middle East cannot be reduced to the victim-aggressor chess game, with any outcome other than red rivers of tears and bruised roads of crashing hardships. Even the chess game itself is subject to annihilation.

So who will look down the road? Who will plot a course? Who will guide the ship? Who will lift the eyes of insanity into the sight of salvation? Who will tend the vineyards of tomorrow's wine? Who will light the path of tomorrow's possibilities? Who will see today's enemy as tomorrow's friend or business partner or perhaps even savior?

The young King of Jordan, who is following in his father's footsteps, is telling the US, "Don't escalate. Use wisdom. Stop the war. An entire region of the world is dependent upon peace. Bring all sides back to the table." He will no doubt go down in history for his wise and cautionary advice.

When I met with the Ambassador of Jordan last spring he said over, and over, and over again, "Peace is the only solution. Peace is the only option. Peace is the only way..." over and over again. He said this while we sat having a late afternoon lunch in a hotel dining room that overlooked the Citadel of David. I nodded and echoed back his words.

We did our best to rise to the occasion of finding a common road on common ground. We both had exhaustion in common; that was one thing for sure. He was a very busy man in the midst of so much trouble. What else could he say? What else was left to say? And I say, "Look down the road. See the turns. See the bends. Don't blow the road up altogether. 350,000,000 people live in the Middle East and all must learn to walk peaceably on the same road." Building a better road is the point.

Hoping that a road for humanity will still be there for my grandchildren is why I come from America, spending my last penny to host peace symposiums. Roads and Jerusalem are soul mates it seems. That is why there are so many great arched gateways that embellish the stone walls that run in a rampart around the Old City. All roads from all directions lead to Jerusalem. Roads from the sea, roads from the desert, roads from Egypt, roads from Jordan and Syria, roads from Lebanon.

Once the kingdom of David and Solomon reached all the way from Egypt to Syria and beyond. Who would have guessed 3,000 years later, that the roads from so many places would still be headed to a single center of things, long after the empire that claimed Jerusalem as the center of its universe had come and gone?

Whether I'm standing here at the center of the conflict, or whether I'm back home in America, I know what awaits me each day as I get out of bed and take my morning shower and read the news or turn on the TV. The onslaught of tragic reports will begin.

The Palestinians are like the world's orphans. Their plight is symbolic for most Arab countries, even though the good and bad of the oil issue leave most Arabs living in either the most wealthy families in the world or living in the most destitute. These are two sides of a road that is affecting every nation on earth as well as the Palestinians. Where does that leave the destitute of the Arab world who eat the dust of the Mercedes automobiles that streak across the desert in high gear from oil field to oil field?

As long as senseless and inhumane disparity between the rich and the poor is denied, trouble will be in the headlines, trouble will be on the road and trouble will be at the checkpoints. It is this senseless denial that makes a quiet day in and around Jerusalem and the Middle East rare and a little suspicious because everyone knows it won't last. A horror of some kind will shatter the stillness. From what I have seen, trouble's face is sculpted solely by the human hand and none other. It is sculpted by insensitivity to the obvious. It is not a thing of God. The hand of God is nowhere to be found on the road to trouble.

And yet even with time bombs ticking like the echo of a cruel joke, if I look beyond what seems to be a hopeless situation, if I look past all the trouble, I can see that this horrible mess has within it an unforgettable lesson buried deep at its center. Beneath the appearances of this utter mess is the golden heart of future days and the lessons learned. Beyond blindness is sight.

Somewhere down the road, after a few bends have been turned, is the promise of peace, still shining, still hoping, still waiting to be seen. God is shining a light on the long stretch ahead, on where that road will lead if we walk together in wisdom, if we recognize that we share the same road, all of us, every one of us worldwide. We sure enough share the same God. And if we don't, where will it lead? Who can guess? Who can know?

One of our speakers, at a recent symposium, gave a presentation on the concept of the "condominium." He was a brilliant man of wisdom and dedication, a renowned scientist who had worked for NASA in Houston, Texas some years back to put a man on the moon. I met with him for lunch several times and he told me his story.

In Houston, he began with nothing but an empty desk, an empty pad of paper, and a pencil. But his heart was full of ideas. He was a part of NASA's "wonder team," and they did what had never been done. They surmounted all obstacles; they did the very thing that had previously been deemed impossible. They put a man on the moon.

Now he's a university professor and wants peace; he wants peace more than anything. He spends his time helping Bedouin tribes receive medical care and education. He is a Jew who is willing to sit down with Arabs and anyone else who has half a flicker of willingness to look down the road.

He loses sleep over all the trouble, like I do. Our friendship is growing, although he is tormented by his worry, and wishes I would do more. I tell him to have faith and patience. He tells me people are dying; people are suffering. The aberrations of human values and barbarisms are an embarrassment on all sides. More recently he has turned his hope to women, and even to women like me.

His proposal for a "condominium" is as brilliant as he is. It reminds me somewhat of the peace that has been struck between the Native Americans and the relative newcomers who have come from around the world to call America their home. He talked about overlapping circles of life, and condominiums of communities. He talked about coexistence; he talked about co-creating nations; he talked about the way things should be. He talked about the preservation of cultural identity within a shared land concept that cared for all of the children of Abraham. He talked about changing the road signs and barbed wire and guard stations that warned of checkpoints on the roads to Gaza, Jericho, Jenin, Bethlehem, and Ramallah.

You would think that someone would listen to a guy who was instrumental in putting a man on the moon. He put his trust in the invocation and inspiration of intelligence, rather than the emotion of tempers posturing as politics, a wise man indeed.

His proposal is not much different than the organic evolution of the cowboys and Indians, except that their integration came about the long way around, through the power of Mother Nature, which changed the course of their mutual history. Dues had to be paid to rebalance the imbalance of power, but in the end everyone lives side by side and walks the same road, the road of peace and co-existence.

Things are far from perfect with many grievances still being tried in American courts to bring justice to the Native peoples. But the heritage of diverse cultures is respected and even admired, and a "live and let live" peace accord is the shady rest stop that welcomes weary travelers, no matter where they come from or where they might be going.

His proposal could very well be the "golden gate" through the land mines of the past. It might be the arched expanse leading to the road of peace and paradise. In his plan, the children of Abraham share the sandbox and get on with the business of building sand castles and eating ice cream together.

His plan is a proposal of intelligent solution that could make it possible to avoid a backlog of overdue debt, which is meted out in severe measure two hundred years down the stretch. Through common intelligence we can choose to coexist, or we can be herded like sheep and cows by circumstance gone out of control.

In his plan, the heritage of culture is respected. An Arab is an Arab and a Jew is a Jew, but they are first and foremost human, walking the same road. In America, two hundred years after the bloodshed between white people and Indian people, it's a matter of personal choice whether or not to ride a horse and wear cowboy boots or, on the other end of the spectrum, to ride a BMW and wear high heels.

Coexistence gives everyone the best of both worlds; it gives us the power of choice. I could go on and on, the story of whites and blacks, and the fight between the North and South, but I think as it all relates to Israel and Palestine, the point has been made.

But now, with the hefty weight of backlog already tipping the boat, the coexistence of the Israeli and Palestinian people peers like a timid and vulnerable child from behind the formidable waste of human bloodshed and the long, long road of broken promises. It looks for signs of trouble at every corner and bend. Hardened skepticism abounds. Arab nations look at Palestine with a combination of sentiment and denial.

I just received a memo from my head of security for the conference, that terrorists will not hesitate to strike a peace symposium, a harshly vivid reminder of the atmosphere in which I am seeking the bliss of revelation. Some terrorists consider Arabs who seek coexistence or peace as the enemy. Even so, there is a solution that prevails, hidden from present view though it might be, perhaps so far down the stretch as to be unseen and unknown and unimagined. But it is there.

Peace is possible and peace is the high road. I saw the truth in the three school children I passed on the walkway that runs beneath the rampart wall. I was witness to the decision to connect as human beings and the moment when a turn in the road could change everything. I felt the truth in the smiles that they passed in my direction.

That is why I feel that Jerusalem is like a child with a troubled past, a child that can still be redeemed, a beautiful thing of human intelligence, a possibility of human potential that could one day become a New Jerusalem, a New Israel, a New Palestine, a New Middle East, a new and better world for everyone. I am convinced of this. I'll empty my pockets and beg on the streets to keep the peace symposiums going, if for nothing else than to pay homage to the brilliance of a mind that formulated a plan to put a man on the moon 35 years ago.

I remember when the space program first began. I watched in awe the impossible on a television set, which sat in my fifth grade classroom, and knew then and there that the impossible is exactly what calls us to reach for the stars and moves us on down the road beyond ourselves. It was a moment of revelation that I cherished as a child, and now my work in the Middle East has brought me into friendship and collaboration with a contributor that had inspired my young mind. The three kids I passed on the street need a vision of what is possible to inspire them to choose the high road to a world worth living in.

Through that same inspiration of possibility, I can hear voices on the wind. Even the oldest holy places, silently speak of a New Jerusalem. The Damascus Gate knows her; the Golden Gate waits for her; the Lion's Gate protects her; the Jaffa Gate welcomes her. And all roads still lead to the center of her heart; all roads come to her; all roads converge like laugh lines on her countenance, to pass through the Golden Gate of destiny, where children can be children in the beauty of their innocence.

I try to conjure what a New Jerusalem might be like. She is waiting to be born from the dust of the past, but is no less than what she is in the gestation of waiting, even if her birth will come in unlikely conditions and the twist in the road deemed unimaginable.

New Jerusalem must be a divine manifestation of what eternal patience must be. New Jerusalem will be the standard-bearer for patience incarnate, and perhaps peace among nations. No matter how long she must wait, she shines from within the surface of outer appearances. She shines from another world into this one. She walks on footsteps of patience and dances defiantly on the edge of survival. She shelters children in her midst.

She is always casting a pale but present light into the possibilities of future worlds, no matter how many bombs are detonated in her midst, no matter how many bullets ping off her enduring walls. The paleness of her luminous presence is not a weakness; quite the contrary, it is simply not of this world.

Jerusalem was a thought, born in a blaze of promise. That is why I am here. All the highways and byways of circumstance have led me here. This is where the road of life has taken me, dropping me like a bundle of sack cloth filled with dates or olives at the doorstep of destiny, a destiny that will gather all the roads that go nowhere into the Circle of Life, as if there has been a master plan from the beginning that leads everything to her center, to her bosom, to her heart, and could, in the end, be the face of redemption on the road to world peace.

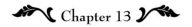

Chapter 13

The Corridor

Doors of Light, Doors of Remembrance

I sit for a long while, staring out at my old friend the Tower of David that looms above the Citadel. Spotlights shine on the tower throughout the night. For me this brings comfort at the end of a demanding day of heated arguments among the pecking order of peace workers, crazy rides through the back alleys with a terrified taxi driver and facing myself over and over for the clearing out of the heart that comes with this work. The rampart wall and the Citadel are like a safe harbor in a hurricane that gives calm to my nervous exhaustion. Still, in all it has been a good day. It has been a good day; realizations of truth have been demanding but good.

Feeling somewhat gathered in and in control of my senses, I head toward the inviting anticipation of hot water streaming down my back. A good shower will turn it all around. A good hot shower is perhaps the best answer I can hope for. Lifting myself up from the chair, I am relieved to see the sunset starting to break across the evening sky, ushering forth a soothing calm to the human fray beyond my balcony, a calm that I welcome into the solitude of my room.

Plodding heavily towards the bathroom, I remind myself not to be so dramatic. There has been enough drama for one day. In the stark light of the vanity mirror, I take a good long look at who is reflected back at me. More gray hair and more strength of character stare back.

With a firm flick I turn on the shower faucet. The cold, white marble of the bathroom takes the hot water and turns it to steam, fogging up the mirror and bringing to a close my inward dialogue about the gray hair and wrinkles that are steadily gaining ground along with realizations that eventually distill into wisdom.

I gratefully surrender to the purifying power of soothing wet heat, staying under the rushing spray long enough for the transformative effect of the water to give me a sense of letting down and letting go. Reluctantly, I step out of the shower, savoring the sense of replenishment, and taking care not to slip on the tiled floor. The glossy surface is cool to my feet and I dry off with a brisk rubdown and wrap the towel securely around my head. I wrap it tightly a second time for good measure, feeling much better than before. Like a rite of passage or an ancient ritual, I offer up in supplication the spoils of the day, and I can finally feel where I begin and the day itself ends.

Switching off the ringer on the telephone, I fall back into the pale blue striped chair and notice that a new moon is low on the mid-horizon, as the first faint stars signal the approach of nightfall. This is a time with no incipient interruptions, no ringing requests, no last minute or otherwise urgent demands from anyone. I am grateful just to sit, relax and forget about everything that seems pressing.

Closing my eyes, I am grateful to leave the world of politics and quarrels and world crisis behind. I am happy to leave it all behind. I'm too tired, too spent to hold onto anything but a welcome emptiness. Dreams, waves, light, misty floating, gentle rocking, long sighs, letting go, as I sink deeper into the chair's cushions and deeper into the space between relaxation and fatigue. It feels good and well deserved to just lift off to nowhere and nothing, just lifting, resting and nearing the edge, where consciousness and dreaming walk hand in hand.

And then I sense something cherished. I sense something that I remember. I sink deeper and drift further into an awakened dreaming only to resurface to distant voices. With a complete sense of ease, I feel like I'm lifting into another world far from this one. Like taking a ship out to sea, I leave the walls of my room behind, following my heart to a familiar sound like waves lapping at old worlds and ocean currents carrying me effortlessly into the deep water of beginnings.

The Ancient Mothers are calling me. The Grandmothers are calling me. Sarah herself is calling me. Like an ebbing tide, I feel the pull of the matriarchs of creation, the Mothers of the Beginning. They are as much a part of me as the tide is a part of the ocean and the moon and the orbiting of planets. Wearing robes of wisdom, they call with moon-pearled voices and sea-spray songs and high lilting harps and deep-throated drums.

I have been sensing their presence and begging for entrance into their world of wombs that hold the long sought answers, the complicated companions of my endless questions. They stand together, these Mothers, on the edge of time. I know that they will not fail me, because I cannot fail myself. I have reached a point of destiny. I can feel it.

They watch and they wait from their ethereal island of knowing. They know that I have been standing on the edge of my own cliff for weeks, willing to jump, but still waiting. They know that during the mind-boggling maze of this endless day's extremes, the cliff edge has been shaking under my feet with the tremors that come before the edge breaks away and falls into the abyss. They know that my feet are bleeding from the razor-sharp ragged stones that have cut into my flesh with deep precision. They know that the stones have a rage all their own, demanding answers that pierce to the bone.

The Grandmothers weep for all women who must endure this world, and they celebrate each small triumph of endurance. But they long for all women to remember the beginning of time and creation, and to carry that goodness into their world where our lives unfold. You can hear them trilling at the first whisper of dawn. I heard them this morning, in-between the pink and faint blue that first moves out of darkness.

They go all the way back to the beginning of all beginnings, this lineage of matriarchs, to the tears that once flooded the universe and caused the mists of the primordial to rise up from the void. This is why they are wisdom keepers. And it is also why I stand on the edge without fear, finally in my own true skin of remembrance.

I have waited a long time for this day, this evening, this sunset followed by a star-filled night sky, this moment. In my archive of seeking, I have wrestled with sweat-soaked sheets on the Sea of Galilee where Jesus taught his first followers, standing on the edge of the shore, wading in deep, sailing across the Galilee's gentle surface, wandering in the narrow streets, praying in the churches, feeling the earth, touching the children who still smile at strangers.

I counted my blessings among the caves of Qumran, studying the language of light that pours off the desert walls in the heat, scaled the cliffs that overlook Jericho, sat silent in the caves where ancient scriptures were written to listen with my soul for the Dead Sea Scrolls, which the Essenes inscribed and gave to the canyons of Qumran for safe-keeping: the Dead Sea Scrolls which spoke of the Mother, the Divine Mother, the Holy Mother, and the teachings of the saints and angels.

I have stood at the Wailing Wall in the middle of the night, lamenting my sorrows. I have been born again at the summits of the mounts of antiquity. I have watched the "Phoenix" take flight at sunrise on Mount Sinai and flung myself whole-bodied into the river Jordan's power of baptism. I have crawled beneath the Old City in damp darkness through underground tunnels, hoping to inch a little closer to the Ark of the Covenant, and have leapt fully clothed into the Spring of Mary to receive the blessing of sanctified waters.

I have fallen to my knees at the high mesa fortress of the Masada in the shocking heat and history of a last stand of Jews, who chose death through mass suicide rather than Roman rule, their final hours spent in the fierceness that only the desert can inflict. I have followed the Bedouin tribes across the Sinai with dust in my mouth and sand in my eyes, unable to eat for days, because foul water had made me sick.

Nazareth, Capernaum, Bethlehem, Tiberias, Hebron, Haifa, Amman, Beirut, Damascus, Luxor, and Abu Simbel are all a part of me now. Each one carved and sculpted my inner being and my outer world, and allowed me to taste the essence of history and the present day lives of the people who live their lives in these places.

I have retraced my steps, taking stock and praying for signs, watching sunsets and praying at sunrises faithfully, all the way back to Cairo and Aswan, the pyramids of Giza and the shores of the Red Sea. I have sat with queens at elegant state dinners, ridden camels beyond my own endurance, broken bread with the Catholic priests of the Church of the Holy Sepulcher, and rocked in full body rhythm to the Sufi zikr of the Islamic traditions. I have wept with Rabbis over stories of penance, and traced the steps of Isis through the temples of the Nile. This is indeed a journey through the Middle East, a quest I could write a book about, and perhaps I will someday.

I have remembered my dear mother's breath upon my heart. For good measure I have made sure to count my blessings during every inch of my quest, as I have come to the Middle East, a place that is troubled, even hostile, sometimes redeeming, often beautiful, always soul quenching and absolutely essential. I come here innocent and giving and searching and brave. I have come to this arid land asking to be an instrument of something greater than myself.

I have endured the worry of my own three children, my grandchildren and the pleading prayers of my aging father not to be here, to stay home in America where I belong. I have carried the ridicule and even the scorn of my dearest of friends, who think I have lost my wits, going to Jerusalem again and again. I have suffered the insults of the native sons of Israel, some of whom see me only as a foreigner, a dilettante, and an expendable nobody, despite who I really am and what I really hold to be true. I have paid my dues here. I have stayed and returned and held fast, despite everything.

The Grandmothers draw closer as they witness my thoughts, close enough that they understand. O, beloved Grandmothers, hear my lament. Will you not take pity on me and take me in?

They nod. They know. I am ready. Today I am ready. I can go no further. I have made every sacrifice. Behind the Grandmothers the sky is blazing blood red and dripping with gold. I feel like I'm sinking into oblivion, into pools of clear blue on an infinite horizon, but this is a welcome sensation, and I allow myself to be absorbed into a hot coolness that swallows and diffuses the boundaries of my personal world.

The Grandmothers are there for me; they are under my wounded feet, giving solid ground. They are wiping my tears with their silver hair. They are draping my shoulders with a prayer shawl of many colors of which I have often dreamed, of which I am dreaming now.

Beckoned by the swing and drape of their long robes of wisdom, immersion is effortless into an utterly still and tranquil place that is permeated with a vast and omnipresent intelligence, like the weavings of goddesses who have woven entire worlds out of sea water and salt and clouds and thunder.

The Grandmothers point to a doorway where space and consciousness meet, where nothing and everything seek each other in an intertwining that gestates all life. Somewhere in the far distance of thought, a small swell gathers, and I recall the term "universal field of awareness" passing by like a cloud. I am all alone, but I don't feel at all concerned. I am alone, but I am surrounded by everything, as the Grandmothers of Creation look on in silent watching and wise observance.

I can see in my mind's eye that the door that they hold open is familiar. I have come to this threshold of secrets lost and secrets found before, in the space where my dreams trail off, where I cease to exist but awaken to something far more. This door has always been there. It will remain where it is forever. A brief and fleeting fight in my half dreaming, half drifting state, with the rationale that the door is really nothing more than a figment of my own sub-conscious, quickly subsides. The door offers the seeking soul salvation and endless exploration into the awareness of truth that brings light to the times of sorrow. Everything from fleeting soul fragments to entire empires can be gathered and counted, healed and made whole.

An image of Jesus with all manner of creatures, deer, lions, rabbits and birds resting on his shoulders stirs my hopes and imagination. And now comes Saint Francis in a similar vein, only many more birds are making his pious frame their perch. Buddha appears as well, only he has gathered jungle animals to his feet: tigers, cobras, elephants and such. Sitting Bull and White Buffalo Woman gather flocks of great golden eagles to their feet. Mother Mary joins the procession with the divine child on her lap of compassion and a crown of stars above her head. Behind them stand the spirits of countless sages and prophets and holy men and women, who have given their lives to fanning the flame of all things sacred. I take this as an auspicious beginning. I steady my awe and strengthen my gaze.

A luminous light is emanating all around like a celestial welcome to the fields of the Gods. The Grandmothers gesture again. It is immediately clear to me that I am to walk through this passage between worlds, accept the welcome, and follow their outstretched hands of redemption. As I take several tentative steps forward, I feel like I am being saturated with a miracle through and through.

In amazement and wonder I am a witness to becoming weightless and timeless, as my very existence is being transformed. My body is no longer physical or solid, but I am acutely aware that it continues to hold the memory of physical life, dutifully tracking the timeline back to where I had stood before the doorway, before I stepped through only a few sheer thin moments ago.

Now it seems as though there is a profound life-altering reason why this experience is happening, and I can feel tears of remembrance welling up from some distant and ageless wellspring. It is like I am being invited to take a journey into the meaning of things, and more importantly, into the meaning of my life and the circumstances that inexplicably drew me to the drama of Jerusalem and the mystical saga that grew out of the exodus from Egypt.

It is as though a chorus of divine wisdom keepers is speaking to me through every molecule, inside and out, and I am absorbing new levels of understanding that could only be received in this transcendently golden environment. It is as though empty space has become the prophet of eternal life, in a voice that is singular, absolute and yet collective, a celestial reservoir of all the voices of wisdom: past, present and future.

I am shown a long shimmering corridor that has no beginning and no end. I am eager to enter. Already I can sense that there are vast halls on either side of the corridor. I can't yet see them, but I know that they are there as surely as I know my own name. My own thoughts echo back to me and reverberate. I hear my heart beating, trilling, and calling out "Sarah... Sarah... Sarah... Sarah... You have the answers. Your wisdom is the wisdom that women have longed for since the circle of women's wisdom first began."

Within these sacred chambers, written upon light-filled scrolls of eternal presence, entombed with utmost care for safekeeping, preserved forever within these Halls of Time, I know I will find something that I have searched for all my life. My steps have become certain and filled with purpose as I make my way down the passageway.

There is so much to see and know and experience. All of it is here. I am being shown existence and meaning at the speed of light, as if the origin of all life is seeking to implant itself upon my heart, never to be forgotten. This is the world from which all others emerge, still carried by a blissful wonderment farther and farther into the holy ground of this place, where the drama of all souls is written by the all-knowing hand of time, the messenger of the angels.

Like Alice in Wonderland, I continue down the length of the corridor, knowing that I have begun a journey, one that will change every step that I take in the future. It is the journey that I have waited for and sacrificed all convention for. I cannot tell where one thought ends and the next begins. It is like walking through a gushing flow of intelligence that automatically responds to every nuance of thought.

"My God, My God..." The light from the corridor is causing even my bones to wail in exclamation. "We are born and born again through our living experiences. There is no death; there is only the journey of the soul through the corridors of time and the spirals of creation."

A voice that is known to me and dear to me and sacred to my soul and intimate to my past and essential to my future seems to be showering upon my awareness. The sound is like warm honey on my tongue and like fields of flowers to my eyes. It reminds me of my mother's love when I was still in her womb, and the chanting of faith-bound sisters in the chapels of charity. It flows from the times of tenderness when Sarah and Hagar walked hand in hand out of Egypt, appreciative of each other, before their destiny in the desert would divide the hearts of humanity, before fate would become the peace of understanding. Fate bonds souls into the compassion of being human when they pass beyond the flesh.

It comes from the white desert tents of the wives of Jacob, the matriarchal mothers who prayed to the goddess in the midst of a patriarchal stronghold, lifting up their platinum voices to the full moon and holding onto the wisdom of the Ancient Mother, even though the mother aspect of deity was forbidden.

The voice is many voices and yet is only one voice, ringing from the archives of the known and unknown and blaring with the screams of mothers giving birth to the wetness of new life. Within this voice is everything that I have been and everything that I have longed for.

The sound of a presence envelops me, causing me to remember and to know that women have always been held in the love of our creator, held close in that love and close in the womb of it, intrinsically of that love, and thus as near to that source as flesh can be. It is women who know with a certainty that God is love, just as a mother knows she is the source of love when she first brings a child into the world. It is women who seek the goodness in God and in themselves. It is women who hold an essential link between Creator and creation, and it is women who bear life and thus bear responsibility for that life.

"Come let me show you. Come let me tell you." A voice that I know calls to me. Then, emerging from the light as far as I can see down the shimmering hallway, a woman of regal floating grace and otherworldly beauty appears like an apparition of mercy. She is a butterfly; she is an eagle; she is a tiger; and she is a whale. As she steadily comes closer, I feel that I know her as intimately as I've ever known anyone, even more intimately than I know myself.

The closer she gets, the more I am taken in. The closer she gets, the less I can resist, as if such a wild thought is even possible. She is old and young and fierce and loving. It is as though she has always known me, through and through, as though she is my mother, or my blood, or my destiny. Her very existence renders me into a state of utter simplicity, as if I was naked of all pretenses, reduced and distilled to only the gossamer filaments of the essence of my soul.

I am aware that my heart is pounding now and breaking open to a forgotten and all-powerful love. My chest is heaving under the stampede of thousands of thundering hooves, hooves of desert stallions pulling the chariots of all the Pharaohs of the sun, chariots with spinning wheels, spinning wheels of fire and glory, wheels of Agni and time. Perhaps my heart will explode, pounding and pounding, so forceful is this internal remembrance, so powerful are the gushes of light that are anointing my soul.

My gaze remains transfixed upon her face, like stone wedded to a mountain or sunlight wedded to sun. Her gaze upon my soul is like a magnet that has found its match, drawing me into the soft and tranquil forcefulness of her eyes, deep eyes that convey to me all the love and understanding that I have ever hoped for, and more. It is as if all ecstasy is not enough to hold her power or the stories of life and existence being told through her expression.

I can barely even formulate the very obvious question that the remaining threads of my mind want to ask:

"Who is this wise woman, this goddess, this all-knowing Divine Mother? Is she a saint or a prophet, an angel, perhaps the bride of the stars and the heavens? Is she a guide or a teacher of the wisdom secrets? Does she hold the keys to my future and the answers that have been locked away in my heart of hearts since time immemorial?"

Sweeping her arms in an arching circle, she summons the light-filled essence of her surroundings, as if she were about to perform a feat of never-before-made-manifest wonder. Her slender and delicate fingers motion and curl as if they were cosmic dancers, enticing the favor of the kings and queens, and the lords and ladies of origin. She sweeps again all around her, pure hands uplifted, robes flowing, light-filled raven hair reaching all around her, as she opens the radiance of her heart and all but annihilates my very being with the power of her love.

She is the priestess of the Beginning of Creation; she is the Lady of the Lake and the Mother of Avalon; she is Isis of the Nile and the teacher of neophytes; she is the mother of purity and the desert tribes of a New Jerusalem; she is the good mother who awaits the Messiah; she is Quan Yin of Compassion and the tradition of mercy; she is Mother Mary and the holy sisters who wed the Christ. She is all of these things. She is the collective spirit of women on earth who know their essential place upon the great wheel of life as keepers of the flame and guardians of the flesh.

Sarah the Matriarch, Sarah who endured, Sarah who has returned to resurrect the white tents of old where the wise women gathered into the bond of sisterhood among women worldwide... Together they will remember their sacred duty to preserve life and to convene once again in the councils of wisdom that future generations might once again be blessed.

Vision upon vision of women gathering, convening and coming together as guardians of a good and bountiful earth, flood my awareness. The all-consuming sound of her voice elicits swirling images that engulf my small world. My past is breaking up like polar ice cracking in the thaw, like mirrors slamming to the floor, scattering shards of glass at my feet, never to resume their precious confines of shape and color, time and space.

My heart is throbbing and burning, twisting and squeezing, in the losing and finding of myself. I am dying, I think. I am dying. I am actually dying in the arms of pure love and shattering ecstasy. The Grandmothers are dancing and trilling and raising their hands to the heavens, surrounded by stellar bodies and marching with surefooted grace and steady swaying on the light of the stars, all of them together, all of them unified.

And then she steps forward to stand directly before me like the keeper of my existence. She peers deeply into my soul with the penetrating eye of a condor and the piercing claws of a thunderbird. I long for absolution through her gaze. I am ceasing to be, and yet I am here more than ever, given new life by the presence of this woman of all the suns in the heavens. I cannot follow what I am feeling with rational thought. It is too overwhelming.

I want nothing more than this, nothing whatsoever. Like a fragile and helpless moth being inexplicably drawn into the roaring, fiery center of a volcano, I am drawn to her. She is the mother of my soul and the sister of my heart and the keeper of my bones. Everything that I have ever been is being drowned by her. I am gratefully, innocently and ecstatically enveloped by her light, and I am ready to follow her to the ends of the cosmos if need be. She has brought me back to myself, back to my memory and knowing that as woman, I am love; and as love, I am life.

Then, with a knowing gentleness that no words can even begin to describe, she extends her hand to me and leads me with the silvery shimmer of purest grace through a luminous archway into one of the light-filled chambers off the main corridor. The walls of the chamber echo her name as she commands her entrance: Sarah of yore, Sarah of the Ancient Mothers, Sarah of Abraham, Sarah of the Promised Land, Sarah of the Tribes of Peace. She turns to face me. I have come, and Sarah is waiting.

With feet that sway and feet that prance and feet that step wisely to the rhythm of future wombs and future worlds, the Grandmothers gather, cloaking me in their gracious golden folds. They lead, Sarah beckons; they lead the way, and I follow.

⚜ Chapter 14 ⚜

The Remembrance

Surrender of Ignorance, Surrender of Peace

A new daylight is bold in its pouring of light across my face. Hands are rubbing eyes to encourage consciousness and produce recognition of a new beginning. Arms are stretching to gather in a new goodness. Mouth is yawning in pleased and luxurious inhalation that opens my chest to new capacity. Yes, I feel like a newborn, wriggling in the heart-touching loving, eyes-touching seeing, and life-touching living. This is the morning after revelation, and I am still in the relief and contentment that old prayers had been answered with new insight.

When I went to bed last night I promised myself the luxury of sleeping in and recuperating from the rough edges of the past week, but inspiration had continued throughout the night. Inspiration continued to flow into every crevice of the morning, and I wanted to savor every last drop of this delectable experience. My head swam with the wisdom of my beloved Sarah. My dreams had been filled with her, like a fountain that spewed generosity. And I was thankful and redeemed.

Revelations of the eternal, the universal, the truth of the ages had become the real ground under my feet, that gives wind to my sails and aspirations. I smile at the paradox. I muse at the contradiction, no longer confused, I give thought and thanks to the prophets and teachers of wisdom that have graced our planet, who have given so much but were rarely understood by anyone and, just as likely, were refuted, denied, and ridiculed. They stood their ground on revelations and on the visions of heaven that bring the skeptical mind into a revved-up readiness to scrutinize, discount and defame. And yet they persevered. They passed the sacred; they passed what is really the obvious, the natural integrity of the human spirit when it remembers itself.

Wide-awake, I am standing on the visions that fill the heart and ease the deep soul. I am pleased and smiling from the inside out, reborn and resurrected and definitely not standing where I stood before. My feet are singing; they know the truth; they know what is real. The veils have parted, and I have walked through to the other side, and that is where I find myself.

Swinging my feet to the side of the bed, I look toward the Old City for the dose of medicine that it always gives me, allowing my eyes to rest on her enduring grace, without so much as a trace of hurried concern about the remaining day. I decide to linger over my morning tea longer than usual. I want to nurse my hot steaming brew and bathe in the drinking of it. I want a slow start. Today is different. I am different. Today I can feel Sarah's presence among the stone walls that have shaped Jerusalem.

Somehow everything makes sense: the timing of things, the sequence of things, the great eye, the long arm, the vast heart of the way it is, and the way it will be.

And something else is different. I am not gazing upon Jerusalem as I have in the past, pleading, seeking and longing to receive something intangible. My gaze pours effortlessly from my heart and I am seeking nothing. Instead, I am standing on new ground. I am giving something back to Jerusalem through the wisdom of the Grandmothers that is taking hold through every molecule of my awareness. This is more than tangible. And the Old City is smiling.

What more could I ask for? The room that surrounds me is full with the strength of long standing spires and the wisdom of arched gateways, the shimmer of ancient towers and the bright gold of domed temples. Smiles and Grandmothers grin broadly wall-to-wall, across the room and across my life, whispering and chanting and breathing songs of creation. Today is different. I can see what has been there all along.

Now it is time for me to also pass the sacred, to add something of my own to the songs that began in the ancient of days, to the secrets of wisdom that were passed around desert campfires, lighting up faces, passed on from mother to daughter in lilting whispers, from elder to youth in guiding example, from parent to child in the lessons of the heart. What was passed on in the billowing sanctuary of woven tents, as the wives of Jacob, the matriarchs Rachel and Leah, gathered to tell their children stories of the Grandmothers who smiled down upon them on star-filled nights and full moons and gave them faith. The stories that carried Sarah's heart into the future and assured the endurance of the blood in their veins must not be forgotten.

These were the stories that were sung from ample breasts well laden with milk. These were stories that never found a place in written history, but fed families and nations no less, stories that called wisdom into plain view, passed it on and roused remembrance. More will come;

more will be given. I'm sure of it. Sarah had promised that there would be more, that our work together would now begin. This is only the first glimmer of the revelation of the welling wealth of the Grandmothers and the loving legacy of Sarah. More will come. Remembrance is awakened.

Another wide yawn spreads hope to the seeing and knowing. Anticipation fills the altar vessel with the oil of anointing and caresses my throat as I swallow new inspiration and breathe deep into my lungs the promise of the journey. The journey continues. Remembrance is seeking new expression. I am eager to embrace the day, all of it, without complaint, counting my blessings each step of the way, knowing that all things happen for a reason.

And so the word "endure" is the treasure that I will add to the new creation, which is tangible, like a prayer shawl on my shoulders or a blessing on my soul. But more, much more than just the word, is my offering. Today I will pour the essence of endure into everything that I do. Enduring, endurance, to endure, to last, to sustain, to continue. Yes, endure. The word sounded sweet on the substance of thought.

With a grateful lightness, with cool steps, careful steps, steps that respect the cold smooth marble beneath my feet, I move through the hallway to the kitchen alcove to make my morning tea. Tea, meditation and prayer go hand in hand, and this will be a good morning and a good day. I can feel it in my bones. I feel rested for the first time in ages. I feel solid and refreshed. I can endure. I can continue the journey, renewed.

A wave of fondness falls from my mind upon all the wise ones who have guided me over the years as I put the teakettle on to boil and think back. What a journey each soul creates, leaving a wake of testimony for each life, each path of converging moments that become the archive of an existence.

An image near and dear to me surfaces in prominence, as I recall the wise old face of a Buddhist leader who has guided me through the years. The Rinpoche's wrinkled, 80-year-old eyes, gathered me into the folds of his gracious fortitude and taught me the practice of calming the mind, taught me to seek silence. How fortunate that I received so much from the Rinpoche father and elder, this revered Buddhist leader: Rinpoche being the revered name for priest or saint or teacher or religious leader.

Waiting for water to boil, I open the honey jar and smell the pleasant fragrance of it, and pour milk into the rounded form of the tiny glass pitcher that gives an elegant shape to tea making. Laughing under my breath with an easiness that I had forgotten, I think back to my naiveté and how little I understood back then about the value of what I was being given.

I was unable to tell the difference between a lump of coal and a nugget of gold. The Rinpoche showed me the difference, which began my ability to discern what is real and what is not real. I emphasize the word began, as discernment is always ongoing in the ultimate quest to seek a state of all-encompassing certainty.

But, at the time, I was so entranced by the mesmerizing twinkle in his deep set shining black eyes, that I was often frozen like a sculpture, unable to think or move. The high altitude Himalayan sun poured from his eyes, with a tiny but powerful brightness that gave anyone who cared to notice a sure and constant stream of the pure silence that he spoke about.

He had weathered many storms, this old teacher, fierce storms among the high peaks of the Mount Everest basin, and all the villagers and tribesmen of the region loved him. They had weathered storms together. The kind of storms that generate 200 mile an hour gales and temperatures 90° below zero Fahrenheit, as Chinese armies encroached upon the remote abode of their sanctuary in the high Himalayas. He radiated the light of a spiritual elder, and I, in my youth and innocence, was intoxicated.

I wonder what he would think of desert Grandmothers? I wonder what thoughts are his, as he looks upon our present world condition of conflict and strife. I wonder what he would think, if he were to come to Jerusalem and join the other spiritual leaders who contemplate the future of the region, and by association, the future of the world? I wonder what he would add to the stewpot, to the campfire, to the tradition of passing the sacred, a Buddhist in a land of Christians, Jews and Muslims?

Considerably up in years, he is probably too frail to travel, but I jot down a note to invite the head monk of the monastery, whom I had befriended over the years, to one of our peace and humanitarian symposiums next spring, when he comes down from the top of the world to Kathmandu to wait out the monsoon. He has come to the US a number of times, and I have always received so much from his gentle but certain power, and the chants and the devotion to silence that surround his presence.

Meanwhile, here I am in Jerusalem, ten years later, wandering in the luxury of milk and honey thoughts and pouring my morning tea. I, too, have weathered at least a few storms, dry dusty ones with fierce heat and bleeding feet. And from the ten-year vantage, I am far more able to realize the extent to which he impacted my thinking.

I will never forget the humble beauty of the monastery abode in the clouds or the astounding monolithic presence of Mt. Everest, rising majestically into the fast-moving sky just outside the Rinpoche's window. Much of what he passed to me took place in his private quarters, as he sat cross-legged on piles of colorful Tibetan carpets that shouted in the loud clear patterns of their weavers, and he would be perched on a ledge in front of an expanse of windows, with the even greater expanse of the Himalayas serving as his backdrop.

Drinking tea together was more like a sacred ceremony, where drinking wisdom was really the exchange. He was the wise old vessel that poured the light of compassion into my cup.

The view of him sitting there, his face framed by snow-capped pinnacles, was something you might find on a postcard, only far more surreal and awesomely exquisite. The snow reflected a soft light all around his head, as if he was a saint of high places and snowy temples. And truly he was.

In his case he was a laughing saint; he was always grinning, throwing his head back and laughing. He poured me tea like a master painter putting the finishing touches on a lifetime of Mona Lisas and Sistine Chapels, not unlike the Arab grandmother who had poured the sweetness of lemonade into my soul not long ago.

When I came under his supervision during the first of many forays into the Himalayas, I was utterly clueless as to the far-reaching effect he would have on my life. His monastery sits like a sentinel of the sacred on a trail that leads to 24,000 foot passes that cross into Tibet. The tribesmen still traverse these heights on foot, bringing their annual tithes of barley grain to the monastery in burlap sacks on their backs, passing the sacred in a very literal sense, knowing that it is their duty to "fund" the good works of the monastery.

At over 29,000 feet in elevation, Mount Everest, a massive spire of rock and ice, and the tradition of spiritual eldership and oral teaching, stood behind the life of the old Rinpoche. It was almost too much for the mind to take it all in at once. Well, it was another life changing, "turn everything around" moment for me. Sacred scrolls, teachings that had been handed down for thousands of years, lined the walls.

As is the Buddhist tradition, he has been the recognized head of the monastery since he was discovered as a three-year-old boy to be the reincarnation of the previous Rinpoche. This was an auspicious setting to receive his teaching on the art of vipassana meditation.

His patient presence, however, is what changed everything. His simplicity changed my approach to everything from my relationship with my children, to my work here in the Middle East, to the simple act of pouring and drinking a cup of tea.

He had endured, and thinking back, this is what he too had passed to me. He told his story of what his eyes had seen, how the monastery and the monks had lived in isolation, how there had been no contact with the modern world, and then how everything had changed when the revered Mount Everest, their sacred "Sagarmata, head of the ocean," became a sporting destination for questing expedition climbers, this on the heels of China's desire to devour all citizens of the Buddhist faith into modern Maoist thinking.

Even now Maoist rebel groups are the force of force in many rural areas of old Tibet as well as present day

Nepal, as the monasteries, from what I observed, do their best to stay out of the way of politics. And yet, the aggressive tendency of the human mind and its thinking and its actions continues.

But he had endured. He continues to endure as thousands of hikers march past the old monastery, barely registering the profound sanctuary that it is, often leaving arrogant and careless footprints in the snow, burning up all the firewood, trampling the sacred medicine plants, and tossing garbage off to the side of the trail like monkeys throwing banana peels one after another mindlessly to the ground. In some places oxygen canisters used for mountain climbing are piled up shoulder high and scattered all over on the ice. It is a sad and irreverent testimony to the western mind.

He endured and passed the sacred to me, a white faced, naive, full-of-herself and half-ignorant westerner, a woman, sincere, but still a female occidental sitting in an all-male monastery, no less.

Then I remember, in the spare but spacious moments that it has taken to pour hot boiling water into the teapot, that I have revisited a turning point in my life. I am standing on the ground of a new phase of my life, calmly watching amber colored tea stream into my cup. Everything will change.

I have connected the weft and warp of the woven path from then until now. The wizened old Rinpoche had a strong hand in shaking loose the scattered pieces of my life, creating a prayer bowl that could hold everything, as it reassembled itself from the unconscious to the conscious. An unbroken line of wisdom, from chanting Himalayan monks, to singing desert matriarchs, to midnight talks with politicians, sealed a new fate.

The memory of when he shattered my small reality and made it bigger begins to flutter through my mind like a flock of geese headed north to the high country. He said, "Every moment is an unending continuum of possibility. As we endure the journey, we become all that the journey has been. As we endure the journey, we become full, so that we can become empty. We Buddhists call this the Great Emptiness that prevails beyond all things. All solutions, all questions and all answers exist in a single unending spacious moment of fullness that becomes empty, an emptiness that becomes full. Begin to train your awareness to see the infinite within the finite, and the finite within the infinite, the full and the empty. All is present in each unending spacious moment. Meditation is the art of finding the spacious and unlimited, the full and the empty, the nature of the infinite within which there is peace."

And then I remembered something else, something that was important, something that raced and rang through my heart that the old monk, the old wise one, had passed on to me. We were sitting cross-legged on the upper floor above the main hall of the monastery, with the crystal-spiked Himals staring down at us like patient wisdom keepers through the row of paned glass windows above our heads.

I was among a group of aspiring minds that encircled his prayer rug and couldn't help but lean toward him, even as they straightened their spines to sit tall and erect, and assume the proper posture to receive his talk on meditation. I was one of them, and back then I was still eager to prove myself. I was full of the knowledge of what I thought I knew, and unknowingly short on wisdom, and certainly not empty in any sort of profound way.

He had just completed a guided exercise, a meditation technique that he called the Blue Lotus and was ready to enter the usual dialog at the closure of the teaching. He taught in the tradition of asking questions, "koans," that stretch the mind like rubber bands to go past wherever the mind had lived before. "What is the purpose of meditation?" he inquired of his charges in a quiet knowing that commanded surrender and respect.

Several students offered up smart answers, which he declined to acknowledge. And I in my ignorance offered up what I thought was sure to gain approval, perhaps a blue lotus sticker of class recognition from the Rinpoche to wear on my sleeve, to boast the prowess of the ego mind. I walked straight into the trap, like a hungry dog.

He shot a look at me, knowing what he did, but I was blind to his signal. I didn't see his flag pointing to the obvious, and I didn't see myself. Instead I puffed up and piped out my confident retort, an impetuous mixture of the childish need for attention and boldfaced arrogance. "The purpose of meditation is to find inner peace, Rinpoche." I bowed respectfully as I quipped and smiled on the way down, pleased with myself. My face flushed red with embarrassed memory, just to register my habit of impossible arrogance.

And then he lowered the boom. It wasn't so much what he said but the force that he hurled in my direction, as if he had wielded thunderbolts to straighten me out, to whittle me down, to humble my heart. "No," he replied with a sharp edge that cut deep, "No, that is not the purpose of meditation."

And then he held a masterful court in a long and skillfully empty silence, shot back to the pain of my embarrassment and to the death and demise of my ego.

That was, after all, his job. The power of silence racked my self-esteem, and burned the facade of pompous know-ing that only shadowed true wisdom.

When the burning of embarrassment and the Zen stick of truth finally subsided, he took a measured breath to which everyone immediately straightened up in an even greater rapt attentiveness, myself included. Duly reduced, now I was ready to learn. From suffering to readiness, I was in an alert receptivity, whereas before I thought I had the answers.

And then he pulled hard on the bowstring of truth and let the arrow fly. "The purpose of meditation is to bring peace to the world," he uttered with all the light that poured through him. Back he went into his silence, as my world changed forever. To put forth effort for some-thing greater than yourself was born and given life.

From this retrieval of wise counsel, the act of pouring tea has gained precious ground, not just any ground but sacred ground, and as real as it gets, even though it has entered a new dimension. I am filled with a new sense of communion as the old memories of Rinpoches and Tibet-ans find coexistence with the newfound gifts from the Matriarch Sarah and the Grandmothers of Creation, the reality of a world gone mad, and the daily work of serv-ing the healing of madness.

And although I may speak with the fluid language of idealistic artistry throughout most of this book, to give meaning to the essence of what I am exploring, plain lan-guage will also find itself in the hour of need to be given in the way that it is needed.

Not long ago, I was invited to join with an alliance of other NGO's, to submit to the United Nations a vision and mission statement. Each organization was asked to submit its own document, which would be included in a dossier that would then be sent to ambassadors and influential persons connected to the UN around the world.

This effort represented a joint effort to bring attention to the issue of Jerusalem and to get the issue back on the podium of consideration in UN discussion and decision-making. Even though the volatility of world crisis was on every doorstep, the resolution of the Holy Land and its epicenter was long over due.

Time must be made to use this city of ancestral importance to the entire world, a city which has been torn apart again and again, as an issue that could serve as a new landmark in global cooperation.

Time must be made to give earnest thought to the immediate and diligent transformation of world thinking and the governance that can begin to assure a sustainable future for all world citizens. Jerusalem could be the highlight of launching the wide sweeping initiative of global guardianship.

The United Nations is a pivotal and optimal agency to mediate and direct the global considerations that affect all nations, a new and unprecedented opportunity for the sane management of our planet. No nation can stand alone in isolation in the millennia to come. We have in every nation the wise elders who in their wisdom can bring about positive solutions that go beyond the self-interest of politics, the unethical corporate practices and the unsound economic manipulation that has all but brought into ruin the stability of our shared global community.

Whenever I have been called to make a contribution to the endless litany of conferences, seminars and such that I have attended or led over the past ten years, I have always heard a small but steady vocal whispering in the background, "Let us hear from those liberated souls whose lives have been given to the service of their fellow human beings, without the ulterior motives of personal position, monetary gain, political influence, or malice to any person, place or thing." It is time for nations to surrender their greed for domination and "favored nation status" and drink from the same cup of universality, if indeed we expect our planet to still be a place that nations can call home for millennia to come.

Rustling through some old files, I managed to unearth the document that had joined the dossier of documents submitted by the collective of NGO's. As I read it again, just to refresh myself on some of the overall objectives that I had held dear for so many years, even though the actuation of those objectives seemed so distant in the future, I gained renewal. I realized that those same whispered voices were present as I wrote the contents of our vision for a United Nations presence in Jerusalem as follows:

Vision for a New Jerusalem

Respectfully submitted by the Peace Promise Initiative:

"It is through the release of the human spirit from the confines of poverty and oppression that nations will choose of their own free will to seek cooperation and alliance for the common good of all world citizens. Let the United Nations convene for this greater purpose, and let all self-responsible persons, organizations and governments rise to the noble vision of a planetary life of contributive diversity and unified commonality. Let us together, in a world call for a higher order of life upon earth, convene in a new era of Good Will governance and global achievement for the benefit of all nations and all peoples."

Devra West, D.D., Ph.D.

Founder/Director, Peace Promise Initiative

The Peace Promise Initiative was conceived as a response to world conditions, as an agency that assists and supports regions of conflict to uphold and assure human values. Its premise moves from the intention to work cooperatively with all global peace and humanitarian organizations for the assurance of human values as the basis of conflict resolution.

Its vision and goals are based upon the inherent value of the human spirit within every being and the productive and contributive nature of that spirit to naturally seek its own betterment. The Peace Promise Initiative upholds the belief that when the outer factors of poverty and oppression are transformed to opportunity and freedom from aggressors, that the full potential of the human spirit will be naturally forthcoming.

Our programs seek to ally with existing NGO's in regions of conflict, to provide the practical bridges and region specific programs that will implement the means by which conflict driven issues are transformed into cooperative coexistence. Our programs seek to align with and orchestrate those avenues that will enable equal access to economic opportunity, health, education and productive enterprise.

Realizing the necessity for a real reordering of our world on the foundation of higher principles, the Peace Promise Initiative views the emergence of the United Nations as the center for international diplomacy and coordinated humanitarian activity as a powerful force for a new human synthesis. As such, our role as planetary citizens is to evoke the potential of the United Nations and its possibilities for the transformation of separatist self-invested national consciousness to integrated service and equal opportunity oriented international consciousness.

In this regard, the Peace Promise Initiative whole-heartedly supports the work of its partner organizations in their commitment to address global issues, and in efforts to create a heightened awareness and increased sensitivity in people for the tasks and importance of the United Nations.

As the world becomes ever more conscious of the power and determinations expressed through the UN Charter for the elimination of war, the Peace Promise Initiative offers its solidarity and support for the efforts of all individuals, groups, and organizations that are truly working for inclusive solutions. In its resolve to help replace war and violence with new conflict resolution strategies, the Peace Promise Initiative will utilize its innovative pragmatic concepts to promote investments for peace and trauma education, preventive diplomacy, and measures for securing and sustaining peace through mature and proactive political procedures.

In particular, the Peace Promise Initiative joins its partnership of altruists from all traditions and religions, to reaffirm its understanding of the need for a new vision of conflict resolution strategies that go beyond the mere improvement of old methods. The Peace Promise Initiative concurs with the perspective that Jerusalem is key to this vision and that it presently represents, as does the Israeli-Palestinian conflict, the visible manifestation of the unresolved social and political patterns of humankind.

Precisely because of Jerusalem's history as the epicenter of a multitude of traditions, no other city holds such potential to be a model of cooperation, diplomacy, and appreciative recognition of the potential of unity within a diversity that can inherently contribute to the benefit of the whole. Drawing on its adamant belief in the unfulfilled promise of the United Nations to serve as the catalyst for the emergence of a truly compassionate and just new world order that can transform Jerusalem into a center for world peace, the Peace Promise Initiative proposes that:

- *Jerusalem be preserved as a world historical site*

- *the city be governed by a council of peacekeepers from the United Nations, who oversee the preservation of sites of both historical and spiritual import*

- *all world citizens have equal access to sites of historical and spiritual import*

- *a grand monument and edifice to the "triumph of unity within diversity" would be built to house a United Nations for peace on earth, for the federation of global nations that will jointly convene for the purpose of creating a new premise of governance for world good*

- *all nations enjoy equal representation in a Council of Leaders in Jerusalem, whose purpose would be to guide and safeguard the sustainable future of our planet*

And now, some time later, after having written this small but viable contribution to a greater collective cause, I sit in reflection, looking out over the grandness of what Jerusalem could be, if we as her stewards would attend to her emergence as if we were making possible the gift of life for all beings and the possibility of a good life for everyone.

This moment of retrieval, return and reflection, takes me back to the vision that burns at the center of my efforts and gives me strength to endure. Somewhere in this gathering of words is the twinkle of the eye of the old teacher who sits on top of the world in a monastery far-removed from Jerusalem. He is one of many teachers who has guided me, and countless others like me, on their way.

He is a "way-shower" who is passing the mantle for a new era of global guardianship to the rest of the world. That mantle is the light of new and innovative wisdom, born of the timeless and unchanging ancient wisdom that convenes deep in the heart when no one is looking and emerges at just the right moment of readiness and need. Every tradition has its way-showers, its elders and its leaders of the value of humanity.

Every religion has those who have endured the proving ground of absolute sacrifice and have stayed the course in service to their people. And then there are the change agents who are destined to go down in history, the Nelson Mandelas, and the Mother Teresas, who are the Sarahs and Abrahams of modern times.

This process of reflection cascades upon itself opening new doors of synthesis in my thinking and being. The slow morning that I had assigned myself has become a rich day of rapid realization.

It is as if I have found a key that will open the archives of existence that were once in my safekeeping but had been lost to me for a painfully agonizing time. I am pouring my tea with a keen and clear awareness. The Rinpoche's brown and weathered hand is firmly on the handle of the kettle. The Grandmothers' wrinkled smiling eyes are hovering in the steam that rises and brushes my face with a warm mist. My mother's voice, as she gently reminded me to count my blessings, is in the smell of milk and honey, finding the union in soft white liquid and clear amber.

Just watching the steaming stream of hot water fill the cup is calming. The sound of the water hitting the bottom of the cup and swishing upward is comforting to my ears. More steam is rising. More is being given to the bold bright daylight that has flooded my room, and the dreams from the night before washed my mind clean of worry. It's almost as if the simplicity of making the tea is as important as the meditation itself, like doing a ceremony that assures safe passage.

It comes to me how important this contemplative time is. I have never been satisfied with the superficial or conventional sides of things. Inasmuch as the ordinary is the hungry consumer of our lives, it is the extraordinary that has always called me.

For over twenty years now, I have always set a contemplative tone in the morning before I pray and meditate, by nursing a soothing cup of hot tea as a way of bringing myself into receptivity. Holding the warm cup in both of my hands, I am reminded how I have been held in the caring hands of those who have shown the way of wisdom.

The monks of the monastery always drank tea, too, in the grace of ceremony, taking periodic breaks from their rhythmic swings between chanting and silence, to sip a hot brew of wild mountain herbs, picked from the steep slopes that surround them. For one thing, the great expanse of the meditation hall was always icy cold in the summer, and dreadfully cold in the winter when the temperature would drop far below zero and the winds would blow at gale force. There was no heat in the hall, so the monks practiced a technique called "the inner fire." Perfect solution.

I remember sitting among them on the sidelines of the dimly lit four story hall as the wisps of steam from their wooden cups rose gracefully into the thin raw air of the Himalayas, causing a small cloud of wafting wisdom to hang around the maroon-colored capes that were wrapped about their shoulders. Brown shaved heads barely poked up from the maroon cocoon of robes that kept them sheathed in the doctrine of selflessness and sacrifice.

With warm tea in their bellies, they prayed and prayed, and chanted and chanted... "May all beings be safe, may all beings be healthy, may all beings be happy, may all beings have peace, may all the worlds and all the beings know peace. Peace, peace, peace."

Finally, the insidious tension in my shoulders that has gripped at my spirit for weeks gives way. An inner dam is breaking free, as the remembrance of Grandmothers and monks flows into the same stream and becomes the same ocean. The prayer bowl, the chalice, the altar of my life is smiling with fullness. A new level of contemplation, of empty presence, rises to engulf me.

Years of meditation have brought home to me enough emptiness to open the doors of the soul, to gain the wisdom that the ordinary mind simply has no eyes to see. Perhaps the mantle of universal wisdom will indeed find its way to a United Nations for peace on earth with many, many more Sarahs and Abrahams, the men and women who will be the way-showers of the future, serving as the bridges to a new planetary possibility. With this summary of contemplative thought and wishful thinking I turn my gaze to the ordinary and all the details of living that call for attention and demand their due.

Chapter 15

The Archives

Teachings of Truth, Teachings of Love

As I proceed farther and farther down the corridor in this rhythmic procession of wise women, I feel gathered into their midst as if I have always been with them. Old wisdom and new wisdom flash through my mind, the primordial and the present seem to overlay upon a single awareness. I can see how certain things in life should never change. The principles, premises, laws and ethics of existence remain at the core of all things wise and enduring, even if form and application change to fit our modern circumstances.

Glimpses of what is true and eternal and how it can be brought into so many aspects of world remedy rapidly light up as if I have entered a higher mind than my own. Solutions, formulas, answers and far-reaching vision are laid out like an all-knowing vista that allows the eye to rest and absorb a higher order of living and planetary cohesion.

Many things that I have searched for all of my life are retrieved in an instantaneous homecoming that puts everything in place, as if the pieces to a puzzle had been scattered high and low and are now perfectly placed, exactly how they should be.

Great archways, reminiscent of the arched stone gateways in the wall that holds Jerusalem in its upturned palm, begin to appear on either side, like veins of wisdom moving from a primary artery of essential existence. Each one is an entrance to a sacred chamber. Each chamber is a sanctified vessel of benevolent intelligence. Each chamber is like a spiritual archive, a vault of illumination that holds the journey of the soul and the experiences that have uplifted the soul's understanding of itself and its true reality of existence.

"Perhaps this is some kind of universal library," I think as I keep step with the sway of wise women and find that my own steps are finally finding their rhythm. The chambers are resplendent and vibrating with living truth pouring in from all directions, as universal intonations meld together vast and eternal intelligence. Each thought that has ever been given life by a thinking mind, sentient being, or conscious entity continues to reverberate in this consortium of blended animation. Every note or chord of thought that comprises the deeds and decisions of souls is merged with all others in these great halls of the sacred records.

It is like a memory bank of information, perhaps what the mind of God might be like, wherein all is sounding forth in a unified undulation of impulse and impression, all of it coming together in a celebration of living existence.

Sarah turns and beckons again. Her gaze sends a surge of shivers through my soul and my body, and I can't tell the difference anymore, where the soul begins and the body ends.

I am aware that what I am experiencing is being absorbed on many levels of sensory intake. Every molecule, every cell, every everything that I am, is being permeated with the vibration and sound and meaning. All the key-notes that resound in this miraculous unity of orchestral wonder are in perfection. One can lose oneself in the totality of the orchestra and be swept away into its grandness, permeated and filled with the ocean of mind. Or one can fine-tune one's awareness and selectively find a specific resonance of consciousness as one wishes to be inspired or uplifted or informed.

Like a virtuoso who plucks each string of the violin with skilled and sensitive precision, so can the seeking soul find points of reference, themes of thought and impressions of experience and take them in through multiple levels of awareness.

The Grandmothers continue to sway, Sarah continues to smile, and together they envelop and nod toward each discovery. Each turn on the great wheel of all minds, from the most faint and barely perceivable, to the greatest declarations of existence, has made its mark on creation and is registered in these sacred halls. It is all gathered into divine alchemy.

Rhythmic pulses of thought and feeling merge, strike new chords, and then continue on their way, creating infinite combinations and limitless diversity of awareness, of wisdom, of possibility.

The promise of emerging creation is everywhere, all of it moving and merging and appearing and receding and appearing again. It is glorious and beyond grace. There are no words that can describe what I am witnessing. It is almost more than I can register, even on a sensory level. It is as if I am becoming thinned out or transparent, definitely less physical or spiritually physical in a new way, a new way that neither my voice nor my mind can give shape to.

Waves of vibrational imprint seem to break upon my understanding and as they do, they foam and surge in an all-knowingness that leaves its mark on the receptive surface of the unformed ether of the mind, like sand that has become intelligent and responsive with the omnipresence of origin. As the waves recede, a language of light is left behind to become yet another wave of comprehended existence.

Symbols like sacred letters of the cosmic alphabet of creation are rising up from the reverberations, like fiery thoughts from a supremely fiery mind. In a flash, I recall the experience of the blind people who are not blind and the Great Books of Time that my mother's memory passed on to me as insight and wisdom.

Again they nod, again Sarah smiles, only now they unify into a single blazing light, a great and brilliant sun that consumes all thought and even the effort to define. My head feels like it could explode. There is white fire moving through me like a racing torrent, like a firestorm, coursing and thrusting, burning away all of my previous thoughts, as powerful letters of pulsing light pierce like arrows of demanding blazing truth into my very flesh, letters of the beginning of time, the first thought of creation, the sounds that formed realms and worlds of being.

This supreme fire commands my body. My eyelids have become invisible. My eyes have turned upward, involuntarily seeking on their own an even greater intensity of light. My lips are numb with electric force. My blood is filled with intelligence, and I can see inside myself as infinite points of light are ignited in countless explosions of

300

ecstasy. My body is shuttering and shimmering, giving itself over to the ultimate power of cosmic fire.

The letters and symbols keep pouring into my bloodstream, becoming an indefinable sea that is the chalice of liquid intelligence of uncountable points of light; points of light that are unified, individual but unified, single lights but also a Single Light, The One and the Many. The roaring sound of Fire, Agni... Agni... Agni... is everywhere and everything. It is booming and cascading and fierce.

It is all the golden chariots with wheels of fire in the heavens; it is all suns in the cosmic sea; it is all light within all life; it is all power, the Will of God. It is cascading and gentle. It is all the waters of primordial nurturance; it is a delicate breeze, the bending movement of a single blade of grass; it is the trusting wonder in the eyes of a newborn baby.

Then I understand something that I have always known, like a chorus of coppery brass cymbals clanging together at a precise moment, in a crescendo of impact, in an immediate knowing and all-knowing that... all things are known by God. All things are God. This is why it is said that God knows every breath that we take and every thought that we think and that the deeds of the soul are recorded for all time. All I have to do is reach out and touch the shimmering walls of this corridor of time transcendent to know this is absolute.

The thoughts are rushing to the center of my being forevermore, as if the Milky Way is spinning for the last time. So many wispy ponderings and faint glimmers of awareness are suddenly becoming solid rock. I am made to see and hear and feel and know and even taste this vastness of truth that moves from the profound simplicity of the inherent gift of life. The inherent is always there; it is simply a matter of seeing it, remembering it and honoring it. From that seeing and honoring, the life that is lived takes shape. This is the great test of all souls, every single soul, every religion, every culture, and every nation.

I understand fully now, that opening the doors to the soul is like entering a living library of multidimensional experience, where time is overlaid upon itself. Consciousness expands like streams of light woven into a sea of many creations, all the experiences shedding light on the soul's origin and divine purpose. It is from this array of endless color and sound that the soul receives its eternal and unique nature, its special characteristics and qualities, in an individuality that is sacred to its Creator, a perfect composition of keynotes forever remembered by God.

I am shown how each soul emanates into a physical life, propelled by a divine power, a path of select purpose, but ever belonging to the greater field of universal awareness of which it is an integral and enduring part. Sarah is my teacher, my prophet of wisdom. The word "endure" moves through me, as I gather its wholeness of meaning from when I first woke up early this morning; the concept, quality and context of the word cascades through my thoughts.

The soul is enduring by its very nature. "Good Will to All Life" is its keynote of ultimate glory and freedom of existence; the note that is struck echoes back in jubilation, from the realms of the angels who celebrate the divine creation of humanity, God's creation. Light is pouring from Sarah's luminous eyes, as if I could bear receiving any more light, and it occurs to me that I am in the grace and glory of a revelation. The truth of the ages has become the floodgates of realization.

The unreal has become the real, as Sarah reaches out and touches my heart with her hand. An eternal pain is instantly eased, soothed, healed and anointed. Her touch is electrifying in its power and like liquid flowing nectar in its love. It is as if she knows my every anguish, my every longing, and my deepest of disappointments. Over and over she whispers, "I know, my daughter. I know, my child. I know." Her words are an icy blue balm upon torn and burning skin, a cooling waterfall upon bleeding memories, upon charred gray ashen bones.

The past seems to be melting away, and I feel bathed in healing redemption as if immersed in the fountains of eternal healing. This must be like what the mystics say about the fountain of youth, or the spring of eternal life, or the primordial wellspring of healing waters.

"I wanted you to see, Dear One, I wanted you to see," she said in the low tones of a near whisper. "With this seeing, my child, comes wisdom, wisdom that can anoint the whole of the world, wisdom that will feed the hungry heart and bring solace to the sorrowful. Dear One, do not regret your life or anything that you have been called to endure.

Everything has a reason and a purpose. Not one experience is in vain. All that you do merely sets the stage upon which the Great Presence is seeking to be seen and remembered. Therefore be thankful for all that you experience.

Through our travails, the veils that cloud our sight are slowly lifted, that each of us might see with the eyes of the soul. It is then that the seeing becomes the lens of perception that ignites the spark of the Flame Eternal in your life. It is then that you become a vessel for the oil of anointing that gives itself and returns itself to the Fire of

God, which burns for all eternity, and thus is renewed without end."

"Come, now. You are ready. Come." she says and gestures for me to walk by her side as she makes her way through a succession of light-filled chambers and glowing pathways. With steps that are as certain as all certainty, as the Most Certainty, she pauses before an arched alcove of radiant, luminous, glowing compartments. They remind me of a distant place of quiet memory, not lost as I had thought, only distant, but still there.

The walls and chambers of sacred writings have been with me since my soul was first prepared to enter a physical life. Somehow, I know this place. Somehow, I really know it. I remember it from the Temples of the Nile; I remember it from ancient Tibet; I remember it from the caves of the Himalayas; I remember it from Qumran; I remember it from the Temples of the Sun in the Andes of South America.

The sacred wisdom has always been passed on; it has always been preserved. The flicker of its flame still burns, even though it burns here on earth heavily shadowed by our ignorance. This time of war, of confusion, of opposing sides will play itself out and come to an end. We will find our way. This light at the end of the tunnel has already begun to shine on the present. Hopeful minds are receiving the answers; the pure of heart will in the end endure.

Swimming in a flood of heart-rending thankfulness, I feel as if I have been gathered up from a torrential river of fear and doubt and left standing on the shores of redemption. Now, as if awakened from an eerie sleep of unreality, I am seeing the crisp certainty of reality at its best. I am seeing the truth of life; I am seeing the divine nature of our Creator.

Sarah smiles and throws her head back in a playful, joyous recognition. "See," she said, "I knew you were ready. The Grandmothers are always right; they are the wise ones who know when each soul, each daughter, has passed through the great test of the ages, has walked through the burning sands of reckoning, and has in the end sought only to know the truth and bring that truth into their lives as an offering to the sacred that lives within all things.

It is at this crucial turning point that the wisdom teachings can begin, and a life of sacrifice can redeem all past into a future of beauty and creative service to all beings. This is the gateway to the future and a new era of Global Guardianship on earth."

With her hands sweeping in an ever-reaching arch, waves of understanding begin to pour forth from the chamber walls, as symbols and shapes open, turn and spin like the spindle of a spinning wheel yielding an abundance of yarn for the celestial loom of woven wisdom. Now Sarah speaks to me in a voice that is silent; not even a whisper passes through the smile that turns itself gently upward on her lips.

Her eyes fill, glowing with a benevolent all-encompassing intelligence, and shine like bright twin stars. In my amazement that there could be anything more, she speaks to me with her mind. Receiving the Teachings of Wisdom from the vast vault of archives that awaken to her touch, she passes the sacred on to me as if it had come through the silver flute of an avatar.

No words can convey the thoughts that she shares as the symbol-draped walls speak through her and she in turn causes my mind to know. Comprehension is beyond the confines of thought and the finite time of words, beyond any human language. Love is the enduring flow of life between us. Love is the language of light.

If thoughts could speak in the totality of their conveyance, this would clearly be her intention. This is clearly what she wants from me, not merely to receive, but to pass this wisdom on to others as well. Seeking to follow her every thought, her slightest shift in being, I ask with an innocence that easily rises up from inside myself, in response to the desire to know her will and feel her love.

I begin to attune myself to her wavelength of being, her nuance of nature. This is like finding the clearest signal on a radio or the clearest picture on a television. I feel like a tuning fork seeking to match every tone and every chord of her vibration. And as I hone in and find myself at one with her, the flow of teaching begins in full.

There are truths that never die and never change and can never be altered. They are truths that sustain life. It is also the absence of these truths that withdraws the sustaining factor of life, like a river that becomes dry and barren and leaves the life that once dwelled upon its banks bereft of life-giving possibility. When the life force of a river is diverted away from its destiny to reach the ocean, when man alters the flow of the river, when it is diverted in a direction other than that of the natural laws of existence, the river cannot flow and cannot sustain itself or the life that depends upon it for sustenance.

Forever and always we are each the creation of our Creator. This is the first light of consciousness that sparks a soul into existence. Secondly, we are the light of the soul, and that second light is the life of the soul's journey. And thirdly, my daughter, we are human beings, the vessel in which the soul lives out its quest for attainment of the qualities that have been given into the safekeeping of the soul.

First we are the light of God; second we are the light of the soul, and third we are the indwelling spirit of human being. This is the Divine Order that can never be changed or altered. And this Divine Order of life that, when respected and upheld, will bring not only peace upon earth, but also a bounty of wealth beyond your comprehension. It is this triple premise that is the Universal Law of Life. It is this premise that will in the years to come be the light that shines upon the legacy of peace and cooperation among nations and goodwill to all.

No soul is supreme to the Creator. No human being is supreme to the soul. Neither religion, nor nation is supreme to God. Neither religion nor nation is supreme to the soul. Neither religion nor nation is supreme to the innate value of a human being. When this Divine Order is in disarray, you will see the fall of a nation and the fall of a soul and the manner by which the fall will be incurred written in the sands of time.

If you were to cast your eye upon all nations, whatever is held above God in value, will be the point of distortion that begins the descent from greatness. Whatever is held above the value of the soul will be the path of demise. Whatever is held above human value will be the fall from grace that spirals the potential of life to its death. Life is God; soul is God; humanity is the expression of this and is the sacredness of intelligent mind and heart upon earth. When this "Law of Values" is recognized, war will become a distant remnant of a past age of hard-earned lessons never to be forgotten.

After these three values come the value of religions and philosophies to inspire each human being to seek a higher expression than is perceived as possible, and thus assures an eternal spiral of life, seeking an ever greater expression of itself. When the function of governments serves this premise, they will become stewards of the greatest wealth upon your planet, the wealth of human value.

Money has no real and lasting value, no ability to have meaning or purpose, if its use is not given to the value of being human, the quest of the soul, and the promise of unending potential for all life. Money can come and go and take many forms, but what of humanity? Can it really come and go from the face of this earth?

Humanity's walk upon this earth is the quest, the potential and the promise of the true value of life. Dear One, this was the lesson that I learned in the desert. This was the lesson that became my moment of redemption as I lay upon my deathbed and saw into the future.

My regrets were many, and my mistakes even greater. For wherever I failed to value life is where I failed to remember the promise of existence. And wherever I failed to remember the promise of existence, I became the hand of suffering, and this in the end of my life I could not bear.

When I in my haste and ignorance sent away my handmaiden, Hagar, in accordance with the belief of the day, that my own son, Isaac, would be assured of favor and fortune, I sent away my own soul, bereft of the true wealth that lives on with the promise of meaning, and the wealth within meaning that makes life worth living.

Had I loved the light within her flesh as I loved my God, my religion, my tribe and my tribal customs, the fate of a nation would have been sent upon a different path. I would not today be seeking souls like you to pass on the wisdom that I myself failed to see. But now I have seen, and now I know what I did not see or know then.

And it was my promise to all that I loved and cherished as I passed from your world to the realms wherein I now speak, to *never lay myself to rest in the arms of my Creator until I have corrected my mistakes of the past. And so the promise of a lifetime was made; the promise of my soul was sent forth. The promise of my light of lights, of spirit and being, is given to you and to all mothers, to all women, to all daughters.*

To turn the tide of time, to turn the chain of events, to make right what has been wrong from the beginning; here in the land where many prophets have walked, this was the desire that consumed me in my last days. In the desert tents that billowed all around me, I cast my soul to the winds, vowing never to rest until the truth was known and cherished to become the Way of Life; for it was my promise to restore the knowledge of the Divine Order among the daughters that live on through my lineage. This is why I walk among the sand dunes and olive groves, the rivers and the mounts, the thorns and the burning bushes of human life.

My promise is a promise of all time, to a people that I love and to the husband that cared for his people and showed me the way of sacrifice as the way of life eternal. Had I sacrificed my pride and my fear to the higher wisdom beyond my own thinking, so would I now be at rest. The value of the light of God, the light of the soul and the light of the human spirit is the truth of the ages, timeless and universal, enduring and unchanging. All else comes and goes, rises and falls in meaning and purpose.

But the value inherent to the gift of life is the meaning within all time and all existence. This is our Creator speaking through the expression of the living word of existence. Let all be sacrificed to the supreme value of all life, for this is the Divine Order of true wealth that the prophets spoke about, the wealth of humanity in realization of itself. It is this wealth that will herald a higher order of life on earth and the land of milk and honey that all souls dream of.

Let it be your promise to me that you will pass my story on, for in the passing there will be hope. And through hope, perhaps one day I will take rest and return to my Creator, redeemed and restored of my own value to myself. What I now pass to you will be passed to others. Let this be my legacy. Let a higher order of life on earth be my child, and let that child drink from the rivers of a land of milk and honey. For this is the sweetness of life, life that is cherished, life that endures.

This is the lesson that I learned as I left the side of my beloved Abraham. Lying in his arms, he whispered the secrets of his heart and passed the sacred on to me. Lying in his arms, I asked to know. Lying in his arms, my promise was made. Let this remembrance be yours. For, this is my promise to every woman on earth who seeks her origin and her destiny. Let the passing be the food of wisdom and the manna of future generations."

For a long time I remained silent and unmoving, savoring all the impressions that had moved through me. This thing that Sarah called the Teachings of Wisdom would live in my heart forever. All that she showed me, expressed to me, conveyed to me was an awesome premise, and for a moment I felt a sudden creeping fear that I would lose everything that I had gained, that I would forget the blessing that was bestowed upon my life through Sarah's presence.

"No, my daughter, ease your mind. I will always be with you, as I am with all women who seek the eternal truth. You are my very blood. I am your grandmother. My soul lives on through you and through all women who seek wisdom. Now is the time on earth that I am needed, and I am in response to this need. It is the calling of all the world's children for the protec-

tion of their innocence, to which I respond, 'You are my daughter. You are myself. Let my wisdom flow though you. Don't be afraid. The time is now to give all that can be given.' The light of God in the soul of every child of every nation is calling you, calling all sisters, all daughters home to the heart of the original and enduring truth of existence. And there is so much more, Dear One.

The wonders of creation await your seeking heart. This is why I called you to Jerusalem, and this is why I called you to all of the places that you have journeyed. It was to prepare you for your awakening. I am a messenger of our Creator. I am a servant of God. I am a mother of a new nation. I will always be with you now, in your dreams, in your thoughts, and in your desire to create a better world, bring peace to the suffering, and the birthright of the soul to the children of the world. I will live and speak through all women of every faith and nation and through a new wisdom born of the hearts of women. The world will endure, and a new era of peace and prosperity will indeed be born on earth. The seeds will be many; the harvest, infinite.

Come, we must go; there is much that we must both set about doing. You must return to your world; I must continue on in my journey; but never are we apart. We are one; we are unified; we are one life, held in the hands of God. Come now, let us return to our places in the worlds of Life and Being."

The Grandmothers beckoned in Sarah's direction, letting her know it was time to complete. Turning together in a fine-tuned arc, they headed straight into the crimson horizon as Sarah followed. When I woke up, coming back to ordinary time and ordinary senses, the soft lights of the Old City glowed sweetly into the night. I sat in my chair, my gaze transfixed by the beauty of Jerusalem, even in the dark. The Grandmother guardians still seemed close by.

And then it hit me, when we place money or power or even religious doctrine before God we have misaligned divine order. When we place nationalistic pride or cultural identity before God, we cut off our connection with divine presence, with spirit, with deity, with origin.

The soul and the birthright of our humanity have precedence over all things of a material nature. And then it became clear to me. When we try to put religious or national identity, or social or economic identity before the truth of original being, we compromise our own nature, our own birthright, our own origin and roots, our own soul of souls.

When we get the divine order of life convoluted, the locusts and plagues begin; war and strife begin. When we are straight with our divine alignment, we are straight with our source and the origin of life. This is the life stream of the prophets and the pathway of a unified heaven and earth.

My body has drunk in this Teaching of Wisdom. My blood has received the fire breath of the language of love. My mind has received a universe of blazing light. My heart has received redemption and the revelation of the eternal.

With this, I gently rise, turn out the lights, fold down my bed, and ease myself into a grateful surrender. Sleep comes effortlessly. Sleep... like the grace of angels and tenderly suckled infants. Sleep... the sleep of wisdom taking rest to dream a deeper fullness.

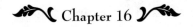

Chapter 16

The Decision

Questions of Faith, Questions of Practicality

Looking over my secretary's notes, I see that my day stretches well into the evening hours. I remind myself of all the demands of my office and the numerous logistical fires, demanding to be put out. The details to be organized and finalized by the end of the day are more than daunting.

I also remind myself that my staff has been working tirelessly for months now, and they may very well be reaching the same edgy cliff of exhaustion that I, myself, had teetered on for most of the past week. They are deserving of new inspiration and all that I can give in the way of sustaining leadership, basic optimism and good spirits.

I decide to wear a bright turquoise dress today to match my much-improved mood, to reflect the color of the sky that soars untouched above the fray of human clamor and worry. Taking a few more luxurious sips of tea as if it were wine from the last supper, I carefully follow it down as it is swallowed. I set my intention for the day, clear of mind and deliberate of duty.

I relish in the comfort of staring out at the peaceful roll and ancient curves of the Old City one more time, as I turn with rock-solid determination to face what lies ahead. Getting dressed, watching fingers button, watching hands smooth and bring order, I think about what I can do to cheer up my staff and help them to remember the driving impetus that led us all here.

Teacups and teapots and thoughts of Himalayan teachers get put away until another time and, feeling bolstered, I close the door to the refuge of my little room. The cool ambiance of the white marble floors and the glazed expanses of the hotel fall away as I head out into the stark brightness of the desert morning, into the fray, into the bowels, and into the heart of Jerusalem. There the winding cobblestone streets are always full of surprises and twists and turns that change your life.

I am late, two hours late arriving at our makeshift headquarters of a largely volunteer effort. This is unusual, extremely so. I am always the first to arrive and the last to go. Most everyone is already near buried, engrossed in their assigned duties, but they stop to acknowledge my late arrival, heads turning, faces questioning, shoulders shrugging as I make my way to the usual pile of files, letters and correspondence, people and projects awaiting my attention.

I beam a bright expression to all of them that I am in good shape, wonderful spirits, just had to take care of some things. Plunking myself down, I can't quite bring myself to plunge in, and instead I survey the tiny but very real reality that I have in a very large part created.

Phones are ringing in rapid fire and answering machines are reciting the messages that come in from the States during the night, like flocks of talking parrots jabbering at high speed.

Instead of tackling my day's workload as usual, I sense the need to come together, all of us, my entire staff, in a new way. Calling everyone to an impromptu meeting was met with unhappy faces. Eyes roll back to voice displeasure, and spirits drag across the room as chairs drag across the floor. What now is the unspoken sentiment? "What could she possibly want from us now, with so much to complete by 5:00?"

Reluctantly my beloved companions gathered around my desk. Much discussion centered around the decision to focus our efforts in Israel and the Middle East on four simple but essential proactive initiatives: increasing women's leadership, the environmental issues, trauma recovery and human values education, and interfaith dialog to bridge and heal past prejudices.

Clearly if regions of conflict were given adequate global support, the problems resulting from conflict and instability could be resolved more quickly, so that normal lives could be resumed. How can we expect a shift in the psyche of a nation either during or after traumatic conflict and war, unless the matter of public education is addressed?

I continued to outline our original premise for being here. Teaching children to go beyond the vendettas of the past is crucial. Helping families heal shattered lives is another. We simply must address the positive contributions that can be made, and we as an organization must be specific as to exactly how to direct our help.

I felt it was crucial not to spread our resources too thin, not to scatter funding in too many directions, not to try to save the world single-handedly. I would still do fundraising for approved grassroots groups with good proposals and programs. We would help umbrella some of the administrative load that upstart organizations struggle with.

We could mentor them in the process of learning to manage their projects. I would still accept speaking engagements to raise money for relief work, hospitals, and for the larger more established non-profit agencies. I would still work around the clock.

Not everyone was happy. Not everyone felt this was enough. "More support of peace marches and rallies should be on the top of the list," some said and were adamant. "How can we sit in an office planning programs while everything around us is going up in flames? Shouldn't we be at ground zero filling in where the relief efforts leave off?"

I disagreed and offered my viewpoint. Picking my battles was something my father taught me. And now with an endless possibility of issues to address, the essential must be separated from the peripheral. I tried to swing opinion in new directions. "After the peace marches, then what? After emergency aid is given, then what? Peace rallies that send the message to strive for more humane international relationships, are a part of the times we live in," I conceded, "but the worst is still to come. We can give aid to one crisis after another, but where do we go from there?"

Concrete programs that focus directly on the people and the land they live on and how they coexist is where the building blocks of the future are needed. I held firm. For me, peace marches are not enough, and I have no desire to contribute to the kind of vigil that becomes a soapbox for hotheads, and after all the demonstrations the real work must begin. After the aid is given, the real work must continue. "All this good intention needs to go somewhere. The voice for peace must become the hands that build," I said. "Radical 'flash in the pan' ideas must become sustainable solutions."

"The whole world is radical," someone offered.

"Rebuilding people's lives when they're falling apart is a priority," I added.

I wanted to disappear. I wanted to bolt out of the room. I wanted to run all the way back to my childhood and the safety from my imaginary battles that my father always provided. But the thought of my wise, aging and beautiful father brought me all the way back to the grand intentions and firm resolve that began my day.

A part of me simply couldn't tolerate fighting about peace. Peace is such a far-reaching and abstract concept. Helping real people to survive the lack of peace seemed far more urgent, standing in the thick of things. Perhaps years from now, I'll look back on this time with far more wisdom gained in the fine art of making practical headway in the midst of humanitarian ideals, when conflict seems to devour everything in sight

I notice that a small crowd of people is starting to form a bottleneck in the hallway in front of the entrance, some kind of mix-up over which group was scheduled for an interview today. We seem to have three groups waiting for intake, all hoping to be included as either presenters for an upcoming conference, contributors to our book project, or prospective recipients hoping for funding for approved projects, one of which has been waiting for a half hour already.

"What do I want to do?" my assistant asks. "Who should have priority?" Necks are craning; eyebrows are lifted for my response, as the chaos builds to a crescendo of absurdity. Our spontaneous meeting is out of control like the rest of the circumstances that we are here to remedy.

All set to offer good cheer and optimism, all dressed in striking bright turquoise and chic sky blue, all ready to deliver the power of ancient songs and newfound emptiness, it is a good time to dive into the ordinary with a tank full of the profound from the night before, when the wonderment of the Teachings of Wisdom were upon my soul full-throttle. I gathered myself and made ready.

But someone else beat me to the need of the moment and just blurted out plain and simple, spilling a half drunk cup of coffee across his desk, as he gestured emphatically to give impact to the thought that had been grinding away at everyone all week. "What in the world are we doing here?" he half questioned, half exclaimed wide-eyed and exasperated.

There it was: the question of the week. The question of all the ages was cast into broad daylight, boldfaced like a boomerang returning on the power of its own pent-up motion, loud and clear with a voice that pushes logjams downstream, echoing all the way out into the hallway. The monumental decision to be made, "What are we all doing here?" the question the whole of humanity must ask.

Movement stilled, phones stopped ringing as if by a supranatural order from a higher command, as all eyes turned to me. All ears waited. Necks still craned and heads extended even farther than before. The straining to hear the humble truth brought us en masse to a dead halt, as the morning pressed on in exponential intensity.

The people in the hallway kept up their buzzing, humming banter, while the rest of us were suspended in time. It hit us all at once, his question of questions, as if a telepathic bomb had gone off among us, silencing the usual din of mundane conversation, the clamor of constant mind chatter and the incessant ringing of telephones gone mad.

The expression "time stood still" conveyed the oddly eerie nuance of the moment that we shared, when everyone looked up from the truly gruesome onslaught of our workload and simultaneously stared into space, speechless. It was like our frustration had reached a critical mass. Nerves were raw. Reserves were spent. Minds were overwhelmed. My previous grand intention to spur everyone on to new heights of altruism paused to assess its entry, questioning its own existence.

I looked around the room that was piled high with stacks and stacks of brochures and program guides, leftover bag lunches from the deli down the street, and heaps of personal effects of all sorts. Slouching backpacks and sleek briefcases, woven cloth tote bags and classy Gucci purses were scattered about, representing all the walks of life that had joined our humble effort. The surroundings that I found myself in had begun to resemble some kind of campaign headquarters, battle bunker or command center in contrast to the tidy streamlined offices that we commonly worked in back in America.

We were "dug in," would be the words to describe the human heaping of paraphernalia that seemed to ooze in every direction. We were stockpiled into corners and pressed to the ceiling, wedged in among one another. Boxes of promo literature and posters were stacked shoulder high, like stores of ammunition, mimicking the supplies that were made ready for an ancient battle. Our little make-shift office stood among many such efforts at the center of a brigade of peace and humanitarian organizations, and bringing them all into a common focus was often a thing of chaos.

We were achieving a metamorphosis that resembled images of soldiers of fortune, Knights of the Holy Grail, marchers claiming the streets with Martin Luther King. We were dug in and clothed with our cause. Stunned, I realized in a flash of embarrassed reckoning that we were beginning to take on the chaotic characteristics of the Middle East conflict itself, with its riddle-ridden insanity and cast of colorful characters that played out the drama of quarrels that perhaps began with Cain and Abel, or perhaps Adam and Eve.

The word fanatic could easily be applied to us by at least some, especially our parents, children, wives and husbands who wonder why we do what we do, and what would cause an intelligent person to hold court in the midst of a global target.

And as the wide-eyed, open-mouthed moment stretched on, there was still no break in the frozen silence or the "all eyes on me" situation. As my staff locked on, and looked hard in my direction, I called up to Divine Providence and silently asked, "Where is the eternal wisdom of the Grandfathers and Grandmothers in all of this? Where is the Judaic blood of Abraham and Sarah right now? Where is the Christ benediction from the Mount of Beatitudes? Where is the Buddhist emptiness from the high Himalayas that flows into fullness and peace... peace... peace to all beings?"

Here we sat, amuck in a hectic whirlpool, spinning in the aftermath of the past several weeks of organizing extreme disorganization, of trying to pay big bills on a tiny shoestring budget, of meeting with hundreds of possible allies and deep talking well into the night on the subjects of religion and politics and the upcoming elections, and what the United Sates might do or not do in Iraq or Israel, or any number of hotspots, and then waking up red-eyed on the mornings after.

The endless litany of details... And be sure to finish the fundraising proposal for the new medical clinic out in the desert near Beersheba. And don't forget to return the call to the Ambassador of Jordan. And be sure to see if there isn't some way to get permits that would allow allied contributors from Gaza to participate.

And remember to check deadlines at the printers. And don't forget to invite the nice man who sang so beautifully the last time, the well-known Israeli folk singer. And be sure to have gifts ready for the young Arab dancers and the Israeli choral youth group that will perform after the fundraiser. And make sure all the sound and recording equipment from the US is outfitted with electrical converters, because the last time the whole thing blew to smithereens. And have we heard from any of the US universities about their environmental programs for the Bedouin tribes? My thoughts were racing with the unfinished business of a single day. And... And... And...

"O, God... It's getting us," my thoughts starting screaming and reeling in wild realization. "The creeping chaos of this place is getting us," my colleague gasped aloud, face furrowed, shaking his head like a horse, this time cracking the tension with the flinging of his angst, arms spread-eagled as if he himself were hanging on a cross.

My mind had already begun to spin into gear with an internal dialog that reached out for angels, messengers, Rinpoche's, Grandmothers, the long-awaited Messiah, or anyone else who would remedy our dilemma. "How can we claim or even try to be peace workers or humanitarians or spiritually motivated social activists, as we are sometimes called? We are pathetic in our own humanity, barely hanging on to our own sanity in this living inferno called the Middle East, in the center of it all, in Jerusalem.

Should we laugh, or should we cry? Should we change everything or keep going as is? Should we hang it up and go home or dig in deeper, past our knees and over our heads?" I offered up all of it, in the most sincere drama that I could muster, head tilted toward the ceiling in divine gestures of supplication.

The ceiling fan was spinning dutifully, precisely above my head for the occasion, comically mimicking the state of mind, making it difficult to take myself seriously, at least for today.

The tension builds. The air is even tighter than before. No one responds. Everyone looks at everyone else. Eyes meet. Hearts touch. Minds melt. And then as if a rolling moving film shifts to slow-motion mode, heads begin to throw back. Faces begin to accept the first traces of upturned lips forced to respond on their own.

The low gurgles of impending laughter begin to rustle through the room like wind on crispy leaves. Giggles begin to sprout, breaking through the hardpan of old worry. The flash of eyes suddenly being given sight, volleys from person to person. Revelation takes hold, spreading like an infectious disease that has suddenly been given the power to reverse its effects: to heal the sick, to make the blind to see, and to cause the dead to rise.

And then, as if Grandmothers are dancing for their lives, and all the elders of wisdom past, present and future are taking hold of the great wheel of cosmic creation, as if they have answered our prayers and solved every last problem, there at the height of pure undiluted absurdity, insanity becomes the decision of the heart.

You could almost hear the tension snap and break free of itself. A hearty round of good-humored jokes spontaneously moves around the room, aimed at our predicament. Unstoppable laughter peels off the walls and explodes out the windows. I swear the force of it made the curtains next to where I was sitting billow like the tents of the ancient Tribes of Israel.

I was laughing tears and blubbering humorous innuendoes at the same time. Several of my teammates had tears streaming down their grinning cheeks, unable to control themselves. Emotions were having a time of it, having been let out of a locked box of tense protocol and chest-heaving pressure.

A sense of triumph filled every cup and every heart and squeezed the love from lost places, like the fruit vendors extracting the juice from pomegranates, or hands drawing sweet nectar from prickly pear pulp, or the wooden presses squeezing plump olives and causing their healing greenness to pour forth the anointing oil.

A decision had been made in a single instance, all together, all at once. The natural goodness of the human heart had endured all the challenges that brought us to this moment. We had made peace with ourselves. We had come to accept the insanity of this place. We even came to cherish it. We came to love it, just as it was, unchanged, the way it has always been. We had made peace with it.

In the place of all places, where promises capture hearts like young children who capture brilliantly colored butterflies, whose wings flutter like flying, stained-glass windows, butterflies that were once larvae wrapped in the dark cocoons of the past, the human heart had endured.

With full-bellied, rolling, guffawing laughter, we had come to celebrate the ridiculous, our own ridiculousness.

We had come to celebrate all the crazy, wonderful, outrageous, incomparable, gut-wrenching, soul-calling beauty of Jerusalem and her wondrous and far-reaching domain as the capital extraordinaire, as the center of our earthly spiritual universe, as the convergence of the countless roads and lives of the desert tribes, ageless, age old and now contemporary.

We were laughing with eyes of love and falling down on the floor of our previous pride, and flinging caution into the wind of a new day of realization. We were throwing our heads back with the joy and wisdom that endures. A sense of childlike freedom became the manna that we passed from one soul to another, like the manna that fed the starving tribes of Abraham 4,000 years ago.

The people standing in the hall began to snicker and then spontaneously passed the contagious effect of unleashed laughter on down the line, even though they hadn't a clue what had broken free to run through the group like children on a playground let out for the summer holiday. Soon they were broadly having a good laugh with the rest of us. The mood lifted in the room as if a curtain had been raised to reveal a new stage.

I called out over my shoulder, "Go ahead and interview all of the groups together; do them all at once, everyone, it's OK, call them in from the hallway; find a place for them." The sound of sirens from the street below was just part of the din of things, the norm here, where sirens can announce the unthinkable on any given day at any given hour.

Back in the command of counting blessings, I called out over the sounds of surrendering souls, "Come on everyone," I yelled mid-laugh. "Let's hustle. Back to work. Get it done and we'll all go home early. I'll be closing the office by 3:00 today. I'm going to visit the Citadel of David and take in the museum, if it's still open these days. Anyone want to come? We need a break. You've earned it. Someone call to see if the Citadel is still open to the public."

With that announcement of victory and reward, the phones suddenly started ringing with the demands of the day, as deliberate hands sure of their purpose reached for the voices on the other end of the lines, possibly the other end of the world. Who knows, maybe the Grandmothers are calling, having taken to the modern convenience of telephones.

Sarah's Promise was wide-awake and living in my soul, feeding my blood with visions of yellow rose gardens and white-doved hope for all of the Children of Abraham. And it was indeed infectious. I think with promise thoughts to all the symposiums seeking solutions that we will continue to convene, to all the projects of hope and remedy which will continue to take shape, and all the dedicated souls who will join us: Arab, Jew, Christian and anyone else of any religious or cultural bent who cares to pitch their tent next to the ancient tent cities that have no walls, before Jerusalem had a name.

They will be robed in the cause of a benevolent world for future generations. They will be bearing the colors and patterns of the histories of their lives, different and diverse though they may be. And we may not always agree on fabric and form, or weave or pattern, but that should make things more interesting, the coat of many colors.

We will not always agree what to do or where to go or whether or not a risk is worth taking; but we will in the full force of sacrifice and conviction go beyond what was possible before. Like the time I brought 25 Arab male youths into a Jewish stronghold and created the bridges of understanding that would open new doors in our shared humanity and new roads to workable coexistence.

In that rather historic personal feat, the previously unheard of, became the accepted and celebrated, a story worthy of recollection, as I sat in the tail wind of an era of new decision that had just taken place, even if coexistence still waited in the distance for rescue or discovery.

My decision of a few years ago had shaped a tiny moment of new possibility and brought fear and refusal into acceptance. As I recalled the day when I invited a troop of teenage Arab boys to perform during an evening session of a symposium, their vivid images leapt from the vaults of my memory. They had triumphed and so had I, as they all but leapt across rainbows and war zones to offer a folk-dancing performance that inspired even the most grumpy, worn-out, or terrified or stolid of souls. Faith was affirmed.

The young men had received a standing ovation, because more than the rest of us could possibly even know, they too very clearly felt they were dancing for their lives. As many in the audience were gripped with the fear of having Arab youths in their midst, so too were the young men terrified to be there.

But they had come, nonetheless, because their dance troop had been convened and funded as a cultural bridge to show the bright side of the kids that held the spirit of desert traditions in their hearts.

But as if delivered from all possibility of evil, as if delivered by the Hand of Creator, as if the power of Sun Gods was upon them, they danced as if thunder and lightening had inspired their souls. They danced as if the Almighty had descended to move among their feet. It was nothing short of awesome to witness the spirit that had been virtually unleashed upon the stage in front of us, and the annihilation of the drama that had held us all in the deadlock of fear.

Gray-haired Jewish women broke free from the age-old feud between Arab and Jew. Children began to tap their feet and clap their hands. A smattering of city officials and politicians in suits and ties began to nod their heads to the beat of twenty-five pairs of feet, drumming and twirling on the stage. Professors from the university, revered Rabbis from the Old City, nuns from Europe and hopeful peace keepers from America all began to be taken into the sway, as if our souls knew the hour had come to let go of the shackles of the past and enter the commonality of fellowship and a simple good time.

People from the audience leaped up to dance right where they stood. In a flooding of remembrance of the desert tribes that first danced these dances, lifting the dust beneath their feet skyward; bodies moved, and fingers snapped.

A few in the audience even jumped up on the stage to join the young men who had the energy of stampeding stallions and the grace and synchronicity of studied protégés, as they strutted and leaped across the stage, in smartly assembled ethnic costumes and black leather boots. The drums and wails of traditional Arab music filled the auditorium.

I had invited them to the conference much to the angst and horror of my security team and the shock of the managers of the auditorium where we held the three-day event. No one wanted any trouble and they couldn't imagine why I would deliberately bring young, male Arab youths into the heart of everything we ever considered worth working for at a time like this, with the city still reeling from the most recent suicide bombings and military insurgence on the rampage.

Why would I risk so much, not the least of which was the lives of everyone present and very certainly my hard earned credibility. But I had done my homework and had researched through and through the possibility, and somehow I just knew that this was the right thing to do.

All the world is living in the grip of a great decision and there is no way to second-guess how the decision will demand to be met, and in what way or by what grace the human spirit will suddenly bolt from its chains and break free of its captors.

In the end, the young boys shared a purity of spirit that is rare in today's world, and won the hearts of all in attendance. Even the security guards were visibly moved and had to give up the fight, at least temporarily.

After the performance, I ordered the dancers ice cream as a thank you for their bravery and willingness to come, and offered a small donation to their effort. It's not easy getting out of Gaza, or anywhere else, even less easy to make it all the way to Jerusalem without getting hassled, thrown in jail or worse, much worse. It could easily cost your life and this fact sat, more than large, on my mind as the conference was ending and the lights on the stage were turned off.

I went out into the lobby to personally thank each one of them, going down the line shaking their hands as they eagerly gulped down ice cream and smiled like happy kids at the carnival, relieved that the scary roller coaster ride was over. Fighting back my tears again, which seems to happen pretty often in my line of work, I wished that I could have given them more than ice cream. As it was, they had to leave through the back of the building with a police escort, because it had been decided that either they posed a threat, or the threat posed itself in their direction.

I wish that I could have given them whatever their young hearts desired that day. I wish that I could have given them what our conference was all about, peace and a future where smiles and ice cream are the norm. But there we all were with nothing but ourselves to offer, and at least for a few small moments all of us could see the beauty of Jews and Arabs standing on the same side of peace, the Family of Abraham enjoying the rights of passage and the simple pleasures of being human.

The reality of suicide bombers and soldiers shooting into crowds suddenly slipped away, as if these atrocities were of another time and another place, not now and not here.

I have tucked that magical moment away like a precious treasure. Every so often I revisit the smiles of their ice cream faces and the restoration of innocence that fell over the group that had assembled itself for the peace conference. I often remember these kids, one by one. They will never become anonymous faces in the crowd. Now years later, I still take this memory out of my archives of hope, carefully unwrapping its perfection for special occasions, as if it were a rare diamond, the "wealth" that keeps true hearts pounding.

This memory will always come to me like a faithful servant on days that are especially rough, when nothing seems willing to bend itself to anything even remotely resembling sanity, let alone peace. In moments like this, the spirit of living for something greater than oneself cascades its power into the midst of things.

Today is such a day, and I am grateful to have this diamond light close at hand, along with Himalayan emptiness, and the passing of the sacred that began with Grandmothers and Grandfathers and moved through the lineage of Sarah and Abraham. This day of astute revelation and delirious decision and uproarious laughter will endure. And some day I know, in my heart of hearts, that peace will endure.

The road may be longer or shorter than expected, and we may be temporarily blinded as we turn the bend, but one day we will see what all of the prophets have seen. We will see what has been there all along.

That glorious moment of dancing boots and clapping hands will endure. The moment of hard questions asked and wise answers laughing in the broad skies of the boundless heart will prevail, as the Grandmothers chant from the other side of the cosmic dust of creation, "Remember the value of the human being. Remember each time you forget. If ever you ask this question, know that the answer is all around you."

Chapter 17

The Meeting

Talk of Plans, Talk of Action

O ne could go on and on with the writing of personal journeys and mystical experiences and the pondering of world affairs, but the time at hand calls for sending out my small story sooner than later. Back home in America, ominous storm clouds gather in response to the collective fears of the entire human race as war, the war of all wars, is falling from the skies of expectation. This time of decision could even be surmised as a path that leads to a fork in the road for every nation and every man, woman and child.

Naiveté and skepticism seem destined to be inseparable companions in much of the US. The stock market continues in the demise of schizophrenia while money doctors seek remedies to save an economy gone crazy; the question of value demands to be answered. Perceived value, deceived value, and true value are standing side by side, waiting for the choice of the human race to step forward.

Whether one sided with the convention that thinks a war in the Middle East can be fought and won with minimal fuss, or whether one thinks that World War III and imminent apocalypse is just around the corner, is a matter of personal perspective. But that perspective is headed

331

down the road of some of the most serious questions that we as a human race have ever contemplated. We seem to be veering down a course that weds the tragic possibilities that lie ahead and the karmic due that is demanding its payment.

Many peace symposiums have now come and gone. Our team of contributors found their way and grew strong. Each one was a success, from the standpoint of essence and content and a coming together of all kinds of people who were willing to be heard. They were not sticking their heads in the sand, nor were they giving up. Intelligent solutions were discussed and committees were formed to set about doing what could be done, given the obstacles that sit hard and obstinate on the path of coexistence.

I'll be putting together a book of the discourses that were presented in the past, so that the brilliance and dedication of the speakers can find their way into the lives of many more people than our little conferences could accommodate. It is my hope that getting the discourses out there will touch a lot of people and let the world hear from the average everyday person, whose opinions are rarely considered. This too will be a labor of love, start to finish, including dealing with all the translations that will bring the Hebrew and Arab and English languages into a synchronized cohesion, and the gamut of personalities that will begin the clamor for benefit that is inevitable, even among humanitarians and social activists.

But the most important thing for those of us who worked behind the scenes to bring the conferences to life and to continue the Peace Promise Initiative thereafter, was that the tests of faith challenged us all and found each of us in need of reconciliation and coexistence at some level or another in our own lives and in our own relationship with the world around us.

332

And so serving as a peace worker automatically sets into motion the need for a good housecleaning internally and externally. By sticking it out and not giving up, we come to face our own demons in short order with the demand to come to terms with why we do what we do. This inner, internal, personal and private peace work makes each one of us better able and more worthy to continue and to give.

But I can't forget the reality that many people in Israel and in Palestine, and in so many places, including the cherished soil of my own country, America, will continue to live with. People that I know and love dearly will stand in harm's way every day, as I return to the land of supposed privilege back in the US. Some of the Palestinians who attended the symposium risked their lives just to be there. Arab peace workers are ostracized, threatened, and sometimes gunned down by their own family members, even hunted down like animals by the Israeli military.

Because of the Israeli security restrictions, getting the required permits to leave the occupied territories is a major feat for our Palestinian speakers, many of whom were distinguished scholars and true spiritual leaders, not radicals or fanatics or manipulators of the truth. But even when we could get the permits, often their own officials wouldn't let them leave the refugee camps. It is high treason to want peace in some circles of the Arab world. The same is true of some circles in the world of Jews. And here in America the war of values escalates.

To want peace, to attend peace conferences, is treason. Sometimes there are protest marches against peace in the streets outside where the peace conferences are being held.

And so I departed my beloved Israel and my beloved Palestine, knowing that the suffering and degradation would continue, and there was no end in sight. Even so, at least some people thought peace symposiums were worth attending, and projects of humanity and hope were worth investing in.

I was grateful and privileged to be in the presence of so many noble souls who offered what they could to bring sanity to the insanity. They came from all directions: scientists, scholars, activists, lawyers, politicians, spiritual leaders, psychologists and peacemakers who were just peacemakers, whose previous professional lives fell away to the work of being full-time peace emissaries.

Many have begun to take their message to foreign countries and are giving peace talks, lifting consciousness, fundraising for war trauma recovery that is so desperately needed by the children who call regions of conflict their home.

One such effort was made by a remarkable twosome, an older Arab man and a younger Jewish man, who had befriended one another and were now traveling worldwide to spread the hope of peace and brotherhood, reconciliation and coexistence. They were standing side by side, Arab and Jew giving peace talks.

At one of the conferences, I sat next to someone who was risking his life to be there. I applauded his courage silently and hoped he would at least take some measure of comfort or affirmation from being among fellow peace workers. He was Arab, and he was nervous and visibly uncomfortable. I didn't speak his language and he didn't speak mine, so our verbal exchange was minimal. But his eyes reached for mine, for help, for hope. His courage and refusal to be silenced gave me hope and helped to strengthen the strength that I needed to live with the fact that he was risking his life to sit next to me. Whether or not he would make it to his hearth and home was a big question.

But the raw reality remains, that people I know may very well not live until my next trip to the region in just a month or so down the road. One young Jewish boy, perhaps fifteen years old, was presented to me just before I departed to return to America. He was still shaking with tremors from having been in a bomb blast that took the lives of his family. He was shaking and his eyes were empty of life. His relatives thought that maybe I could help him. Resting my hand on his heart, I reached for his soul, asking him to remember himself, including the part of him that was literally shocked out of the skin of his own body.

I did what I could to bring calm to his shaking, and return him to himself. On my way back across the ocean, my heart set itself to masterminding a major program for children of war, to heal the horrors of the soul that they had suffered. This young Jewish boy deserved better; it's a value that should be worth its weight in gold, all the gold of the treasures of King David, reputed to still be buried somewhere in the Middle East.

Leaving for the Tel Aviv airport with this as my last interaction with the people of this land that I love so dearly, gives me strength to continue, and the conviction that I needed to spend the nine-hour flight to the US buried in the work that would seek the gold for the kids that deserved it.

If you love, you must do something. And so as I return, how can I keep writing small stories under these circumstances, when SCUD missiles and dirty nuclear bombs are eyeing each other with slit-eyed competitive combat-ready eventuality, both willing to destroy everything worth living for. My efforts must turn from writing this book, to writing yet another funding proposal, to taking greater action.

Whether I am in America or the Arctic, Jordan or Judea, I know that a human hand rests on the red button and black trigger of destiny. It is not God that would create a creation that exterminates itself. We are being watched; I'm sure of it. Our collective decisions will be recorded in our hearts and in whatever manner our creator provides to remind us of our past violations against our own humanity.

The finger of a human soul will be the one to pull a spring-loaded trigger, or push the button down hard on a target, setting into motion a fast spinning and fateful fury, an almighty hurricane of irreversible decision, sending the wretched, whining, wailing screaming screams of the entire human race out into the starry realms of the universe. Perhaps it will be the scream of regret that will be heard for all time.

If the buttons are pushed and the fate is sealed, the world will watch in muffled, sickly impotence and silent, deadly betrayal. No one will be spared. Not even the lonely soul, who takes a red and furious fate or a black and evil destiny into his own hands and points his finger, knowing full well the suffering that will follow, but pointing and pulling, and pushing all the same... to... to... to... nothing less than the apocalypse of the human soul.

My eye has never left, never for a second, the fixed and absolute watching of the hand that would send all of humanity into a massive grave. Undoing that will not be easy and will rest on the consciousness of the human family, with millennia of compounded destruction and an infinite eon of regret. It is not easy to resurrect oneself from the deathbed of nuclear pollution or dig out from under the unspeakable travesty of everything gone wrong. I have watched that finger on the red button, that finger on the black trigger, every second that words have formed in my mind to find their way onto these pages. It is this trigger-pulling, button-pushing insanity that fueled my perseverance to write this book in a single month. This is why I have shared my story and shared my innermost thoughts. This is why I have exposed myself, raw and naked in my ignorance and in my own arrogant assumptions and with whatever feebleness is clearly evident in my character.

I have already decided that people can make of my attempt whatever they will. But I must bring attention to what is going on here in the land of sorrows and promises, on the stage where all the world will stand and be counted, because we stand at the brink of a decision, the effect of which will never end. America will not be immune to the hurricane. The solar fires of the potential holocaust of a planet will surge to the heartland and beyond.

We stand before the altar of our own fate, just as Abraham once stood before the rock on the mount to lay down his son Isaac to a future of spiritual inheritance either through death or life. The heavens poured down upon Abraham and declared that "Life" is the way of the family of Abraham. His son was spared. Life, sweet life... the unknown sacrifice.

Sacrifice can be holy or unholy, a pitiful, blinding, grieving waste of human light, a defilement of the human spirit, or a noble, beauty of regal dignity and everlasting salvation that proclaims the promised land for future generations. I pray that the prophet Abraham set the stage for us in our modern day saga, as we are also called to make the ultimate sacrifice. I pray that Life itself will be spared and that future generations will prosper in the inheritance of peace on earth and good will to all beings.

And so the question is, shall we be redeemers or destroyers? Shall we be grave robbers and death wardens, or stewards and angels of a new and prosperous life upon our sweet earth?

Will the contenders for Jerusalem give her to the world as the great sacrifice that will bring the East and West together and unify the Tribes of Israel once and for all? This question will not go away, dear reader. It will not go away. It will follow every single one of us into the farthest reaches of our being and into the future of all futures. We stand at a crossroads of decision. Jerusalem, the beguiler and anointer, sits like the Mona Lisa at the center of choice.

"There comes a time in history when to remain silent is betrayal." These are the words of Martin Luther King, Jr. who offered himself up in the public eye, had his private life hung out to dry, and was gunned down for the cause that he stood for. But in the gunning down he lived on, larger than life through the horror and the honor of his sacrifice.

And so I ask you; I ask you now. What if silence is betrayal? Each of us will have to answer this in our own way. I don't need to give this any more thought or deliberation, and my sentiment is shared by many, many souls who are perhaps for the first time in their lives, throwing all caution of a conventional kind to the wind, and are standing up for what is right.

There are people who are selling their houses to finance the peace effort. There are people who are traveling to dangerous places to give what they can give. There are people who know that they must stand and be counted on the side of peace, on the side of life. There are people who see the United Nations as something that belongs to everyone, not just the privileged or the few or those with favored nation status.

I have made my decision. My hand has typed the words on these pages. My heart has answered the call to tell this story. It is a story that some will cry over and will be inspired to change their lives. It is a story that some will scorn, perhaps even protest as insane, and declare to be false-prophecies, that I can't be trusted and don't know what I am talking about. But who does know?

In the fleeting month of writing at all hours around the clock that it has taken to put thoughts and feelings to words, much has come to pass in my own life and in the planetary life that is being hurled through space all around me. The headlines tell the story of tragedy everywhere. We are more than likely living in some kind of "end times." If we pay any attention to the prophets and sages of wisdom, it certainly looks that way. Everything is rotting on the vines of human existence.

Children are shooting children in the United States of privilege, wealth and prosperity. Cancer is running rampant, leaving few who are immune to the possibility of the silent taker of life. Women are being mutilated and abused as an accepted tradition in Africa and most everywhere else at some level of degradation or another.

We are polluting our environment down to the last molecule of air and water, earth and soil, fauna and flora. Corporate gladiators are making deals to hang on the coliseums of green-eyed greed, and taking sport in convincing stockholders that the fast buck is their birthright, even as the Wall Street darlings and gurus are being dragged off to serve their terms of office in jail cells instead of boardrooms.

Journalists who only wanted to tell the truth are being shot down in their prime in Afghanistan. Already their stories are best sellers. Look everywhere around you, dear reader. Look and take all of it to heart.

My own grown adult children are scared and losing sleep. My grandchildren are nervous, and wary like little birds on the lookout for predators. I don't say much about what I do in the name of peace and human values to my family members. They just can't take it and want to live normal lives. They want me to live a normal life. But they know without me telling them, that we have come to the point of no return.

Somehow we all know, in the wisdom of our human bones, that the time has come. The question of the ages will not take leave from the putrid sickbed of a lost human society, until we nod to the left or to the right. Thumbs up or thumbs down. Yes or No. Life or Death. Peace or War.

There was a lot I didn't tell in the writing of my story, didn't say and didn't reveal, partly because time is running out, and the story simply must find its way to the few or the many who are intended to read it, immediately, right now. I can't wait another week to send this book on its way; so demanding is the urgency to take action.

And I haven't said everything either, partly because there are parts of my story that are sacred to me and no one else. Putting my personal life into words has been painful and difficult, because there is a commitment to it, that strips away all the normal buffers that shield a person from vulnerable exposure. But I will not be alone, in the tide of willingness to be seen and be heard, as I join all the voices that are willing to speak up, and do so before it is too late.

My hope is that maybe, just maybe, even if it is a feeble, faint and faraway maybe, a few words, even a single word or a single thought will fall upon a human mind or heart somewhere in the dark night of the soul of humanity and make a difference. Dear God, I hope you are listening to the undreamed dreams of my grandchildren and will, in the final hour, spare them as innocent witnesses to yet another holocaust of planetary proportions.

It seems one holocaust wasn't enough to convince us that taking life is not the way to give life or to survive. The roles are reversed, the players are different from the drama that sent millions to their graves, but the horizon will be painted black if the button is pushed. Millions more will perish unless the human heart remembers itself and calls out for divine intervention.

Dear God, I call out for divine intervention. Only you in your wisdom can show us the way, can bring sanity to insanity, can save us from ourselves. Send this book and every other voice for peace into the fortresses of power on this planet. Let the call for peace penetrate the walls of defiance and conviction.

Let the call for peace become so full of life, that fissures and cracks run wild in the walls of refusal and arrogance, bringing the walls of human ignorance down to earth, the earth that we all share and live upon, the earth that is the Promised Land, the table of the Last Supper for all of humanity. Will we rise to the occasion, take action and carve out a new possibility, or will we pull the trigger by doing nothing?

The ending to my story will depend on which direction we, as a human family, choose to walk. Which path will we follow? Will we deny the personal decision to be made, and instead assign the decision to be made for us by someone we never met and never knew, who sits upon a presumed throne of power? Will we in our refusal to decide, allow "him" to decide for us? Define who "he" is for yourself.

Their names are in the headlines. Most rulers rule primarily for themselves. Few rule for the good of the people. Those few must muster that goodness into a power that has yet to be seen and heard, and it is time to do exactly that. I call the round table of noble souls to this moment. I call you wherever you might be.

And so I will ask again, and again and again, will we allow someone else who doesn't know or care about our children and grandchildren to decide for us, because we sat there stupid and silent, limp and lulled, as if we were mute and blind and crippled to our God-given ability to have a voice in the future of our children's children? I love my children and my grandchildren and all the world's children more than that. I call on you to speak up, even if the ultimate sacrifice is asked of you.

I attended a peace summit conference in Geneva, Switzerland some time ago, that invited over five hundred women spiritual leaders to make an initial inroad into the United Nations and to launch new initiatives for human values, and the value of women and children, in particular. This conference was convened in the wake of the summer of 2000 when a World Summit of Spiritual Leaders was held in New York City with over two thousand representatives of our world's religious leaders in attendance. The New York conference was hosted by the UN and convened on an invitation only basis.

Less than fifteen percent of those invited were women. If we want peace, if we want a benevolent society, if we want sanity instead of insanity, it is time to open the doors to women in the halls of leadership.

It is time for all women to recognize their own innate worth as half of the world's population and also as the nurturers and guardians of human life. The old paradigm wherein women have precious little true power in matters of global importance has led us to the brink of irreversible, unprecedented, unimaginable consequences. If we were to compare the number of women holding leadership positions or political offices to the female population globally, the ratio is unthinkable.

I have pondered many "what ifs" throughout my trying experiences in the Middle East, and many "what ifs" have been voiced in the pages of this book. This leads me to one more controversial "what if" and that "what if" is: "What if the imbalance were reversed, and men had precious little true power in matters of global importance, and men held relatively few leadership positions or political offices in relationship to their numbers?"

If this were the case, what kind of planet would we be living on? What would our quality of life be? What would our global condition be? Where would we place our values, upon whom and upon what? Would we have war? Would we have famine? Would we have disparity? Would we have environmental pollution? For the sake of "what if," these questions deserve being asked. Would a woman push the red button or pull the black trigger? Would she? Would you? Who will? Who would?

While I dearly love the male side of humanity and cherish the good men in my own life, these questions must be asked. Our conference in Geneva was attended by women who were not elected officials, but rather, women who have proved their leadership and have earned their badges of courage by working in the fields of spiritual service and human values. These are women who, like myself, head international organizations for peacekeeping, for environmental protection and restoration, for the eradication of poverty and hunger, for the education in human values of our children, and for the teaching of adults not to harm or kill or abuse.

We are the new CEOs, the new change agents, the new movers and shakers. And we have only begun to gather our forces, to convene, to take action. We have given every dime that we have, and every waking hour that can be given, to the welfare of humanity and to the ground that humanity walks upon.

Our Geneva conference was a huge success if we gauge it by the magnitude of what was birthed. In fact it was magnificent. The press didn't find the event worth mentioning in the evening news. CNN didn't stand around asking for commentary from the truly amazing women spiritual leaders who graced the conference at the United Nations.

Even the great emblem up on the stage at the front of the Assembly Hall was draped and hidden, because the UN wasn't sure that they could openly sponsor our event, or so I was told. But we did gather and we did drink from the cup of hope, together, all of us. And we walked away in the light of a new commitment. We are taking action and are convening all around the world in every way possible.

I stand in the company of women who already know that the day of sacrifice has come and are willing to make that sacrifice. They are willing to put their lives on the line, like the mothers who stand witnessing and watching at the checkpoints, as young boys point guns at the dilemma of the ages, not knowing if the gun barrel stares down the throat of an innocent bystander or a perpetrator of horror. Not knowing, but pointing the gun anyway.

What choice is there? Is there a choice? I think there is. I know there is. These women are finding their voices and their power to stand up and say what must be said, and do what must be done. The choice is rapidly taking on new dimensions of possibility, with good men rising to the cause of doing the right thing side by side with the wisdom of women.

I sat in a hotel lobby here in America as war claimed lives indiscriminately around the world, surrounded by what I think of as living Grandmother Guardians of the precious earth. I had met them at the conference in Geneva and now we are joined in the common bond of caring for future generations. They are mothers and grandmothers and great grandmothers. They are ordinary and extraordinary women. They come from Los Angeles and Rio de Janeiro, from the countryside and from the city.

They are self-assigned, good will ambassadors. They are smart and heart-centered and decent and caring. They are strong and fearless, like warriors of a new breed. They are also damned good at making a difference. They have orchestrated amazing feats of goodness, despite the pitiful dearth of funding, despite the odds against them and the manmade obstacles that have stood in their way over the years, the long hard years.

They have watched madmen go to war and bloody the land and pillage the wealth of humanity and even do the unthinkable, raping the women of the declared enemy. These women may very well become mothers to children born of the atrocities of war and the violation of human decency. This is the picture of war that young inspired soldiers should guard against, and this is the picture that women have watched as men spend trillions upon trillions of dollars on solutions that don't work.

We women must change our ways and give the love that is needed and take responsibility for not doing enough to change the way things are. We women must claim our own storehouse of reckoning by putting our own lives in order, the order intrinsic to integrity. We must look at the world we live in, and take care to preserve it for our young. These women that I sit with are gathered to fight the legacy of destruction tooth and nail, and largely unnoticed, and are among the many who are never featured on CNN or displayed in headlines of newspapers, not yet.

These women are fighting to preserve the environment by personally seeing to it that young people all over the world are taught to have respect for the water that they drink, the air that they breath, and the ground that stretches out under their feet.

These women have gathered movie stars and performers to lend a hand in making a difference and have orchestrated major events throughout the country. These women have made it their business to feed the poor, because they need to be fed, and they do it without any religious fanfare or agenda.

These are women who have gone to Afghanistan and have seen the debris of war crimes strewn upon the landscape. They have seen the tender shoots of grass humbly reach up from under the hulking weight of abandoned military tanks, tanks that have been left to rust into the very ground that they gouged open before coming to a dead and final stop. Now amid these wasting, twisted piles of metal, is the cold reality of starving children who climb on the lifeless machines as if they were playground equipment. War junk in the world is the play yard of the destitute.

The mothers with whom I sit are the mothers who can't bear this absurd legacy of children reduced to using weapons of destruction as their play yards, or any of the other travesties of human depravation and negation that have become so commonplace. Human values of all kinds have become lost in the greed and war lust of insane policies that can only lead to a horror of horrors, the perversion of our planet's children. And then what if children who have lost their souls grow up to be leaders?

These mothers and grandmothers have taken things into their own hands. They are not willing to let strangers decide the fate of their children's children. One of them casually commented as we sat together in a peace conference, "situation room" all our own, "We are finally angry enough to do something about all the lies." When she said this, we sat huddled around a large shiny table not so unlike politicians in Washington, DC, who decide the fate of nations and babies yet to be born.

We talked and we planned, staring out through the windows of the hotel lobby at the snowy white winter skyline of a downtown vista in the heartland of America, knowing that the fate of babies was in our hands, too. It really struck me when she said what she said.

She said it half joking but dead serious, serious enough to give her own life if need be, serious enough to go to Iraq and stand among the Arab women and children who will be used as the human shields for a madman, serious enough to join the women of Iraq who will serve as the sacrificial lambs for heartless soulless smart bombs and weapons of super-intelligent perverted power.

This one of whom I speak is a great-grandmother with a contagious laugh, a wide earthy smile on her face, and an even wider smile on her heart that rests like a golden sun in her ample chest. She has invested the whole of her life and personal wherewithal in the human race, and three generations have followed her own. Her children are also peace workers and environmentalists and preservers of all things to be cherished. She has traveled the world for many, many years, speaking words of wisdom that few have had the wisdom to take seriously enough to side with her in the fight for life. Few have been willing to write the checks that will fund a benevolent future.

She too has given me hope. She is a savior of the environment: the jungles, the deserts, the high mountains and the most remote regions, and a benefactor to a host of indigenous peoples and spiritual leaders. She has cared for them all and given them a home here in America, if they want it, inviting them to a place high in the Rockies to convene, to live, to offer their wisdom. She has given her all. She has been willing to do what no sane person would be willing to do.

But that all depends on what you call sane. And these days it's a hard call. It's hard to tell. I myself wonder which side of sanity I am on. It's gotten to the point that in recent months I've changed my mind about everything I thought I knew. As one human being makes the decision to pull the trigger, other human beings will arrive ready to offer bags of food and medical supplies, to join a peace march or demonstration, because they are mandated by the fact that they are women and mothers, or men and fathers, and they must do something.

In the peace council of mothers that convenes in hotel lobbies, we ask ourselves, "If we arrived by the thousands in Jerusalem and stood with the Arab women and Jewish women and all women of every faith and color, would the leaders of nations still push the button and still pull the trigger? Would they shoot down the hopes of mothers worldwide for a peaceful coexistence among nations?

If we came to Jerusalem en masse, by the hundreds of thousands in a united call for peace, would it make a difference? What will it take to get CNN to roll the cameras, or the Jerusalem Post to print the story, or the leaders of nations to notice what the people are saying?

Questions like this were more than small talk, both of us so swamped with the work of "earth service," that going to a peace gathering would almost be a luxury on many counts of reality of comprehension. So we sat together with grandchildren sitting in our laps, playing in our midst, banging pianos in the background. They were being fed pancake breakfasts and had syrup dripping down their chins which needed wiping as we planned. We sat together seeking to rise to the occasion of nothing less than creating a master plan for saving our planet and everyone on it.

We cooked up a pretty good stewpot of possibilities and will, in the weeks ahead, spin the wheel of fortune to put the plan into action. Funding in the millions of dollars will be needed and sought. Hard work into the midnight hours will be called of each of us. Sleeves will be rolled up to elbows, even when dining with dignitaries or pitching a proposal to philanthropists.

But we are not only willing, we are adamant that the time is now. We have decided to join a veritable army of angels, a legion of earth guardians and earth restoration warriors, a growing troop of peacekeepers and mothers of humanity in creating a global peace event that will bring together people who are choosing peace from all over the world.

We join a host of other women who have received the same vision and who are sitting in planning meetings just like our own. We will organize and host everything from small neighborhood meetings, to star-studded gala events in locations on every continent. We will hold a global event never to be forgotten, which will bring billions of souls to the side of sanity, to the side of peace the day peace becomes the choice of nations and the light of the future. The voice for peace will be heard, and it will be one voice, the voice of the human heart.

Before we closed our meeting to save the world, restore the environment, educate the innocent, feed the poor, avert the disaster of a World War III, and crown Jerusalem as the queen of all sacred sites, the great-grandmother among us reminded us of a prophecy from Isaiah in the Christian Bible with a twinkle in her eye. This same quote is prominently displayed at the United Nations. "...and they shall beat their swords into plowshares, and their spears into pruning hooks: nation shall not lift up sword against nation, neither shall they learn war any more." (Isaiah, 2:4)

When I asked her to elaborate on how she saw this, this is what she said... "Well, it's really very simple. We no longer allow war as an option for conflict resolution.

We seek non-violent solutions. We hold our leaders to the truth. We refuse to elect them if they aren't willing to stand for truth. We elect them to legislate a sustainable future for all of humankind.

"We demand that they treat our international neighbors the way we ourselves want to be treated. But more than this, we should melt down all of the weapons of destruction and use the metals and agents that they are comprised of as the materials and building blocks of peace.

"We turn the metal from military tanks into windmills that generate power without pollution. We take atomic technology and create instruments of human benefit that sustain life rather than exterminate it. We build new education centers that protect and celebrate the beauty of our environment. We reverse the balance of power. We teach soldiers to be ambassadors of peace and protectors of all humanity."

Her comments gave way to the paradox that we live in, as I remembered seeing for the first time, way back in the 1960's, the bumper sticker that is popular among peace workers, "What if the Pentagon had to hold a 'bake sale' to raise money for their weapons?" And further, what if the teachers of children, who hold in their hands the well being of future generations, were paid the wages of professional athletes or movie stars or some such, instead of receiving a mere pittance at the bottom of the economic totem pole? What if we turned bomb money into pay raises for teachers all over the world?

What if the entire premise of the military worldwide became peacekeeping of a different kind? What if enlisting meant serving all people, all nations equally? What if young people were given the opportunity first hand to see what life is like all over the world, and soldiers became ambassadors of good will, good deeds, and good intentions?

Yes, turning swords into plowshares is a proposal handed down through the ages from the realms of prophets that foretells a new era of peace and prosperity among nations. What if we all shared our planet's wealth of human and physical resources, instead of investing in prisons and prison camps, guns and more guns, and campaigns to avert terrorism? What if we had listened to the desperation that turned fanatical before terrorism became a part of our modern day reality?

What if we saw it as our responsibility that children do not grow up to be desperate, desperate enough to blow themselves up, taking their own lives to promote their cause, because they simply have nothing left to lose? What if, what if, what if...

The choice must be made and the "what ifs" answered. There is no way we can avoid the time of reckoning for all souls. And so the comparisons of peacemaking and the brainstorming continued among us for some time, and I left the meeting feeling like I could go on.

This is how I will leave my story for now. I will do all that I can to make a difference. Join me. With so much to lose, there is everything to gain. The future belongs to all of us, all of us. Choose wisely. The time has come.

Later after returning home from my meeting with the women, I looked up the quote in the book of Isaiah, because I hadn't read it since I was a child. I found another passage that gave me hope. "And it shall come to pass in the last days, that the mountain of the Lord's house shall be established in the top of the mountains, and shall be exalted above the hills, and all nations shall flow into it."

Perhaps my vision of a great Hall of Wisdom in Jerusalem, a new United Nations of Peace on Earth, will one day become a reality, and all roads that lead to Jerusalem will sing her praises as the Mother of the Ages, the city that endured and opened her heart to the promises of prophets, that we, after thousands of years, might be the children of milk and honey.

Sarah's Promise

Mother's Milk, Mother's Love

From Sarah:

*L*ong *have I waited for this time. Long have I watched and waited. For you see, I am one who loves you and all of the people of this land called Israel and Palestine, this place of sand and rock and olive trees. Know also that I love the people of earth for they are the children that will one day not only inherit this earth but also know its value.*

My heart has always been with you, with all women, with you who are the daughters of my soul. As you live your lives in the skyscrapers of modern cities as well as in the mud huts of disadvantage, the value of the human spirit belongs to each and every one of you. It matters not what you believe or hold true or how you perceive your circumstances. You have within you the substance of our creator, the light that can never die and the spirit that cannot be bound by time, nor by the ignorance that is its temporary captor.

The Promised Land has always been the state of mind that sets the human spirit free. For it is that spirit that can rise above all adversity and claim a new day of future possibilities. There is no thing that is beyond the creative nature of the human spirit, including the fulfillment of the prophecies of seers who guided kingdoms of the past and the worlds to come, from the deep eye that is at one with the great eye of eternal existence.

I call you to a new vision, that all of my daughters might see with the eyes of the heart and the courage that sets free the human soul. For, I am nothing other than this call. I have lingered throughout the ages to call you. To call you home to the wisdom that lives in the inner sanctums of your heart. There you will hear the voices of all who have made the sacrifice of giving oneself to the Great Life that others might live.

As that Great Life is entered, and all is given in the fearless moment of decision, the wings of angels carry you home to the truth of All Life and its value, the essence that animates unending potential. And so I call you to the value of the Life within all living things.

You can hear me in the sounds that are all around you, for I carry the archetype of the giver of Life. I am the creatress, the priestess, the healer, the teacher, the protector and even the warrior. I am that which gives birth to milk and honey. I am in the eyes of laughing children. I am in the chants and ceremonies that hold our traditions. I am in the voice of the faithful lifted up in praise of the true existence. I am in the love that suckles new generations. I am your blood and your bones and the beating of your heart. I am the breath that responds to your breathing.

Oh, you, my daughters, the mothers of all peoples. Oh, you who are the people who have searched and wandered. I am praying for you. I am calling out for you, that you might receive the strength to make the final sacrifice, to walk the final steps, to give of yourselves what must be given. For I have walked long upon this earth in spirit with only my desire for your wellbeing as the light that sustains my being. For, it is your ultimate destiny that is my gateway of return into absolution.

My story is a story of faithlessness and faith restored, the refusal to believe and the decision to trust, the choice to cast out and the retribution and penance that gathers together. My Dear Ones, you are all my children. Even those whom I once denied in the past are my true blood through the light of God who exists in every drop of blood that sustains life in all peoples, all cultures, everywhere.

My story, my tribulations, my suffering is my offering. My journey through darkness is now my wisdom and it is this that I preserve and give to you. My story is your story, my tribulation is your tribulation, and my suffering is your suffering. For is not the journey of forgetting also the journey of remembrance?

Dear Ones, hear me, feel me, for I am present among you, and I am sent across the barriers of time to call you home to the power of your heart, for it is the light of the pure heart that has always been the Promised Land of the Eternal Life. And from the pouring forth of the heart's ultimate wisdom that lives deep within us all, the promised land of earth and water and wind and sky will be that which we witness as the legacy of the Children of Israel.

Wander no more my beloveds, seek not the claiming of your inheritance in physical terms, but seek first the wisdom of your own heart and discover there what has always been promised. For there you will find your goodness; there you will find the greatest of mercy; there you will find the answers that you have longed for, the answers to all questions and all difficulties.

There you will find the true Promised Land, from which the world of an abundant and prosperous physical life and manifestation will flow. For this is the law of all laws. The pure heart will endure and will reign o'er a thousand years of peace. The pure heart will be lifted up to the illumination of the mind that will find the answers that are needed, heal the hearts that weep,

357

clothe the naked and feed the hungry with the promise that I have given you.

Throughout our experience on this earth as the family of humankind, it matters not whether we call the divine concept for a benevolent existence the Promised Land or Zion or Nirvana or Shambala or the Great Emptiness or the Land of Milk and Honey. It matters not, Dear Ones.

Within each of us lives this same Divine Premise. It lives forever and ever in our hearts. For beyond all the illusions that we have cast upon ourselves, our true nature remains. For we are made, created and caused to be, in the image of our Creator and that God lives within all souls, one and the same. It is our Creator that is the headwaters and the source of the land of milk and honey, and this land, this kingdom, this reality, lives now in the depths of your hearts, wherein the human spirit resides. It need only be unleashed for a mighty awakening to move o'er the face of this earth and a new day be proclaimed among the nations of the world.

So now I give to you my wisdom, simple though it is. The Love of God lives within you, and it is that love that will make manifest all that you long for. Inside the long night of searching, you will find the ultimate light, you will find the supreme answer to every question, and that answer will be the face of love, glowing and shining in its benevolence toward all beings. It is this benevolence that will redeem you and bring peace to strife, peace to your homeland, peace to your heart.

The time is come to let the voice of the heart be heard, to seek it and exclaim it and to revel in its wisdom. I join now with all the prophets of the ages, as we together make our prayer for the people of earth, as one prayer, single in its intention, as one in its focus of desire. Peace, peace, peace, O let there be peace among souls, peace among families and peace among nations.

For it is then that the treasures of the heavens will be upon you all the days of your life. O, my children, can you not see what the prophets have always seen, can you not find the light of God in your own eye? O, Dear Ones, can you not sense what shall be given unto you as you seek the purity that is yourself.

For it is this, your own true nature, that will open the Golden Gates to a New Jerusalem and a benevolent future for all beings. Know that it is there. Know that it is this that you should seek above all else. For this is the Will of God, that all souls know themselves as divine creation, all souls, Dear Ones, all souls. Open the gates of the heart and the gates of new creation, and the promise of the ages will also open.

And so I, as Sarah, speak to you as one who now remembers, I call you home to each other, to the tents of old, to the fires that warmed you, to the prayers that protected you, to the love that originally brought you into this world.

For you were conceived in the same love and the same promise. This I know, and it is with this revelation that I passed from the physical world into the spiritual world, as I lay in the grief of my sorrow and my regretting that became the new promise of my heart. O, Dear Ones, I found my heart. I found my love. I found my truth. Through love, you are all my children, Christian and Arab and Jew. Through the Light of God, you are all my blood.

Join one another in new creation my children, my sons, my daughters. Eat as one. Drink as one. Live as one. Share the bounty of this earth, this land as one. To do so is to fulfill your divine destiny. To do so is to set your souls free. To do so is to enter the Promised Land of the Love of God.

For this is what I remembered. And this is what I pass on to you. And so it was that my death as the wife of Abraham was also my liberation. For as the beating of my heart slipped away and came to rest, ceasing the rhythm of its beating, so did

I offer up my existence to my Creator and became whole in my remembrance. And so my promise is given unto all the Children of the Desert, all of the Children of Israel, all the Children of earth and her nations. You who live of the blood of Isaac, you who live of the blood of Ishmael, you are one blood, under one God, under one sky, upon one land. You are brothers. You are brothers. My promise is given unto you as one.

My promise to God is my promise to you. I will pray for you, I will walk unseen among you. I will speak in the quiet of your hearts. I will call you in the silence of your minds. For my promise is my reason for existence. I will offer up all that I am for the union of your souls. O descendants of my heart, I call you home to yourselves.

And to all mothers, I beseech you; rise up into the nobility of your souls. For, there is no child that is not your child. There is no son and no daughter that is not yours to suckle. There is no being that is not yours to care for, and love, and give life to. Be the Great Mother that you are. Know that the Ancient Mother lives in your heart and holds within you the premise of all life... to love... to love... to love... all that is sacred.

For, all life is sacred, and you my sisters, my daughters, are the Mothers of All Life. Be you young and unripe of womb, be you old and withered of womb, you are yet the mothers of future generations. You are the face of love; waiting to awaken to its destiny, for you will be the hand of God in world affairs. The waiting eyes of the children of the world are cast in your direction.

Do not deny them; do not refuse them. For their innocence is in your care. It is now that we as women, as mothers must remember. For this is our covenant as women with our Creator. You will remember, and you will know. For, love is the premise that caused all life to be. And it is through love that all hearts will be healed, and all souls will be redeemed, and all families and nations will be reunited.

My promise lives through each of you. My promise is the promise of the Ancient Mothers of Creation who have given the milk of life, the essence of their own existence to All Life.

Let a new beginning take root. Let peace be manifest. Let love rule the land. For I am Sarah, and I am with you, and my prayers will endure. In this, my faith is absolute, and in this I am one with my Creator. This is my Promise; I will be with you on the wind, in the stars, on the breath of every newborn, in the heart of every woman. My Promise is to you and to God, as one covenant returned to its source in faith that knows itself as the Flame Eternal.

About the Author

Devra West, D.D., Ph.D., is one of the foremost innovative thinkers of our time and a visionary leader in many areas of human endeavor. Her quest moves from a greatness of heart that contributes to a better life and a more viable and creative existence for all human beings. She is the founder and creative director of several non-profit international peace and humanitarian organizations inspiring a new era of global guardianship, philanthropy, higher consciousness and the stewardship of human values.

Her visionary capacity for futuristic thinking has put her consulting firm, Millennia Mind, Inc., in the forefront of leadership development, and made it one of the most sought-after agencies in the field. In addition to the Peace Promise Initiative, her work with the Global Guardianship Institute promises to offer a dynamic influence in the field of ethical corporate, economic and environmental practices. One of her present endeavors is her work with global leaders to create new financial systems based on the ethics of sustainability and prosperity for all nations.

The Rocky Mountains of Montana is where Devra makes her home. She is a dedicated mother of three grown children and the proud grandmother of a still growing third generation. Through her vibrant roles as a dedicated humanitarian, a dynamic transformational teacher, and a corporate and leadership consultant, she demonstrates an inspiring example of living in the vitality of one's full creative potential. Dr. West is the author of a wide range of leading-edge books on higher consciousness and new paradigms for a more benevolent shared global environment, and continues to earn international recognition for her tireless efforts to improve planetary conditions.

⚜ Author's Related Projects ⚜

Sacred Arts Institute, a degree granting program of higher consciousness that brings the wisdom teachings of universal consciousness into contemporary application, with two primary programs in the United States and Geneva, Switzerland. For information, visit our website (*sacredartsinstitute@montana.com*) or call: (406) 961-0007

Millennia Mind, Inc., offers corporate consulting and culture development based on new paradigms in ethical business and financial leadership for global sustainability, Dynamic Creativity Trainings and Essence Branding for progressive professional identity. For further information visit our website (millenniamind.com) or call: (406) 961-8585.

Global Guardianship Initiative, an alliance of philanthropic leaders that engage international programs for human values, ecological ethics and sustainable international corporate practices promoting peace and abundance for all nations. For more information call: (406) 961-0007

✺The Peace Promise Initiative✺

The Peace Promise Initiative is an innovative concept to encourage cooperative alliances between global and local organizations in regions of conflict. Moving from the existing Israeli/Palestinian issues, PPI seeks to develop methods for improving the ability of NGO's to engage a collective support response in regions undergoing political and military turmoil to lessen unnecessary human suffering and ecological damage.

In keeping with its efforts to set action-oriented goals to achieve an end result sustained by responsibility and accountability, all Peace Promise activities focus on four "action categories":

Environmental Stewardship and Reclamation Efforts
Trauma Recovery and Human Values Education
Women's Leadership and Political Engagement
Interfaith Reconciliation and Intercultural Dialog

As it brings the nobility of the human heart to regions of the world where peace in longed for, the Peace Promise Initiative is destined to foster practical remedy by:

Pursuing a major fundraising campaign to assist approved peace, humanitarian, interfaith, and environmental groups and organizations with funding.

Developing PPI's four primary "action categories" into long term, viable programs that bring practical assistance to groups, communities and grassroots efforts.

Offering education and cultural projects to foster human values and the dignity of the human spirit.

Hosting symposiums, active dialog seminars and major public gatherings for peace

Engaging public speaking and major media projects, such as television, concert performances, and documentary events as a vehicle for getting attention to the global efforts of peace workers, PPI and allied organizations.

Your personal contribution is the hand that will change and uplift world conditions. We welcome contributions of time, talent, expertise, networking, donations, and fundraising, including co-sponsorship and organizational alliances. For more information contact:

Peace Promise Initiative, Inc.
736 Fred Burr Road, Victor Montana 59875
Tel.: (406) 961-0007; FAX (406) 961-8877
E-mail: *peacepromise@montana.com*
Visit our website: *peacepromiseinitiative.org*

ISBN 155395519-6

9 781553 955191